From Village to City

The publisher gratefully acknowledges the generous support of the Philip E. Lilienthal Asian Studies Endowment Fund of the University of California Press Foundation, which was established by a major gift from Sally Lilienthal.

From Village to City

SOCIAL TRANSFORMATION IN
A CHINESE COUNTY SEAT

Andrew B. Kipnis

UNIVERSITY OF CALIFORNIA PRESS

University of California Press, one of the most distinguished university presses in the United States, enriches lives around the world by advancing scholarship in the humanities, social sciences, and natural sciences. Its activities are supported by the UC Press Foundation and by philanthropic contributions from individuals and institutions. For more information, visit www.ucpress.edu.

University of California Press
Oakland, California

Library of Congress Cataloging-in-Publication Data   ·

Kipnis, Andrew B., author.
    From village to city : social transformation in a Chinese county seat / Andrew B. Kipnis. — First edition.
        pages   cm
    Includes bibliographical references and index.
    ISBN 978-0-520-28970-3 (cloth : alk. paper)
    ISBN 978-0-520-28971-0 (pbk. : alk. paper)
    ISBN 978-0-520-96427-3 (ebook)
    1. Urbanization—China—Zouping Xian.   2. Zouping Xian (China).
I. Title.
    HT384.C62Z6855   2016
    307.760951′—dc23

                                                         2015033647

25   24   23   22   21   20   19   18   17   16
10   9   8   7   6   5   4   3   2   1

To the good people of Zouping

CONTENTS

ILLUSTRATIONS AND TABLES

FIGURES

MAPS

TABLES

ACKNOWLEDGMENTS

A book like this owes its greatest debt to the people who spoke to me, invited me into their homes, and shared their lives with me. Thanks to all in Zouping who did so. In China, I was greatly assisted by the Shandong Academy of Social Sciences, especially Li Shanfeng, Yao Dongfang, and Julie Zhai. At the Australian National University (ANU), I worked with several people interested in processes of Chinese urbanization. My close colleague Luigi Tomba and I visited each other's field sites, created a detailed survey instrument (which we never used), and discussed issues feverishly as we coedited *The China Journal*. Sin Wen Lau, Beibei Tang, and Jinying Zhao often contributed to these discussions. Ben Hillman and Jonathan Unger organized a wonderful conference on the urbanization of rural China, which got me started on writing this book. Tom Cliff and Chen Liang worked in their own ways on urban projects in different parts of China. Reading and discussing their work helped in the development of my own ideas. Other ANU colleagues, including Børge Bakken, Markus Bell, Anita Chan, Jamie Coates, Sacha Cody, Tiffany Cone, Dong Xuan, Assa Doron, Thomas DuBois, Tamara Jacka, Li Geng, Andrew McWilliam, Kirin Narayin, Kathy Robinson, Sally Sargeson, Philip Taylor, Matt Tomlinson, and Zhu Yujie contributed to my sanity and to my thinking by engaging in intelligent conversation in a difficult institutional environment. Ann Buller and Sharon Donahue provided admirable administrative assistance, and Karina Pelling of the ANU CartoGIS unit is owed special thanks for the hours she spent working on the maps and photos in this book.

Gonçalo D. Santos and Stevan Harrell organized an excellent conference on the topic of Chinese patriarchy in Halle, Germany, at which I experimented with versions of some of the ideas contained in this book.

Christian Goebel graciously arranged for me to try out an early draft of this book as a lecture series for a class of MA students at the University of Vienna. The beautiful city and intellectual environs rekindled my enthusiasm for the project at a crucial stage. Audiences at Hong Kong University, the International Union of Anthropological and Ethnological Sciences conference in Tokyo, the Chinese University of Hong Kong, the University of Chicago Center in Beijing, Nanjing University, and Fudan University reacted to presentations derived from the chapters of this book with appropriate mixtures of criticism and encouragement. Fan Ke, Thomas Gold, James Hevia, Minhua Ling, Setha Low, Fuji Lozada, Helen Siu, and Vesna Vucinic made crucial practical and intellectual contributions to these forums. Guy Alitto, Deborah Durham, Judith Farquhar, Priya Nelson, Vanessa Fong, William Jankowiak, Lorri Hagman, Teresa Kuan, Mayfair Yang, and Roberta Zavoretti either read portions of the manuscript or contributed through their own intellectual exemplarity.

At the University of California Press, Reed Malcolm provided strong backing and a steady hand through the review process. Three readers, two of whom turned out to be Stephan Feuchtwang and Yunxiang Yan, gave thorough and helpful readings of the entire manuscript. Stacy Eisenstark guided me through the production process, and Sheila Berg proved an intelligent copy editor. Jeff Evans prepared the index.

My field research was funded by ARC Discovery grants DP0984510, DP140101289, and DP140101294 and enabled by the patience of my family, especially my wife, Kejia, and mother, Dorothy.

ONE

Recombinant Urbanization

From 1988 to 2013 I regularly visited a place called Zouping in Shandong province, of the People's Republic of China (PRC). Zouping is the name of both an agricultural county and the urban area that is the county seat (map 1). Over these years, the county seat transformed from a relatively impoverished, sleepy town of thirty thousand people to a bustling city of more than three hundred thousand, complete with factories and high-rises, parks and bus routes, shopping malls and school campuses, and just about everything you might expect from a relatively wealthy mid-sized city in eastern China. In the process of its expansion, many rural villages were incorporated within the county seat's borders. In addition to the villagers incorporated into the city's territory as it expanded, many other former rural dwellers moved there from more distant villages. This book is about the urbanization of Zouping: the transformations of the place itself, the transformations of the lives of formerly rural but now urban people who live there, and the interrelations between these two types of transformation.

Urbanization is one of the key concerns of modernization theory, which typically differentiates the premodern "rural" from the modern "urban" in a series of black/white, either/or transformative contrasts. A shorthand version of this theory suggests that premodern, rural people ate what they grew, were enmeshed in the ecologies of their land, lived in face-to-face communities and extended families, raised their children at home, had parochial worldviews, arranged their children's marriages, and suffered from patriarchal oppression; in contrast, modern, urban people are said to work in factories, obtain their food in supermarkets, be enmeshed in the economic webs of the world market, not know their neighbors, live in nuclear families, find their own spouses, turn their children into national and global citizens

MAP 1. China, Shandong province and Zouping county.

by sending them to school, and suffer from various forms of alienation and anomie. In anthropology and other disciplines, this theory has been dismissed precisely because the contrasts it draws are too standardized and too stark. Rural people often produced for wider world markets, sent their children to school, and thought about world affairs. Urban people still find communities of belonging and think locally (Smith 1979), and patriarchal ideas about family life and marriage are not dead (Harrell and dos Santos forthcoming). Moreover, what the rural and the urban consist of has continually evolved, with the result that how the urban is contrasted with the rural has also changed, in different ways in different eras and places (Williams 1973).

While I agree with much of the standard critiques of modernization theory and certainly will not be championing a return to the sorts of teleological, hackneyed forms of modernization theory imposed by development agencies on third world countries, I have two related concerns about the manner in which subtler ideas of modernization have been dismissed. First, the dismissal has resulted in turning the topic of urban anthropology away from questions of the social transformations related to urbanization. In urban anthropology, new and interesting concerns such as urban citizenship, urban renewal, and urban social movements have replaced urbanization itself as disciplinary foci. These topics take an urban environment as a given and focus on struggles within it. While such issues are important, changing the topic does not result in forms of theorization that are better able to address the problem of conceptualizing urbanization and the related social transformations themselves. Second, while I devote much of this book to showing how transformations in patriarchy, in lifestyle, and in lived experience are never black and white, it is the case that urbanization in Zouping has involved shifts that resonate with the classic concerns of modernization theorists. In Zouping, people have increasingly moved from courtyard-style homes in villages to apartments in complexes of high-rise buildings; at the same time that they have moved into new dwellings, the number of years that children spend in school has drastically increased, and as the number of years spent in school has increased, the ability of people to speak the national dialect has improved; consequently, the ease with which they can travel to different parts of the country and even the world, in search of fortune or love, has grown. At the same time that the number of years of schooling has increased, a demographic transition has emerged, with the vast majority of households having only one or two children; as Zouping has urbanized it has also industrialized, and as it has industrialized it has become more wealthy, and as it has become more wealthy, people have begun to purchase all manner of modern consumer goods, including automobiles, motorcycles, mobile phones, and computers; these purchases have greatly facilitated "time-space compression," and the country and the world have become a smaller place (Harvey 1989); and last but not least, rather than grow what they eat, or even shop in local outdoor markets, Zouping residents now mainly obtain their food at supermarkets that are branches of provincial or national chains.

The dismissal of modernization theory has caused a wide variety of social theorists to ignore questions of social transformation in places that are simultaneously industrializing, urbanizing, and developing. Some see the rise of the industrial city as an eighteenth-century European phenomenon (Short 2012). Such a periodization elides entirely a place like contemporary Zouping where interlinked industrialization and urbanization have taken place outside of Europe during the twenty-first century.

Jennifer Robinson (2006) surveys the entire field of urban studies and concludes that two major types of research dominate. The first examines "global cities" (e.g., New York, Tokyo, and London) as sites of power, innovation, and cosmopolitanism. The second focuses on "third world cities" as sites of social problems, poverty, and developmental failure. Robinson usefully points out that the "global cities" also suffer social problems and that "third world cities" are also sites of innovative living and urban policy. She concludes that all cities should be viewed as "ordinary," as sites of both suffering and innovation. But where does the global city/third world city dichotomy leave a place like Zouping? On the one hand, as "ordinary" as almost any place could be, Zouping could never count as a global city. On the other hand, despite the fact that, like New York and London, Zouping is not exempt from poverty (later chapters introduce the very real problems confronting many of Zouping's inhabitants), neither is it a site of extreme deprivation or decline. For the period of my research, it was a site of rapidly expanding wealth, development in the classic sense of the term, and increasing (but rarely satisfied) aspirations. Robinson's work suggests that lack of attention to places like Zouping is widespread across urban studies.[1]

In anthropology, modernity is often dismissed as myth, mirage, or ideology. James Ferguson's (1999) exploration of urban life in the Zambian Copperbelt is one of the most influential works to do so. When Ferguson did his research, the Zambian Copperbelt had suffered through twenty years of severe economic decline. For Ferguson, this decline laid bare the faults of modernization theory. He takes the central myth of life in the Copperbelt as that of "modernity" itself and explains that the term *myth* has a double sense: "a false or factually inaccurate version of things that has come to be widely believed . . . [and] the anthropological use of the term, which focuses on the story's social function: a myth in this sense is not just a mistaken account but a cosmological blueprint that lays down fundamental categories and meanings" (Ferguson 1999: 13).

Ferguson (1999: 42–43) furthers his dismissal of modernization theory by invoking Stephen Jay Gould's well-known critique of viewing evolution as a "tree" that progresses through distinct stages.[2] The "tree of evolution" begins with bacteria, proceeds through insects, fish, reptiles, and mammals, and ends with "Man." Such an image masks the fact that the bacteria, insects, fish, reptiles, and mammals are still with us. Rather than see evolution as a tree with a "main line," we should envision it, Gould argues, as a bush with many branches in which change is not linear and in which many forms of life might be imagined to coexist. Ferguson applies this argument to his discussion of forms of social life in the Copperbelt. He demonstrates that both before and during the period of economic decline multiple forms kinship practice, multiple styles of inhabiting the world, and multiple strategies of migration to and from rural areas existed. He calls the coexistence of these multiple forms the "full house." This book likewise shows how a full house of patterns of family life, migration strategy, and even styles of inhabiting the world coexisted in Zouping over a period of marked economic change. However, though I can agree with Gould and Ferguson on the faults of tree-like depictions of evolutionary or social change, I am not entirely satisfied with the metaphor of a bush either. As bushes grow, the intertwining of their branches becomes ever more complex, but they never undergo anything like a transformation. There may be subtle changes in the size and shape of the individual branches, but there is no sense of the intertwined nature of the changes. And herein lies the gist of the matter. While Ferguson admits that there have been changes in the types of social strategies available in the Copperbelt and the frequency of their appearance (79), he grants little atten-tion to these changes, does not explore the interrelations among changes in various arenas of social life, and refuses to name any before or after state that would discursively highlight the interrelation among the changes. To speak of social transformation is more than just admitting that change exists. It requires a sense of the interrelatedness of a wide variety of changes, even if, as Ferguson, Robinson, and others would emphasize, we must never imagine that transformations occur in exactly the same way or at the same rate in different places.

Another problem with Ferguson's book from the perspective of Zouping is his focus on decline. Certainly it would be easy to declare that Ferguson examined a place experiencing economic decline while I examine a place that underwent rapid economic growth and that different places in different times can experience different economic fortunes. But as in the case of Robinson and the entire literature that Robinson critiques, I believe that Ferguson's preference for exploring and generalizing from cases of decline over those of growth reveals theoretical biases. He concludes his book by pointing out that decline occurs not just in Zambia, but in all of Africa, in Russia, in Indonesia, and in Korea. He states, "Decline, though often hellish to live through, is 'good to think'—at least for those who would critically interrogate the certainties of modernist metanarratives" (Ferguson 1999: 257). I would counter that for those who want to envision how social trans-formation can be imagined without resorting to a treelike metaphor, places undergoing rapid economic change are equally "good to think."

Finally, there is the manner in which Ferguson dismisses theories of modernity as myth. Imagine the uproar that would occur if I were to dismiss "theories of decline" as myth in the double sense of being both simply false and a cosmological generator of the discursive imagination of the world. I could point out that ideas about decline and failure, about the imminent collapse of the local or national economy for this or that reason, circulate among academics studying China, media pundits discussing China, political leaders in China (Patricia Thornton [2009] depicts how talk of crisis is manipulated by the Chinese political elite), and people conversing in the streets (later chapters discuss street rumor in Zouping) almost with as much regularity as narratives of the historical inevitability of China's rise and coming world dominance. I could also point out that simultaneous industrialization, urbanization, and economic growth has occurred in many places other than Zouping. If the fact that Zambia has experienced serious economic decline makes theories of modernization simply false, why does not the fact that Zouping has experienced rapid economic growth, industrialization, and urbanization make "theories of decline" simply false?

I will not go so far as to assert that "theories of decline" are simply false. But neither will I accept that theories of modernity are simply false. As in Zambia, in Zouping modernization can be a myth in the anthropological sense of the term. It can also be an ideology used by elites to cynically dismiss the concerns and interests of the less powerful in the pursuit of personal profit. It can also be a discourse that informs the plans of governing officials in their honest attempts to make Zouping a more prosperous place. But various theories of modernity, as espoused by social scientists, also, to greater and lesser degrees, illuminate aspects of the social transformations Zouping has undergone. As critiques of modernization theory have led to its outright dismissal and then a lack of interest in examining places that actually are "developing," it strikes me that a treelike imagination of the evolution of social theory has led to a disregard of the full house of social processes unfolding in today's world. The ambition of this book is to contribute to theorizations of social transformation by critically drawing on certain aspects of theories of modernity. Which theories, exactly, do I refer to here?

THEORIES OF MODERNITY

Consider three perspectives on the question, What is modernity? The classic answer sees modernity as the period after the all-encompassing historical break in which agricultural societies become industrial societies. Postbreak societies are marked by industrialization, urbanization, capitalism, the rise of the nation-state, new governmentalities, bureaucracies and biopower, national systems of education, a concomitant increase in the number of years children spend in school, and a demographic transition. Exactly which aspects of this break are considered to be most important shift with the theorist examined and even the particular book of a given theorist. Wage labor and capitalism (Marx and Engels 1886), the division of labor and nation building (Durkheim 1956, 1960, 1973, 1979, 1992), industrialization and bureaucratization (Weber 1978), and discipline and punishment (Foucault 1979) are all important enough. As Arjun Appadurai (1996) suggests, theories of modernity as historical rupture or "break" implicitly pose the "traditional" as the antithesis of the "modern": societies or countries or places that have not yet industrialized or urbanized or established an education system take the label "traditional." This label becomes an epithet in the mouths of government officials in charge of "modernizing" their countries. Appadurai's solution to the dilemma of posing a modern historical rupture without disparaging the nonmodern as traditional is to redefine modernity in terms of recently globalized media imaginaries. The planetary reach of new technologies of communication and the worldwide dispersal of imaginary "scapes" suggest that no place on earth can still be called traditional.

Appadurai's book was one of a series of works (e.g., Bauman 2000; Beck, Giddens, and Lash 1994; Beck and Grande 2010; Castells 1998) that attempted to redefine modernity in terms of a new, second wave—that is, post-nineteenth-century European industrialization—break or rupture. Despite also theorizing the modern in terms of a historical rupture, these redefinitions contributed to the demise of classic modernization theory. As the moments and causes of rupture multiplied in the imaginations of social theorists, the general importance granted to classic modernization declined. But more important, the continued positing of ever newer historical ruptures to fit the present moment raised the question of whether any single historical rupture was important enough to define an unchanging line between "tradition" and "modernity." Newly posited forms of modernity proliferated to include reflexive modernity, liquid modernity, socialist modernity, and so on.

Scholars who use the term *alternative modernities* likewise shook the view of modernity as a single break. While admitting that the entire world took something from "Western modernity" (at the very least this would include the now-universal governing form of the nation-state), they also argue that regardless of what was taken, the modernity of a particular non-Western place is not simply Western because it depends upon the social (national) context in which that modernity is received.[3] This perspective gives a slightly different twist to the discussions of theorists like Appadurai, Bauman, and Beck. While the "second wave" theorists suggest that social transformations continue to occur *after* the urbanization and industrialization of the nineteenth and early twentieth century (in Europe), theorists of alternative modernities imply that the history of what happens or happened *before* industrialization and urbanization also matters. The history before forms the national social context that differentiates various modernities. In positing a singular rupture, classic theories of modernity erase both what happened before and what happens after the rupture of modernity. Taken together, theorists of second wave and alternative modernities thus provide an important corrective to classic theory. However, taken to an extreme, these theories imply that all transformations are equally important and that the concomitant rise of industrialization, urbanization, biopower, large state bureaucracies, national education systems, and demographic transition is no more important than any other moment in history. Thus this second perspective on modernity is one that effectively deconstructs the entire category.

A third perspective on modernity focuses not on the modernity/tradition dyad but rather on the modern/postmodern opposition. It sees world history not in terms of a single rupture but as a series of long-term cycles of capital accumulation and flight. This perspective is most forcefully articulated in the work of Jonathan Friedman and Kajsa Ekholm Friedman (2013; see also Friedman 1994; Friedman and Friedman 2008), but it also comes across in the later work of Andre Gunder Frank (1998) and his arguments with Marxian world system theorists over when capitalism began. For Friedman and Friedman, cultural moments of modernity—that is, of belief in the powers of planning, of progress, of singular national cultures, of the ability of governing institutions to improve the lives of those who live in a given place—occur in places and times where capital is accumulating and being invested. In contrast, capital flight gives rise to two contradictory cultural articulations: expressions of postmodern cosmopolitanism by elites and xenophobic nativism by the masses. The elites favor cosmopolitanism and multiculturalism because they are able to move with capital to wherever it is flowing and thus embrace cultural difference and mobility. The masses are not mobile in the same way and thus take refuge in xenophobic movements. Neither group believes much in progress, planning, or the powers of government. In the perspective of Friedman and Friedman, the rise and decline of theories of modernity in the West, along with the more recent rise of theories of alternative modernities and postmodernity, reflect the nineteenth- and early twentieth-century accumulation of capital in the West followed by its dispersal to various Asian centers, most notably China, beginning in the later decades of the twentieth century. In short, Friedman and Friedman attempt to trump the other two perspectives on modernity not just by coming up with an alternative theory, but by constructing a theory that can explain the rise and fall of the other perspectives.

The relation of belief in the powers of government to cycles of modernization goes against certain neoliberal theories of modernization, which suggest that for development to occur the state must minimize its role and stay out of the way of Capital. In East Asia and much of Southeast Asia, heavy state involvement in the economy has gone hand in hand with rapid modernization, at least in its initial stages (Robison and Goodman 1996). I would differentiate my position from Friedman and Friedman here. It is not just the fact that an influx of capital allows for a larger government and a belief in the powers of planning but also, in the case of the "late" and "compressed" modernizations of East Asia (Alpermann 2011; Beck and Grande 2010; Han and Shim 2010), that at the start of the modernization process there was plenty of room for governments to learn from the experiences of other places. As a consequence, processes that took centuries to work out in England, and involved considerable trial and error, could be "rationally" planned and implemented by authoritarian governments in a few decades. The compressed modernizations of places like Zouping also make their modernizations seemingly fit idealized models of modernization more closely than European cases actually did. That is to say, the degree of the simultaneity of industrialization, urbanization, growth of government, development of an education system, and so on is greater than it was in places like England.[4] The notion of a compressed East Asian modernity expands on more past-oriented theories of alternative modernities by suggesting that the present historical context as well as legacies of the past contribute to differentiation within modernity.[5]

These three perspectives on modernity, while contradictory in their purest forms, are not necessarily impossible to combine. One can insist that there are simultaneously linear and circular (cyclic) aspects to history, and one can argue that while no single historical transition is all-encompassing, some transformations are more important than others. In this manner, I apply all three perspectives to Zouping's urbanization. I draw on classic theories of urbanization when I discuss, and insist on, the importance of the social effects of Zouping's simultaneous urbanization, industrialization, and growth in consumption, infrastructure, urban planning, education, and biopower, but I constantly strive to show how history matters to Zouping's modernization, as well as leave some place for technological transformations such as the Internet and new communication technologies, which came after classic modernization in the West. From the cyclic theories of modernity I take the insights that Zouping's (and China's) rise is in some sense related to declines elsewhere, that I cannot assume Zouping's rise is permanent, and that the belief in planning and progress in Zouping's government as well as the lack of attention of contemporary Western theorists to cases of "modernization" are perhaps related to patterns of capital accumulation and flight. However, in contrast to Friedman and Friedman, I also explore how forms of cosmopolitanism and xenophobia are also apparent in a place like Zouping, where capital is accumulating.

RECOMBINANT URBANIZATION

How, then, do I combine such disparate theories? How can I insist on both social transformation and the relevance of prior (and future) histories. Several strategies assist with this portrayal. The first comes from the realm of the social imaginary and more particularly the notion of social memory and the manner in which memory informs dreams of and plans for the future. Børge Bakken (2000) begins his masterpiece on Chinese modernity with two chapters on "memories and dreams of social order" (ix). Acknowledging that memories of the rural past, that is, the particular rural past of Zouping, are present in its contemporary urban milieu, and continue to inform the ways in which Zouping residents imagine and shape the future, is an important step to overcoming black/white, either/or portrayals of urban transformation.

As Marcel Proust portrays it, the daily cycle of sleeping and waking continually intermingles past and present:

> When a man is asleep, he has in a circle round him the chain of the hours, the sequence of the years, the order of the heavenly host. Instinctively, when he awakes, he looks to these, and in an instant reads off his own position on the earth's surface . . . but [for me] then the memory, not yet of the place in which I was, but of various other places where I had lived, and might now very possibly be, would come like a rope let down from heaven to draw me up out of the abyss of not-being, from which I could never have escaped by myself: in a flash I would traverse and surmount centuries of civilisation, and out of a half-

visualised succession of oil-lamps, followed by shirts with turned-down collars, would put together by degrees the component parts of my ego. (1923: 3–4)

Proust's depiction is apt for a number of reasons. The memories he depicts are those of an (urban) Parisian who once lived in the countryside, in a period when modernization, of a classic sort, was proceeding rapidly. More important, for Proust it is not just that the pieces of the "centuries of civilization" inform his memory, but that these memories are further needed to construct his ego itself. This construction is informed by concrete objects, like oil lamps and shirts with turned-down collars, which serve as mnemonic devices. A Chinese meditation on the place of concrete objects in processes of memories can be found in Jia Pingwa's novel *Remembering Wolves,* in which memories of a not so distant time when wolves roamed the hinterlands and of the people who hunted them are caught up with memories of communication through the recently outdated technology of postal mail (Jia 2000: chapter 16).

Memory is both a complex process in itself and a metaphor for processes of historical reproduction that extend beyond individually bounded human bodies. Human memory is not simply a computer-like process in which "bytes" of information are dryly stored away. As Maurice Halbwachs (1992) argues, processes of human memory are selective and enmeshed in collective narratives that are consciously manipulated in the simultaneous processes of narrating the past to create the present and using images from the present to narrate the past. Human memory is emotional, can be caught up in the semantics of words and the structures of language, and can be embedded in nerves and muscles that unconsciously remember how to walk, how to talk, how to hold one's body in certain social situations, and how to perform complex skills (Chakrabarty 1998). It can be part of a social habitus that is re-created through the reproduction of the social situations in which an individual is embedded (Bourdieu 1990). Beyond the individual human person, "memory" can be embedded in institutional structures, contained in documents and computer files, and reproduced in architecture, in bus routes, in place-names, in parks, monuments, and the layout of the city itself. Accidental forgetting, the politically motivated silencing of rejected (perhaps even previously dominant) narratives, and the physical erasure of previously lived urban environments are negative processes that intertwine dialectically with processes of memory.

Here, some of the works on urban theory discussed above become more useful. Drawing on the work of Walter Benjamin, scholars like Robinson emphasize how the urban spectacles of advertising, as well as the constant building, deconstruction, and reconstruction of urban space, give rise to states of consciousness in which the old and the new, modernity and tradition consistently intermingle. Especially powerful here is the work of Steve Pile (2005) who focuses on the phantasmagoria of urban life: dreams, cityscapes of the imagination, magic, vampires, and ghosts. Pile links the dialectical interaction of the old and the new in the urban imaginary to the transformations resulting from urbanization itself. Common urban features like monuments and monumental architecture, advertising and neon lights, rapid urban renewal, and spaces where mingling among strangers of different ages, ethnicities, and genders takes place inform the dreamscapes and memory work of urban people. In short, Pile neither denies the importance of urbanization as a form of social transformation nor ignores the ways in which the "tradition" of the past is brought into the modernity of the present but rather links the two. Throughout this portrayal of Zouping's urban transformation, I detail particular forms of both remembering and forgetting, of both reconstructing and erasing. Like Pile, I attempt to show not only that modernity and tradition forever intermingle in practices of memory but also that the transformations of urbanization in fact create the conditions for the intermingling.

The second theoretical strategy for portraying Zouping's convoluted urbanization builds on Daoist philosophies of transformation. In an exchange with Judith Farquhar, Qicheng Zhang contrasts the metaphysics of the Taijitu with that of black/white dualisms (Farquhar and Zhang 2012: 283–84) (figure 1). For Zhang, images of black/white dualisms imply two things that exist in a state of mutual opposition, that are entirely separate and independent from one another. With such a metaphysics, the only kind of historical transformation that can occur is the complete replacement of one formation by the other.

Consider the ways in which various forms of classic modernization theory have yielded black/white pictures of social transformation. For Marx and many Marxists, social transformation only occurs as the result of a revolution. Once the capitalist revolution occurred, then all categories of thought and practice became colored by the imprint of capitalist society. No reform to capitalist society could be useful as only a socialist revolution could overturn capitalist evil. Andre Gunder Frank's question—when does capitalism begin?—is thus quite uncomfortable for Marxist thinkers because it focuses attention on the impossibility of both a sudden and totalizing transforma-

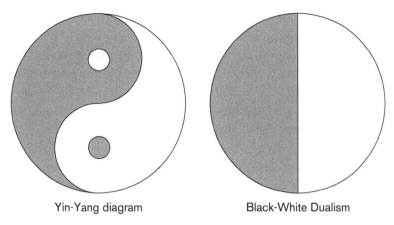

Yin-Yang diagram   Black-White Dualism

FIGURE 1. Taijitu and black/white dualism.

tion to capitalism and a sudden and totalizing transformation out of capital-ism.[6] For Durkheim, the transformations of modernity constitute "social facts." In his analysis of divorce and anomic suicide among men (Durkheim 1952: 259–73), for example, correlations between increases in the divorce rate and increases in suicide among divorced men are taken to demonstrate that the moral structure of society in general had shifted and that this shift must be considered a shift from one type of society to an entirely different type. Left out of the explanation entirely are points of continuity between the two "types" of society, including the cases of divorce and male suicide in places with relatively low divorce and suicide rates, cases of divorce and nonsuicide in both types of places, and cases of nondivorce and nonsuicide in places with relatively high rates of both. The focal points and lacunae of Durkheim's argument result from his debates with Gabriel Tarde and Durkheim's result-ant desire to define social facts as sui generis. But all the emphasis on sui generis social types prevents him from illuminating points of continuity and similarity between historically or geographically contiguous societies.[7] The work of Michel Foucault also often relies on stark contrasts between the modern and premodern periods. Foucault's *Discipline and Punish,* for exam-ple, famously opens with a contrast between a public execution, the drawing and quartering of the regicide Damiens in 1757, and the daily timetable of a boy's reformatory in Paris during the 1830s. Foucault emphasizes that though less than a century separates the two forms of punishment, they each define very different penal styles. The period between them was when "the entire economy of punishment was redistributed" (Foucault 1979: 7).

In contrast to black/white images of social transformation, the yin/yang diagram suggests mutual incorporation and interdependence. There is a bit of yin in the heart of yang and vice versa. Transformation involves different dynamic juxtapositions of the elements, not simple replacement. When I introduce the transformations of Zouping's urbanizations in this book, I strive to depict the reorganization of the new and the old rather the simple replacement of one thing by another.

Returning to the dialogue between Farquhar and Zhang, consider how Farquhar agrees with Zhang about the metaphysics of transformation but cautions against essentializing the two models as East/West cultural contrasts in the manner of the black/white dualism he is rejecting. She relates yin/yang metaphysics directly to the topic of modernity through the writing of Bruno Latour (1993):

> Latour has made a similar argument about modernity, arguing that a dualistic "modern constitution" that distinguishes nature from culture, objects from subjects, and (arguably) "tradition" from "modernity" has formed the modern understanding of history and culture, but has never been a very useful way of actually accounting for the realities of "social-natural" life. So he says "we have never been modern." The simple dualisms of the modern constitution have not explained anything, and what we need is closer attention to the nondualistic mixtures of social-natural and traditional-modern in worlds of practice. (Farquhar and Zhang 2012: 284)

The traditions of theorizing transformation that have emerged from Daoism can be quite complex. In Chinese medicine, diseases are not simply present or absent but evolve through multiple stages as imbalances of yin and yang constantly recalibrate in reaction to treatment and move around different systems of the body. Health is a matter of a proper dynamic and vulnerable balance, not the simple replacement of yin with yang or vice versa. When Farquhar and Zhang (2012: 251) turn their discussion to practical problems of the maintenance of health and "the nurturing of life," they often refer to the doubled phrase "living, living, changing, changing" (*shengsheng huahua*). Life, in this conception, is a process of unceasing, multiple reproduction and change. Transformation and reproduction are intimately linked.

Carla Nappi (2009) affirms this position in her reflexive discussion of analyses of natural history in "early modern" China. She simultaneously examines how Chinese naturalists understood processes of transformation and how these modes of understanding themselves transformed in the social dynamics of early modernity in China. Natural processes of reproduction, metamorphosis, and development, of the digestion of food and the decomposition of death, were analyzed so that their transformative powers might be applied in medical situations. Resemblance was an important aspect of transformation, as it allowed the identification of both parallel processes and continuities over time. Like Farquhar and Zhang, Nappi identifies an epistemology that takes transformation as ceaseless. She translates the favorite poem of Li Shizhen, the famous sixteenth-century naturalist, as follows:

> Transformation of the universe goes on without respite.
> Cycles of ebb and flow—now advancing, now retreating.
> Image and essence evolve, a transforming magicicad.
> Boundlessly subtle, beyond language's pale.
> Ruin, Fortune's mistress; Fortune, Ruin's flame.
> Misery and joy crowd the gate, blessing and disaster seed the soil.
>
> (Nappi 2009: 138–39)

Applying such an organic perspective to Zouping's urbanization requires close attention to the multiple, crisscrossing paths of various forms of memory. It requires seeing how practices, ideas, ideals, fantasies, dreams (and nightmares) are displaced, reinvented, or shifted rather than simply eliminated. At the same time, when so much that is new arrives in so short a period, it requires acknowledging that the rate of shifting and displacement has been extreme and that a transformation as large as simultaneous urbanization, industrialization, and growth in governing apparatus is historically more significant than just any form of social change. Finally, it requires a focus on the place of social production and reproduction in the processes of transformation. How have the modes of reproducing the household themselves changed even as they continue to reproduce this central social unit? What social processes of valuation are entangled with the reproduction of households, and how have these changed? How have the social processes of producing people themselves evolved, and what processes of valuation are caught up with these? Both the centrifugal and centripetal aspects of these processes must be acknowledged.

To continue the organic perspective and to give a label to the particular view of urbanization I wish to adopt in this book, I have settled on using the adjective *recombinant* alongside processual nouns like urbanization, industrialization, modernization, and transformation. I derive the term from the notion of recombinant DNA, which is used in genetics to refer to the exchange of strands of DNA resulting in a new genetic combination, but it could be used to describe almost any physical, biological, or social transformation. In chemical reactions, electrons are recombined in a way that yields a new chemical substance. In metamorphosis, nutrients are absorbed from outside of the body as cellular material is recycled, reproduced, and grown to yield a transformed organism. In ecological succession, complex ecological "communities," or systems, are transformed over time through the in-migration of outside organisms, the differential reproductive success of existing organisms, and the recycling of various forms of organic material. Note from these examples that recombinant transformations can involve the combination of both materials originally present at a given site and those introduced or absorbed from outside of the place where the transformation began. Even in processes of cellular genetics, material may be transferred between cells and proteins can be absorbed across cellular membranes. In addition, transformations do not always have to take place in the same manner or at the same rate; however, common patterns can emerge. In this book, Zouping's urbanization and industrialization and all the related social transformations are depicted as recombinant. Since I conceive of processes of transformation as involving the recombination of preexisting elements (whether present at the site or absorbed from outside) into a new mixture or pattern, when depicting Zouping's recombinant urbanization I strive for a rhetorical balance between explaining what is new in the posttransformation pattern, examining how the pattern draws on preexisting elements, and analyzing how various aspects of social transformation interrelate.[8]

CHINESE URBANIZATION

The speed of urbanization in China over the past quarter century has been mind-boggling, and urbanization has occurred in many forms. Large national cities such as Beijing and Shanghai have grown into global megacenters, doubling or tripling their populations and expanse of built-up space. Provincial capitals have likewise rapidly expanded, and those in the western provinces are becoming increasingly dominated by the ethnic majority Han population (see Gaubatz 1996 for a history of five such cities until roughly 1990). Along the eastern seaboard especially, even many prefectural-level cities have grown in population to over a million people (Airriess 2008). The Pearl River Delta (PRD) has transformed from a largely rural area into the world's largest single contiguous metropolitan area, covering thousands of square kilometers from Guangzhou in the north to Hong Kong and Macau in the south, with Shenzhen, now housing a population of over ten million, growing from scratch. Medium-sized cities have become large, towns have become cities, and villages have become towns. Not all of this urbanization is "real." A spectral refraction of the growth of Beijing, Shanghai, and the PRD appears in the construction of "ghost cities"—places where cadres and developers have erected buildings and constructed infrastructure but to which no person or industry has moved (Shepard 2015).

As a single case, Zouping's urbanization cannot represent all of China, but it can be seen as mediating and combining contradictory aspects of urbanization found in different types of Chinese cities. To begin, Zouping is in no sense a ghost city. Industrialization and population growth have accompanied the replacement of agricultural land with roads and buildings. Yet, as is the case with perhaps all instances of urban growth, every new building and every new enterprise carries the risk that people and activity will not be drawn to it. In marketized regimes of urbanization, this risk is caught up in processes of speculation and all of the gossip, promotional activities, anxiety, and bargaining that such processes generate. Many upwardly mobile Zouping urbanites, like those elsewhere, enjoy and fear their own participation in these processes.

In terms of size, Zouping is much larger than many of the surrounding towns or villages in the same county, some of which have gained the look and infrastructure of an urban area without the population growth. With roughly 350,000 people, Zouping might count as a midsized city in a global comparative scale. It is roughly the same size as two other cities I have lived in, Cincinnati, Ohio, and Canberra, Australia. But in China it cannot count as a middling urban center. China has well over one hundred cities with a population of over one million (in August 2014 Wikipedia estimated 160). Administratively, China officially ranks cities into four tiers (directly administered or national, provincial, prefectural, and county level). Zouping is only a fourth tier, or county-level, city. Nevertheless, as such, it at least has a place in the governing hierarchy. Consequently, it has many advantages over villages and towns that have grown, industrialized, and urbanized without gaining a place in the administrative hierarchy. Zouping has its own bureaucracy, its own claim on industrial tax revenues, its own city planning agencies, and the ability to influence the distribution of government services like schools, police, and hospitals under its jurisdiction. Zouping's physical size and place in the administrative hierarchy would not deserve much attention if it were not for the particular biases of the existing literature on China's urbanization. While scholars have paid considerable attention to China's large urban centers and the urbanization of the PRD, and also to China's rural areas, very little work explores either processes of urbanization or lived experience in China's county-level cities or cities with a population range of 100,000 to 1,000,000.[9] There are hundreds of county-level cities in China in the same size range as Zouping, most of which have also seen massive growth over the past fifteen years. This book hopes to give such cities the attention they deserve.

More interesting than its in-between size or administrative status is the way in which Zouping is located between differing models of urbanization within China. Writings on Chinese urbanization during the 1980s emphasized how China provided an alternative model to Western, capitalist urbanization. Martin Whyte and William Parish's thirty-year-old classic, *Urban Life in Contemporary China*, suggested that the urbanization that occurred under the planned economy of the Maoist era took a different shape from the urbanization that had occurred in Western countries. Families and neighborhood communities remained close-knit, they argued, while crime, drug addiction, and prostitution seemed rare and slums or shantytowns nonexistent. The interlinked systems of household registration (*hukou*), work units (*danwei*), and neighborhood committees (*juwei*) enabled both the administration of the planned economy and the tight control of urban life. The household registration system made it difficult to migrate from rural to urban areas without official government sponsorship and approval. The work-unit system reduced the distance between the private sphere of household reproduction and the public sphere of work by making the provision of housing, health care, schools, and more the business of the employer. Many work units hence became "total institutions" that provided widespread welfare benefits and in so doing were able to regulate most aspects of their employees' lives (Bray 2005; Henderson and Cohen 1984). The street committees regulated those who were not employed by work units. In short, under the Maoist or work-unit model of urbanization, everyone and everything urban appeared to be heavily regulated and tightly governed (Whyte and Parish 1984).

During the 1980s and 1990s, as collective farms in rural areas were split up and space for the marketing of industrial products outside the national economic plan grew, township and village enterprises (TVEs) emerged in many former rural communes. In China, this process was known as the "leave the soil but not the countryside" (*litu bulixiang*) model of economic development. Greg Guldin (1997) called this China's "rural urbanization," and Guldin and others saw this process as a form of in situ industrialization and modernization (without urbanization). In both the planned economy/work-unit-driven model of urbanization of the 1980s and earlier and the rural urbanization of the 1990s, tight-knit communities were maintained or reproduced and the social processes modernization theorists typically associated with urbanization, including alienation, individualization, increased interactions with strangers, and rising anomie, seemed absent.

As the prominence of TVEs faded during the late 1990s, new models and processes of Chinese urbanization emerged. Large numbers of rural migrants began leaving the countryside and finding employment in cities and in the factories of the rapidly urbanizing Pearl River Delta. The places where they lived and the terms of their employment were much less regulated than had been the case with work units, and the resulting processes of urbanization began to more closely resemble those that Whyte and Parish had previously seen as more Western than Chinese. Migrant workers were ruthlessly exploited, and their employers paid as little attention as possible to either their welfare or the regulation of their lives outside of work (Jacka 2005). Unregulated "shantytown" areas emerged, and within these areas drug addiction, prostitution, and petty crime became easy enough to observe (Zhang 2001; Zheng 2009). Anthropologists studying the lives of the residents of these areas often emphasized themes such as alienation (Pun 2005; Yan 2008), anomie (Liu 2002), individualization (Yan 2009, 2010a, 2010b), and cosmopolitanism (Jankowiak 2004b) that classic theorists of modernization associated with urbanization in general.

As later work by Whyte (2010) and many others have emphasized, though during the 1980s the household registration policy was loosened enough to enable migration to occur, it still plays a major role in ensuring that migrant workers remain second-class citizens in the places where they work. The household registration policy links people to the particular place (village, town, or city) where they are registered. Since government services and benefits are distributed through local governments, people registered in wealthy places often receive much better benefits than those registered in poorer places. People registered as peasants (*nongmin*) in rural villages are eligible to receive allocations of land in their villages and were treated more leniently by the birth control policy than the urban registrants.[10] But people in urban areas often have access to much better schools, much better health and welfare benefits, and even preference for certain types of (government-controlled) jobs and licenses to operate certain types of businesses. People migrating from poor areas to wealthier areas for work are usually ineligible for social benefits in the places where they work. The exact nuances of how the household registration policy works are quite complex and vary from place to place, as local governments have great leeway to determine how the policy will be implemented under their jurisdictions. There are various intermediate categories of registration, including "temporary household registration" for migrant workers and "collective household registrations" for people who move to a given locale under the auspices of a particular institution, such as students moving to a large city to attend university. Collective household registrations are administered by the organization in question (e.g., the university) rather than the local government.

In Zouping, as is the case in many other fourth-tier cities, the household registration policy does not discriminate against in-migrating workers as much as it does in larger cities. Some of the larger employers in Zouping have collective household registrations for their in-migrating employees. For those working elsewhere, temporary registrations are available to anyone with steady employment. Crucially, in Zouping, anyone with a temporary or collective household registration may send his or her children to the local schools under the same conditions as those with an urban Zouping household registration. That is to say, the children can attend the local primary and junior middle schools in their district for free and can attend academic and vocational senior middle schools for the same fees as local residents.[11] In addition, welfare benefits in Zouping are extremely low,[12] and licenses to start new businesses are granted as freely to migrants as to locals. As a consequence, even though Zouping offers migrants with a steady employment history the right to transfer their household registrations entirely to Zouping (i.e., not just in collective or temporary form), very few take up this offer. Completely transferring one's registration to urban Zouping would entail giving up both one's land rights in one's village home and the more lenient treatment the birth control policy in one's home may offer.[13] In practice, the only people who transfer their household registrations completely to Zouping are middle-class workers who come to take white-collar jobs in Zouping's schools, hospitals, banks, and government. For these people, accepting an urban Zouping household registration is a condition of employment.

For many scholars, the Pearl River Delta has become the starting point for understanding China's urbanization, but the patterns of urbanization emerging there are in many ways extreme. There urbanization has been driven by foreign investment and the arrival of migrant workers from distant parts of China. Local governments have worked with foreign investors to use the household registration policy to ensure that the profits to be gained from industrialization are split between the local (also formerly rural) population and the investors, with as little as possible going to migrant workers from distant rural locales. Though there is variety among them, these local governments use the profits from urbanization and industrialization to shower welfare benefits on the citizens of their localities while denying even the most basic benefits or even rights to migrant workers from elsewhere. Local "villagers-in-the-city" (*cheng zhong cun ren*) become a privileged minority, often a rentier class, sometimes living in gated communities among hordes of outsiders in newly urbanized settings. The vast majority of factory workers are migrants from afar, and the fate of these two groups of people diverges sharply.[14]

Against the extreme of the PRD, Beatriz Carillo (2011) describes the gradual urbanization of a town in Shanxi province. The town is slowly industrializing and expanding into a small city, but it is not doing so by attracting migrant workers from distant rural locales. Rather, the workers come from the surrounding countryside. Since the workers are locals, as in Zouping, the local government does not use the household registration policy to discriminate against them. Moreover, these workers are much less alienated from their rural roots and their extended families than the migrant workers of the PRD. In comparison to the PRD, this form of urbanization can be considered a type of in situ development, much like the earlier "leaving the soil but not the countryside" model, but in this case the new factory workers often do leave their rural homes to move to a city but one that is quite close by.

Zouping sits between the urbanization of the PRD and that described by Carillo. On the one hand, many factory workers come from nearby rural areas and factory workers are not discriminated against by the local government. Most of the major factories in Zouping sprang up from local government-run TVEs, which saw providing jobs and benefits for local workers as a significant aspect of their raison d'être. Some of these enterprises now provide work-unit-like housing and other benefits for many of their workers. On the other hand, industrialization in Zouping has been rapid enough to also attract large numbers of migrant workers from more distant locales. Despite their access to local schools, these workers are in many senses more alienated than those from nearby. Many Zouping factories split workers into the categories "contract" (*hetong*) and "temporary" (*linshi*), with the former receiving more work-unit-like benefits than the latter. While this split does not necessarily map directly onto the local/nonlocal division, there is significant overlap. In addition, the speed of the physical expansion of Zouping's urban area has created numerous "villages-in-the-city" (*cheng zhong cun*), and many of the people from these villages have been able to parlay the terms on which their land was confiscated into an advantageous class position, though not to the same extent as is widespread in the PRD. There are both shantytowns on the urban fringe and work-unit-like housing complexes provided by the new factories for their workers.

In sitting between the PRD and the town described by Carillo, Zouping also mediates many of the other extremes described above: between a model of in situ urbanization and one that relies on migrant workers from afar for population growth; between the well-regulated, work-unit/government-controlled form of urbanization depicted by Whyte and Parish and the unregulated free-for-all they saw as representative of Western urbanization. It also lies between the extremes of anomie, alienation, and individuation that some modernization theorists saw as universally connected to urbanization and that anthropologists have been finding increasing evidence for in the PRC and the reproduction of practices of kinship, dreams, and lifestyles from a rural past/present to which many Zouping urbanites remain intimately connected.

RESEARCHING RECOMBINANT URBANIZATION

A city, even one of moderate size like Zouping, is not a single face-to-face community that may be easily scrutinized with traditional ethnographic methods. My understanding of Zouping's urbanization derives from multiple research methods and many visits to Zouping over a long period. I first visited Zouping county in 1988 but did not spend much time in the county seat until the mid-1990s, just before its rapid expansion began. I completed a major project on education reform in Zouping during the 2000s (Kipnis 2011a), which, in addition to enabling me to understand the local schools and educational system, allowed me to witness the transformation of built- up space, to conduct interviews with nearly one hundred households in the county seat, and to form relatively close relationships with ten families whom I would visit at least once every time I came to Zouping. From 2008 to 2011, I undertook further research specifically with the idea of writing this book.

During this latter period, I targeted what I saw as two major gaps in my knowledge of the city. First, I felt I did not know enough about the Weiqiao Pioneering Group (Weiqiao Chuangye Jituan), which is by far the largest employer and taxpayer in Zouping. The Weiqiao Group began as a cloth-producing TVE in a town in the northwestern corner of the county and grew into the largest cloth producer in the world. It has diversified into aluminium refining, clothing, and electricity production. It moved into the county seat as it expanded during the first years of the twenty-first century and by 2006 employed more than one hundred thousand workers there. Since the early 2000s Weiqiao has proved impossible for me to investigate directly. I had conducted interviews with its leaders and taken tours of some of its factories when it was relatively small, but by the mid-2000s Weiqiao had become so large and famous in China that it was besieged with interview and tour requests. To maintain good relations with the government, it consistently offered investigation tours to visiting groups of Party cadres from other parts of the province and country, but it no longer had time to accommodate the interview requests of a sole foreign researcher.

Fortunately, three indirect research strategies proved more fruitful. First, because of the earlier education project, I had good relationships with the schools that the children of Weiqiao workers attended. Working with these schools, I managed to complete another fifty household interviews with families who worked at Weiqiao in various capacities. These interviews involved households with a child in either the second or the fifth grade, which gave me access to parents who themselves, on average, belonged to slightly different age cohorts. The parents of the fifth-graders were mostly born in the mid-1970s, before the onset of the birth control policy. The parents of the second-graders were mostly born in the late 1970s, with a few born as late as 1981. Because of the onset of the birth control policy, these parents averaged many fewer children than those of the fifth-graders.

Outside of the schools, I pursued a more youthful vantage on working in Weiqiao through two sources. First, by hanging out at the roller skating rinks and other entertainment venues where some young Weiqiao workers spent their free time, I was able to conduct unstructured interviews with twenty unmarried and childless workers between the ages of 18 and 23. Second, I completed interviews with a class of thirty-five 16-year-old students in a Zouping technical school whose major was designed to enable its graduates to work in Weiqiao and other Zouping factories. Finally, because of the size and fame of the Weiqiao Group, I was able to collect hundreds of newspaper articles, yearbooks, and other documentary sources on Weiqiao's growth. These sources, alongside similar ones for Zouping's second largest employer, the Xiwang Group, constitute the background of the narrative of economic development in chapter 3.

The second gap in my knowledge of Zouping's development involved the government and the way its planning and regulating activities affected the expansion of Zouping's built space. In 2009 and 2010, I conducted sixteen formal interviews with officials in the government's construction, planning, and land bureaus; in the city district government offices (*jiedao banshichu*); in community offices (*shequ*); and with the heads of villages-in-the-city (*cheng zhong cun*). I also collected thirteen volumes of government-produced yearbooks and other written sources that narrate the planning and growth of the city from an official perspective.

Other research activities conducted since 2008 include interviews with a group of twenty female students who had moved to Zouping to attend a vocational school class on teaching kindergarten; formal interviews with three department heads in the Xiwang Group; dozens of informal interviews with workers in shops, restaurants, and hotels; formal interviews with the owners of eleven small businesses (stores and restaurants); and hours spent exploring the nooks and crannies of the continually expanding city. In all, between 2005 and 2012 I spent close to thirteen months living in Zouping and conducted over two hundred formal interviews with households or single people, formal interviews with nearly twenty government and industrial leaders, and scores of informal interviews; I also collected thousands of pages of documents and statistics and witnessed much of Zouping's transformation firsthand. As an anthropologist, I primarily attempted to construct a view of the city's transformation from below, from multiple worm's-eye views, but supplemented this approach with written sources and interviews that allow a partial reconstruction of this growth from a bird's-eye view.

James Ferguson introduces his own ethnographic methods with a quote from Marcel Mauss: "Ethnology is like fishing; all you need is a net to swing, and you'll be sure that you'll catch something" (cited in Ferguson 1999: 17). Ferguson writes that he did not start out with the intention to investigate decline, but decline is what his fieldwork yielded, and he could not ignore it. He even suggests inverting Mauss's metaphor: it is not so much that the ethnographer catches the fish but rather that the fish catches the ethnographer. While in the last (post-2008) years of my fieldwork I purposefully set out to investigate Zouping's urbanization, I made that decision only after the fish had already caught me. When I first went to Zouping in 1988, I could not have imagined what the place would be like by 2008. As the processes of Zouping's urbanization, industrialization, economic growth, and social transformation unfolded before my eyes, I could not ignore it. Though discussions of simultaneous urbanization, industrialization, and social transformation are rarer than theorizations of decline in contemporary qualitative social science, I doubt that I have caught, or been caught by, the rarest fish in the sea. Aspects of Zouping's story are illustrative of social processes in many Chinese cities, of processes that occurred slightly earlier in many other East Asian cities, and, to a lesser degree, of processes that have occurred in many places all over the world and that may yet occur in still other places. To the extent that Friedman and Friedman's theorization of modernity is correct, there should be a rough balance among places experiencing decline and those experiencing growth at any moment in the world.

ORGANIZATION OF THIS BOOK

This book is organized in two parts. Part 1, "Transformations," comprising chapters 2 through 5, takes a bird's-eye view. It both provides the context for the life stories presented in part 2 and explores historical dynamics with a certain analytic distance. Chapter 2 focuses on the physical expansion of urban space and the always recombinant nature of planning, that is to say, the contradictions and conjunctures between different plans: those of one government department and those of another, those of government departments and private builders, those of yesterday, three days ago, and today, and those of relatively powerful actors and everyday citizens. It draws on interviews with government officials and the narratives contained in government documents, maps of Zouping collected since the early 1990s, and a lived sense of how different parts of the city reflect both the planning ethos of different eras and the unplanned (or nongovernment-planned) reactions to government thinking.

Chapter 3 examines the evolution of productive industry in Zouping (what some might call the economic basis of the city's growth). It relies primarily on written documents to narrate the growth of the city's largest economic entities, the present-day Weiqiao and Xiwang Groups. It depicts this evolution as simultaneously constrained by the imperatives of global and national markets and the roots of these enterprises in the TVEs of the late

1980s. The path dependency of these groups is shaped by both their local histories and the telos of Capital.

Chapter 4 examines the consumer revolution that has emerged in Zouping. It considers how new products and services—automobiles, computers, mobile phones, supermarkets, restaurants, nightlife, tourism, and retail—transform human possibilities and create new desires in ways that react dialectically to the scope of possibilities and desires that existed in previous periods. This chapter relies both on my own notes on how the field of consumer possibilities has evolved over the years and the interviews I conducted with Zouping's residents.

Chapter 5 considers how the transformation of public space affects the imaginary experience of living in Zouping. More speculative than the other chapters, it considers both the practical use of public space and the images extant in those spaces—from monumental governmental displays to advertising—to suggest ways in which urban imaginary experience is transformed through recombination during processes of urbanization.

Part 2, "Transformers Transformed," focuses on the people who have come to live in Zouping, constituting its tenfold population growth. It divides these people into groups to reflect both the ways in which Zouping people categorize each other and common classificatory schemes of the social sciences. In all, five groups are examined in five separate chapters: villagers-in-the-city, married migrant factory workers from villages inside the county or from nearby parts of neighboring counties, married migrant factory workers from distant locales (both from other places in Shandong province and from other provinces), middle-class families (government workers, teachers, doctors, and accountants), and youth. Roughly speaking, these five groups represent class factions in the Weberian sense of facing common structures of constraint and opportunity. The major structures of opportunity involve place of origin, which influences access both to certain government derived opportunities and to local kinship networks, and educational attainment, which influences career path. Yet, despite needing to find their way in a hierarchical society, people in these groups cannot objectively be located in any fixed hierarchy; senses of social status in Zouping are both evolving and contested. The rapid evolution of Zouping society requires treating youth separately as the social structures that will constrain and form them are still emerging. The young people I interviewed—in vocational schools, in the roller-skating rink in the Development Zone, in restaurants and hotels (where they were service workers)—were still making choices, and being pushed and pulled into choices, about their careers and familial futures. The processes in which their choices were made reveal both extant structures and ideologies of status and the fluid and contested nature of social status in Zouping.

The second part of the book takes a worm's-eye view of the transformations discussed in part 1. It focuses on the human experience of living in a new and rapidly expanding city. Each group lives and is defined by a different set of contradictions that open up different fields of possible personal transformations. The villagers-in-the-city are caught between the property regimes of their local village communities and the cosmopolitanism that a growing city and a shrinking country and world offer. The nearby migrants are caught between city living and their densely lived familial networks that link to still-farming communities. The migrants from afar are caught between the opportunities of a growing city and the call of a distant home. The middle classes are caught between a desire for distinction and the fact of living in a place that depends on factories for its existence. Finally, young people are caught between an opportunity structure largely shaped by factories and ideologies that disparage factory work. Despite these defining contradictions, experiences within each group vary. The chapters in this part do their best to wrestle with the diverse life stories and opinions contained within each group and to relate these to the structure of the group itself.

Before turning to these stories, however, let us consider the recent history of the place. How has the physical space of Zouping evolved over the years, and what plans informed this evolution?

———

PART ONE

Transformations

INTRODUCTION

During the late 1980s, I did not really enjoy spending time in Zouping. My research was focused on a village about 20 kilometers north of the town. Each time I went to the village, I would have to spend a night in the county seat, as transportation was not as convenient as it is today. The town seemed less clean, less comfortable, and less hospitable than the village. It was not set up for independent visitors, especially foreign ones. The few hotels and restaurants were run by the government or its enterprises. They were old and lacked facilities such as regular hot water for showers or easy access to boiled drinking water; more important, service, at least to outsiders, was poor. The hotel personnel saw little need to attend the needs of "customers" who were not accompanied by the leadership of the county or their immediate boss and with whom they had no personal relationship. Most of the people in the county seat worked for the government or one of the state-owned factories and were too busy with their lives to mingle with a strange foreigner. Admittedly, even then, the county seat had its attractions. On the southeastern side of the city was Yellow Mountain (Huang Shan), which provided a nice space for walking and views over the town. The government offices, in which I would arrange permission to visit the village, were located there, as was the only bank in the county where it was possible to exchange foreign currency. Yet there were few spaces, such as parks, cafés, or shopping malls, where one could easily mingle with new acquaintances. Though I could walk from one end of the town to the other, at times I felt constrained by the lack of public transport. There were no buses or taxis, and I did not own a bicycle at that time. The village was where I knew people, where locals would invite me to drink tea and chat, where I could experience human warmth and more easily look after my everyday needs.

Over the 1990s, as I spent more time in the county seat, I witnessed what seemed then to be fairly rapid growth and also began to enjoy my time there. I became more intimate with the town's street markets and stores, its church and hotels. I also learned about Zouping from the work of many other scholars who conducted research there.[1] But the growth and change of the 1990s turned out to be nothing compared to what would happen in the 2000s. The rapid change of that decade in many ways either erased the changes of the 1990s or made developments that previously felt progressive seem like dinosaurs—both out of place and out of time.

Depicting the contours of this change, as I witnessed it and then reconstructed it from documentary sources, is the purpose of the first part of this book. The four chapters of this part provide a context for the narratives in part 2 about how Zouping residents came to live in and experience the city and also give a sense of the vast web of interlinked changes that a transformation on the scale of Zouping's urbanization requires. Changes in built space could not have occurred without economic growth, and economic growth could not have occurred without an expansion of built space. Both of these forms of growth enable new forms of consumption, which, in return, contribute to economic growth by enabling consumers to live more efficiently, by enticing consumers to work harder, and by undergirding businesses that contribute tax revenues to the city government. The growth in consumption also opens space for new forms of phantasmagoria—the fleeting images, sensations, and experiences that make Zouping feel like a "modern," urban city rather than a rural town. I begin with a consideration of the expansion and development of Zouping's built space and the place of planning in structuring this expansion.

TWO

Recombinant Planning

In his classic book, *Seeing Like a State* (1998), James Scott offers a rather negative view of city planning. He shows that city plans and planned cities tend
to be modeled on a gridlike pattern in order to make them legible and convenient to officials and outsiders rather than livable for insiders. He argues
that regular street layouts and numbers make the population easier to "moni-
tor, count, assess, and manage" and suggests that in authoritarian societies,
"where there is no effective way to assert another reality, fictitious facts-on-
paper can often be made eventually to prevail on the ground, because it is on
behalf of such pieces of paper that police and army are deployed" (82, 83).

There is much in Zouping's development that Scott's book illuminates.
Since the late 1980s the layout has progressively become more gridlike, the
streets have been named in a manner that renders them easy for outsiders
(including leading officials who are often rotated in from other places) to
recognize, and the state in Zouping certainly has been authoritarian. In addition, as Scott anticipates in *Seeing Like a State* (and brings out more fully in
later work [Scott 2009]), it is precisely in those urban spaces where the central
plan is least applied where those who wish to evade regulation reside and
where "anarchy" seems to reign. But there is also much in Zouping's development that Scott's work renders opaque. His work singularizes both the state
and the plan. It explains neither the diversity of "the state," with its many
levels, bureaus, and niches that effectively blend state and society, nor the
diversity of "planners," who both complement and contradict one another
and draw plans to both guide implementation and mask the ways in which
implementation will actually take place. Perhaps most important, in the
context of a rapidly developing and hence changing place Scott's work
obscures the ways in which the latest plans overwrite and contradict previous

plans, leading to a palimpsest even when order is imagined. Finally, Scott's focus on the state's self-interest renders invisible the fact that even in a place as authoritarian as China the state's self-interest is not always opposed to that of at least some of "the people," that it might be in the state's interest to create a livable city (where, after all, the state's cadres will themselves reside) and, hence, that there might be a fair amount of public good that comes out of the state's planning efforts.

To illustrate these contradictions, this chapter presents a detailed account of urban development in Zouping for the period from roughly 1985 to 2010. Readers who are not interested in a blow-by-blow account of Zouping's continuous reconstruction may wish to skim the first two sections of this chapter.

Map 2 displays Zouping town in the late 1980s. It reveals a bit of Zouping's historical layering, as the outlines of the old imperial town, with its walled and gated court, can be surmised from the names of some of the villages. On the map, the four villages East Gate, West Gate, North Gate, and South Gate (Dongguan, Xiguan, Beiguan, and Nanguan, A, B, C, and D) give name to the places that were immediately outside the north, south, east, and west gates of the imperial county seat. The village named Inside the Walls (Chengli, E), refers to the place that used to be inside the walls of the imperial court. We can see that during the Qing dynasty, Zouping as an "urban" area was not only much smaller than during the 1980s but was located northwest of Zouping's 1980s center. The imperial court walls were partly destroyed during the wars of the first half of the twentieth century and completely dismantled by the local populace for building materials during the first decade of PRC rule. In 1970 the county government moved to the location indicated by the star on the map (Zouping 1992: 50).

During the 1980s, the county government headquarters included both offices and housing for the government cadres and their families. Factories were built on the outskirts of town. In 1987 the streets were renamed in gridlike fashion—Daixi (Black Creek) Roads #1–4 (BC1–4, map 2) and Huangshan (Yellow Mountain) Roads #1–4 (YM1–4)—though they did not at this point form a geometrically perfect grid, as compromises were allowed to route the roads around existing factories, housing, and farmland. Running down the eastern edge of the map is Black Creek Road #6. There was no Black Creek Road #5 at that time, demonstrating that a place for it was allocated by city planners. Most of the urbanized area of the 1980s was contained within the outlines of the area contained by the Black Creek/Yellow Mountain 1–4 grid, with the long-distance bus station (F) located at what

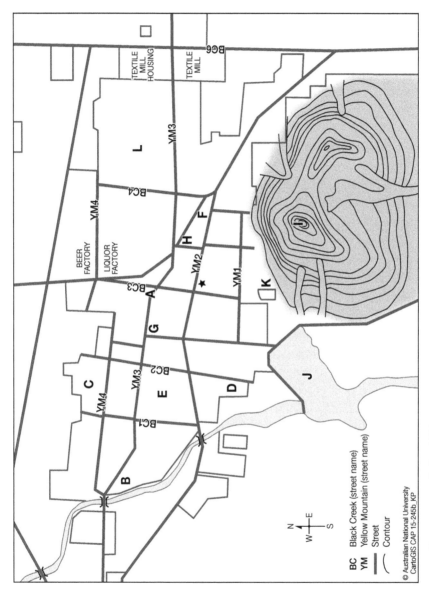

BC   Black Creek (street name)
YM   Yellow Mountain (street name)
——   Street
⌒⌒   Contour

MAP 2. The county seat before 1990.

was then the edge of the town. Most of the town's residents did their food shopping at two covered outdoor markets (G, H), located between Yellow Mountain Roads #2 and #3, to the east and the west of the county government. The main factories of the time, those producing beer, liquor, dyed cloth, and cotton, had housing facilities for their workers on their land. Yellow Mountain (I) along with the March 8 Reservoir (Sanba Shuiku, J), created by a dam across Black Creek,[1] formed geographic barriers at the southern edge of the town.

GRADUAL EXPANSION DURING THE 1980S AND 1990S

In 1935 fewer than 8,000 people lived in the urbanized district of Zouping. By 1982 the population was about 21,500, of which 11,271 had urban household registrations (Zouping 1992: 50). In later years the districts in which the population was counted shifted, so the total figures are not directly comparable, but the numbers for those with urban household registrations are. The population with urban household registrations in the county seat reached 17,653 in 1986 and 28,529 in 1995, more than double the 1982 population with urban household registrations and triple the 1935 population (Zouping 1997: 409). In 2000 the total population of the town reached 50,000 (Jin Ri Zouping 2008: 1).

In 1982 the county government, with the help of the Provincial Urban Design Institute (Sheng Sheji Yuan), created its first city plan. This plan enabled the county government to expand the area of land it could urbanize as part of the county seat and gave the county government some zoning control over the land held by individual government bureaus and state or collective factories in the county seat. It also put the land of fourteen villages within the planning jurisdiction of the town. The plan was officially approved by the provincial government in 1984 and then, after considerable negotiation, modified to include a slightly larger area in 1991 (Jin Ri Zouping 2008: 1; Zouping 1992: 32, 286). The town itself could thus expand to the area shown in map 2.

Growth of the county seat during the 1980s and 1990s relied primarily on the gradual acquisition of agricultural land from the fourteen villages. The ways in which the land from those villages was acquired varied from case to case, though almost all the villages have ended up better off than before. All the villages received thirty years of money to replace grain (*dunliangqian*), an amount equivalent to the value of the wheat that would have been harvested. More important, each village received control over some portion of the newly urbanized land. As its value has increased dramatically over the years, this land has turned into a valuable collective asset, especially for those villages that have developed their land wisely or were located in prime locations. Over the years, some of these villages turned their urbanized collective land over to the county government in exchange for cash payouts. Others developed TVEs or constructed commercial buildings. Several villages also developed collectively or privately owned construction and subcontracting businesses, with the most ambitious offering services that ranged from the supply of construction materials to interior decorating. Through these businesses the villages declared themselves able to construct large buildings from start to finish (Zouping 1997: 4, 11). While all the villages have benefited at least slightly from urbanization, inequality among the villages has greatly increased, with Beiguan, Dongguan, and Anjia (C, A, K, map 2) doing much better than the rest.

In addition to the fourteen villages within the county seat's planning jurisdiction, many near the county seat began converting farmland to other uses. Between 1986 and 1995, roughly 18 square kilometers (over 27,000 *mu*) of farmland was lost in and around the county seat (Zouping 1992: 410). In response to these developments, in the 1991 redrawing of the urban plan, in addition to expanding the official area of the county seat from 11 to 13 square kilometers, the Provincial Urban Planning and Design Institute (Sheng Chengshi Guihua Sheji Yuan) placed nearly 45 square kilometers of land under the planning jurisdiction of the county government (Zouping 1992: 286). In 1995, in part by including Yellow Mountain in the town's territory, the official area of the county seat was expanded to 19 square kilometers (Zouping 2004: 260).

The first years of urban planning in Zouping led to a gradual regularization of the urban grid and the development of urban infrastructure. However, because the funding for improvements in part had to come from the villages-in-the-city (for the bits of land still under their control) and from the urban work units (such as the beer factory), some of these improvements were uneven. The villages that were doing best economically would rebuild their infrastructure before those that were doing poorly. During the late 1980s and early 1990s, the discrepancies were especially evident in housing stock. While many villages still contained adobe houses and left house building to individual families, others collectively built high-quality brick houses for all residents. The village of Dongguan was particularly well-off because of the early success of some of its TVEs. It was relocated in 1987 to allow for the straightening and completion of Yellow Mountain Road #3. On the new plot of land allocated for the village (L, map 2), a spectacular and well-ordered grid of two-story villas was created (Zouping 1997: 287). Dongguan even built a new village headquarters complete with a public square.

The county government undertook some of its own infrastructure projects. Between 1986 and 1995 it gradually straightened, completed, and extended the major roads of the basic Yellow Mountain/Black Creek Road grid. Sidewalks were added to most of these roads. In 1988 the village of Anjia (K, map 2) was relocated to allow the extension of Black Creek Road #3 so that it ran between Yellow Mountain and the March 8 Reservoir, and many new stores, restaurants, and government offices were built along this road. During the early 1990s, the Black Creek Mountain Resort (Daixi Shanzhuang) was built on the slopes of Yellow Mountain overlooking the reservoir. It was the nicest hotel in the town for the next decade. As the 1990s progressed, the town as a whole became more gridlike.

Road building and infrastructure projects outside the county seat also drastically influenced the growth of the town. The most important of these was the completion of the superhighway from the provincial capital of Jinan to the port city of Qingdao in 1994. The highway ran just to the south of Yellow Mountain. An exit was established on Black Creek Road #6. The superhighway drastically reduced travel time between Zouping and Shandong's major cities. Through the port of Qingdao, it also gave Zouping's factories direct access to the export markets of Japan and South Korea. The superhighway also linked Zouping to Jinan's international airport. As the airport was located between Jinan and Zouping, it became quicker and easier to get to the airport from Zouping than from many parts of Jinan. It now takes less than one hour to travel from Zouping to the airport and less than three hours to Qingdao. The county also improved roads between Zouping town and many nearby towns and small cities, both inside and outside the county. Finally, the county government began a campaign to construct a paved road to every village in the county in 1992. With a few exceptions, this goal was reached by 1994. In addition to greatly reducing travel time within the county, these roads altered the nature of the "rural" territory against which the "city" of Zouping could be contrasted. Since 1994 many of Zouping's villages have become more like suburban commuters' communities than independent farming units.

Some of the work units located in the city invested in improving employee housing. During the 1990s I visited new apartments built for employees of the beer factory, construction bureau, courts, and several schools. Although the plans for these buildings had to be nominally approved by the county government, the outcomes varied widely, from independent houses to three-story and even six-story apartment buildings. The building materials and availability of utility hookups varied considerably from place to place, to an extent that would not have been permitted a decade later.

The city drilled new wells and laid enough pipes to provide water to almost all parts of the town by 1995. New storm drainage and sewage pipelines were also laid, with particular attention to industrial drainage for the factories on the north side of town. The government also began piping the steam produced by the electricity plant to many of the work units in the town, thus providing free heating in the winter. Natural gas pipelines were also installed. But as is often the case with infrastructure improvements, the latter projects relied on a combination of county government and local inputs, meaning that only the wealthiest villages and work units were able to secure them. Almost all the work units that provided natural gas to apartments were part of the government itself.

In short, throughout the 1980s and 1990s, Zouping gradually expanded, improved its infrastructure, became more gridlike, and developed economically but not in a manner that would make map 2 seem entirely outmoded. When I visited Zouping in 1999 I noted in my diary that it had become more like a relatively well-off city than an impoverished town, with infrastructure improvements, neon lights, and new stores, hotels, and restaurants giving it an up-to-date feel. It was the new plan of the year 2000, however, that led to the complete rebuilding of the city, rendering the Zouping of the 1980s unrecognizable and making many of the developments of the 1990s obsolete.

THE PLANNED REVOLUTION OF 2000

By the end of the 1990s Zouping was booming. Local industries were beginning to export their goods and tax revenues were growing, but room to expand the city was limited. In 2000 the Zouping government called on the planning department of Shanghai's Tongji University to help draw up a new urban plan. The plan included a new city (*xincheng*) to the south of Yellow Mountain and the Jinan-Qingdao superhighway and a development zone (*kaifaqu*) to the east of Black Creek Road #6. The original Zouping town displayed in map 2 was designated the Old City District (*laochengqu*) and would come to occupy less than one-third of the total space in Zouping city. The new plan was approved in 2001 but then expanded and redrawn in 2003. The 2003 plan placed 83 square kilometers under the control of the city government (Zouping 2004: 332). By 2007 the built-up area of Zouping encompassed 48 square kilometers (compared to 13 square kilometers in 2000) and the population reached 360,000 (Jin Ri Zouping 2008: 1). According to the last figures available (2011), the built-up area of the city comprised 55 square kilometers (Zouping 2012: 317); after 2008 the city stopped keeping population statistics in the same way, so comparable population figures are no longer available.

Map 3 is derived from a 2003 tourist map of Zouping. The "built-up areas" on the map partly indicate the city as it was and partly indicate areas that were under construction or that had simply received planning approval. The map reveals drastic changes in comparison to map 2. Most noticeably, Yellow Mountain (A) marks the center of Zouping rather than its southern border. The Development Zone (B) and the New City (C) were built from scratch (see figures 9, 10). They were laid out on rectangular grids, but even the Old City became more gridlike. As the map indicates, city streets were built or rerouted to align on a straight north, south, east, and west grid. The Old City's Black Creek Roads #3 and #4 and Yellow Mountain Roads #3 and #4 were extended and straightened. Black Creek Road #5 was added, one of the outdoor markets was removed, and the bus station (D) was moved to the edge of the Development Zone to allow for the construction of more commercial space in the Old City. A large manicured garden and plaza area, Yellow Mountain Plaza (E), was situated on the southern edge of Yellow Mountain, just north of the new superhighway and facing the main government building in the New City. The government itself was in the process of moving from its old headquarters in the Old City (marked by a star) to the new headquarters (F) in the New City at the time the tourist map was drawn. The land on which the old government headquarters used to be was auctioned off for commercial use. A huge new campus for the county's number one senior middle school was built in the New City (G), and the old campus was turned into a private junior middle school. The new campus cost 230 million yuan and contained facilities that rival those of almost any secondary school in the United States or Europe: a hard rubber outdoor track and pristine, synthetic athletic fields; an indoor athletic complex housing an Olympic pool, an indoor track, basketball courts, gymnastic facilities, and other athletic equipment; high-quality language, science, and computer labs; libraries; art and

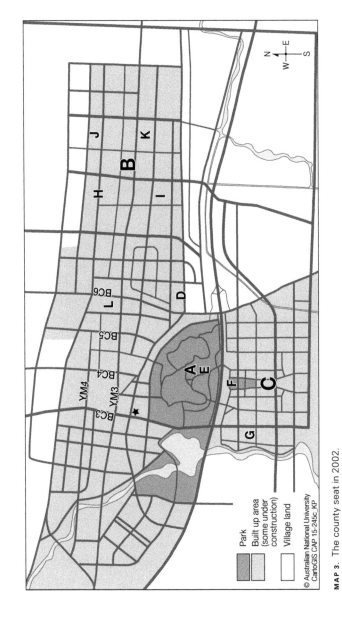

MAP 3. The county seat in 2002.

Park

Built up area
(some under
construction)

Village land

© Australian National University
CartoGIS CAP 15-245c_KP

music buildings with specialized equipment; multimedia projectors and equipment in all classrooms; a completely networked campus; landscaped gardens and green spaces; and dormitories with a capacity for eight thousand students as well as cafeterias, stores, clinics, and pharmacies.

In the Development Zone, the tourist map on which map 3 was based designates two areas for use by the Weiqiao Group (H and I) and an additional one for aluminium refining (J) that was also undertaken by the Weiqiao Group. A fourth area is designated for biotechnology enterprises (K). A fifth area (L), near the border between the Development Zone and the Old City was designated for the Yashi Group, but when the Yashi Group left Zouping it ended up being used by several smaller businesses.

In her work on urbanization and land development, You-tien Hsing (2010: 105–14) draws a sharp distinction between development zones and new cities. She describes development zones as projects in which township and county governments enclosed rural land during the 1990s. She finds that they were often poorly planned, with roads that did not connect to the external grid, and speculative: by declaring the land part of a development zone, for industrial use, local governments hoped that outside investors would come in and improve infrastructure; such hopes often failed to materialize, and despite their name the zones did not develop.[2] In contrast, Hsing finds that new cities were constructed primarily by the governments of large urban areas (cities at the prefectural level and above) during the 2000s. These projects were usually well planned and focused on residential property development. If they failed, it was because property prices fell after construction was completed.

Zouping's simultaneous construction of a development zone and a new city bridges this dichotomy. Both areas were well planned and developed between 2000 and 2006. The construction of both areas was overseen by the county government. Both areas have thrived. After the completion of the initial sections of the New City and the Development Zone, Zouping came to have the tripartite structure of today: Old City, New City, and Development Zone. Officials in the planning bureau and district government offices repeatedly explained to me that the three parts of the city serve different functions; the Development Zone is for industry; the New City is for the government itself, as well as for parks, schools, and residential areas; and the Old City is for commercial services. Though this imagined overview is accurate as a gross generalization, it masks certain realities. The Old City continues to contain some industries, most notably beer and liquor factories.

FIGURE 2. New government headquarters. Photo by author.

These industries were the mainstay of Zouping's economy during the 1980s, and though they are no longer economic focal points, the city government cannot force them to move. In addition, the Old City is still home to many people. The Development Zone has also become a major residential area, as many of the factories that moved there built housing for their workers. In fact, it is the most populated part of Zouping. To service the people living there, schools and shopping malls have been built. In short, despite the differences in emphasis, the Old City and the Development Zone are industrial, commercial, and residential, while the New City is both commercial and residential.

In addition to the new middle school campus, many major public works projects were undertaken during the early 2000s. Between 1999 and 2003, 1.5 billion yuan were spent on infrastructure development in Zouping, with more than 500 million yuan spent on twenty-nine projects in the New City (Zouping 2004: 311–12). Most notably, the basic road grid was completed and underneath each road pipes and wiring for fully modern utility setups, including water, sewerage, gas, Internet, electricity, and heating were laid out. The new government headquarters, a massive twelve-story building, was finished in May 2004 (figure 2). Infrastructure in the Development Zone was completed in conjunction with the large business groups, most notably the Weiqiao Group, which agreed to move there. These groups financed much of the Development Zone road construction and pipe laying, in addition to building their own factories and employee housing. The cost of this

FIGURE 3. Apartments in the New City. Photo by author.

infrastructure was considered an industrial secret and was not publicly reported. But the infrastructure seems solid. At a cost of 40 million yuan each, the Weiqiao Group financed the building of two large new primary schools for the children of their employees. These schools, completed in 2004 and 2007, were built to the specifications of the education bureau for top-flight new schools. They contained science, computer, and language labs; multimedia classrooms; music, dance, and art equipment; and much more—equal to most primary schools in the first world (Kipnis 2011a: 29–31).

Under government contract, several gated, high-rise residential areas (*xiaoqu*) were completed in the New City during the early 2000s (figure 3). Throughout China such areas are designed to prevent through-traffic and to enhance crime prevention and social control (Bray 2008). They typically feature several apartment buildings, green spaces, public facilities such as exercise equipment, and parking areas, all within a walled compound with one or two gates. There may also be guard houses staffed with sentries who can view much of the complex through CCTV cameras. Most Zouping residents see these areas as "modern," comfortable, and luxurious rather than as mechanisms for state control. Not surprisingly, the first high-rise residential areas completed were those for the government employees who previously were housed in the old government headquarters in the Old City. At a subsidized price of slightly more than 1,000 yuan per square meter (which was mostly offset by the compensation received for their old apartments), county government employees purchased units in these new areas. Within a few years the apartments were worth more than 3,000 yuan per square meter. By 2011 they were worth more than 5,000 yuan per square meter. Some non-government New City apartments were built as freestanding buildings, without gated walls.

Infrastructure projects also continued in the Old City, despite the fact that many of them required the undoing and rebuilding of the infrastructure projects of the 1990s. Streetlights were erected, traffic lights were added at many intersections, and sidewalks were widened. In 2005, despite the need to dig up most of the Old City's sidewalks, completely new sewerage, water, and underground heating and gas pipelines were laid.

One of the most impressive parts of the continued development of the Old City, as well as the construction of the New City, was the configuring or upgrading of a number of parks, squares, and public recreation areas (map 4). Yellow Mountain Plaza (A) was completed in August 2001 at a cost of 8 million yuan (Zouping 2004: 45). It was built directly to the north of the New City government headquarters, according to the imperial, geomantic logic dictating that all government headquarters should be faced by impressive and geometrically aligned plazas. To avoid blocking the energy emanating from Yellow Mountain, a large window was constructed in the center of the government headquarters. While government officials will not admit to "believing" in geomancy, or feng shui, they feel that aligning the mountain, the plaza, and the government headquarters in this way enhances the majesty of the government. This planned recombination of geomantic logic and the name of a historical landmark is typical of strategies of urban branding throughout China. It also contributes to what Fernando Coronil (1997) terms "the magic of the state." As Pile (2005: 88–89) notes, geomancy is one of the most common forms in which "magical" beliefs enliven the design of modern cities.

Also completed during the early 2000s were Physical Education Plaza (Tiyu Guangchang; B, map 4), Black Creek Park (C), and Urban Citizens' Park (Shimin Gongyuan, D). In addition to a large paved area used for roller skating and public performances, Physical Education Plaza contains ample outdoor exercise equipment and several croquet courts. Black Creek Park is at the edge of Black Creek Lake (Daixi Hu), which during the 1980s and 1990s was called March 8 Reservoir. This park includes a pier where people fish and rent recreational boats; a green area surrounding the lake; a paved plaza with a statue of Fan Zhongyan, one of the historical personages

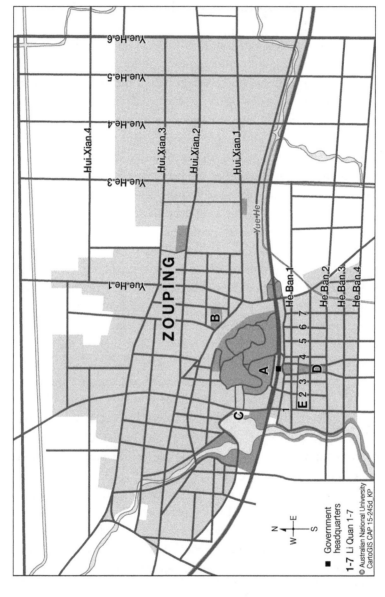

MAP 4. The county seat in 2005.

Government
headquarters

1-7 Li Quan 1-7

© Australian National University
CartoGIS CAP 15-245d_KP

FIGURE 4. View from the end of the pier in Black Creek Park. Photo by author.

Zouping memorializes (Thøgersen 2002); an area for roller skating; and an old people's "university" (*laonian daxue*) where there are croquet courts, meeting rooms, and other recreational facilities for senior citizens (figure 4). Urban Citizens' Park continues the north-south geomantic axis from Yellow Mountain Plaza. It contains an extended water feature with fish, numerous walking trails with bridges over the water feature, flowers, and amphitheaters. Further expansion of both Black Creek and Urban Citizens' Parks is apparent on the 2008 map (map 5, below). Black Creek Park was connected to a walkway and green area that follows the entire length of Black Creek. The creek itself was cleaned up as part of this process. Overall, both the Old and New City Districts have ample green spaces and recreation areas.

Infrastructure improvements and other forms of construction and expansion continued throughout the first decade of the twenty-first century. A few features notable on the 2005 map (map 4) deserve mention. First, the streets of the New City and the Development Zone were named in proper gridlike fashion. The east-west streets in the Development Zone were named Hui Xian (Gathering of the Immortals) Roads #1–4, and the north-south streets were named Moon River (Yue He; the stream running through the Development Zone, visible in maps 4 and 5) Roads #1–6. The east-west streets in the New City were named He Ban (Crane Partner, the name of a local mountain) Roads #1–4, and the north-south streets were named Li Quan

(Fountain of Liquor, the name of a local temple) Roads #1–7 (1–7, map 4). A pedestrian mall (*buxingjie*) was also constructed in the New City (E, map 4). Such pedestrian malls are a ubiquitous aspect of twenty-first-century Chinese urban planning and are found in almost every newly constructed city.

In 2003 a public bus system was established; it has been modified and slightly expanded several times since, and the 2008 version of the six bus routes are displayed in map 5. The routes conveniently link the three parts of the city. From its establishment to the last time I took a bus (2012), the cost for occasional users remained one yuan a trip. During the early years the buses stopped anywhere along the route, and each bus had both a driver and a ticket taker. By 2010 the system was much more regulated and modernized. An electronic card system replaced the ticket takers, buses stopped only at designated places, and routes were organized to leave specific stops at specific times (a taped broadcast told the drivers when it was time depart).

The 2008 map (map 5) shows even more changes. Not only did all districts of the city continue to expand, with new roads, schools, parks, bus routes, and residential areas, but the city government initiated several major projects. The background in this map has been left entirely white, as almost all the area covered by the map was either urbanized or in the process of being urbanized. A new bus passenger terminal (A), near the northern edge of the city, replaced the bus station of the early 2000s. This building was much more spectacular than the old long-distance bus station, which was little more than a series of outdoor bus stops with a ticket office and a bit of shelter. The new passenger terminus resembles a large train station or even a small airport terminal, with gigantic halls, gates for scores of long-distance buses, electronic displays, multiple ticket offices, stores, clinics, restaurants, information stations, and even a hotel.

In addition to the passenger terminus, the government units outside of the county government proper, which answer more directly to bureaucracies outside of Zouping (*tiao zhichui danwei*), such as the tax and education bureaus, began building their own office towers in the New City. Several of these units also went into deals with contractors to have residential areas for their staff built in the New City. Several new markets and malls, most notably the Zouping International Traders City (Zouping Guoji Shangmao Cheng; B, map 5) and the Huixian Wholesale Market (Huixian Pifa Shichang, C), were built in the Development Zone. Though these names suggest they are wholesalers to upscale retail stores, in fact they became shopping areas filled with low-end retailers and service providers catering to the

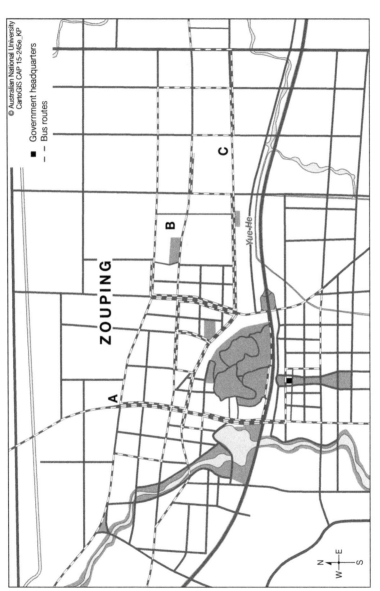

■ Government headquarters
– – Bus routes

ZOUPING

A

B

C

Yue-He

N
W —•— E
S

MAP 5. The county seat in 2008.

huge population of factory workers who lived in the Development Zone. Finally, not content with developing parks and recreational spaces in the county seat, the county government also developed several tourist sites (hiking areas and temples) in the mountains to the southeast of Zouping town. These include the Tanglian Scenic Area (Tang Li An Fengjing Qu), the Liquan Temple, Heban Mountain National Forest Park (Heban Shan Guojia Senlin Gongyuan), and the Baiyun Mountain Scenic Area (Baiyun Shan Fengjing Qu) (see map 7 below: G, H, I, and J, respectively).

Since 2008 Zouping has continued to expand. Each year I visited I discovered new residential areas, shopping areas, and factories and improved public facilities. Perhaps the most impressive aspect of the post-2008 expansion took place outside of the zoned area of the county seat. The city has expanded so much that it is beginning to form a single contiguous urban area with the surrounding towns, including Zhoucun in the neighboring prefecture. Over the course of the early and mid-2000s, the town of Handian (A, maps 6 and 7), just north of Zouping, has been expanding rapidly because of the Xiwang Group headquartered there. In the mid-2000s one of the city bus routes connected Zouping to Handian. In 2009 car dealerships secured land rights along the stretch of road between Zouping and Handian, north of the new passenger terminus. By 2012 these dealerships lined the entire stretch of road between Handian and Zouping. Similarly, to the east the expansion of the Development Zone began to reach the edges of Changshan town (B, maps 6 and 7), which was the most industrialized part of the county in the 1980s. Another city bus route was extended to Changshan in the late 2000s, so that Handian, Zouping, and Changshan have become part of a single public transportation network.

To the south, new residential areas were constantly being added to the New City, so that it started to stretch to Xidong town (C, maps 6 and 7). Moreover, green areas, including the expansion of Urban Citizens' Park, new schools, a public Olympic sports center, and an exhibition hall were added to the New City. To the southwest, toward the town of Haosheng (D, maps 6 and 7), a new road was built and a large railway freight terminus completed (E, map 7). Several new furniture factories sprang up near the freight terminus. The construction of this terminus meant that Zouping has gained excellent rail, road, and air links to the rest of the world. As Haosheng itself has also expanded in the direction of Zhoucun (F, maps 6 and 7), it appears that Handian, Changshan, Zouping, Haosheng, Xidong, and Zhoucun may one day become a single urban area with a combined population of nearly one

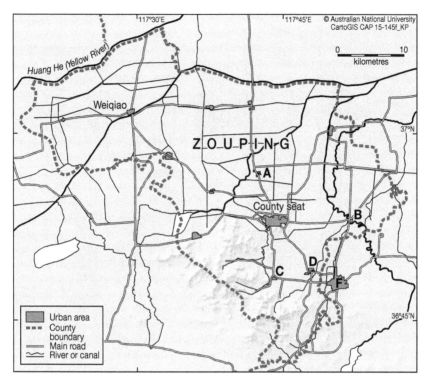

MAP 6. Zouping county in 1990.

million. Roads connecting these places to each other and the rest of the county have been continually upgraded. Comparing the maps of Zouping county in 1990 and 2012 illuminates the extension of urban space in southwestern Zouping county.

EXTRAGOVERNMENTAL DEVELOPERS AND PLANNERS

As the New City and the Development Zone expanded, more parcels of land were auctioned off or allocated to various private companies and village governments. The county government took less responsibility for direct supervision of urban construction. Three processes dominated. Sometimes negotiations with villages over the appropriation of their agricultural land left village governments in control of pockets of land. How it was to be developed would then also be subject to negotiation, though the county government would try to ensure that certain zoning requirements were followed. In the Development

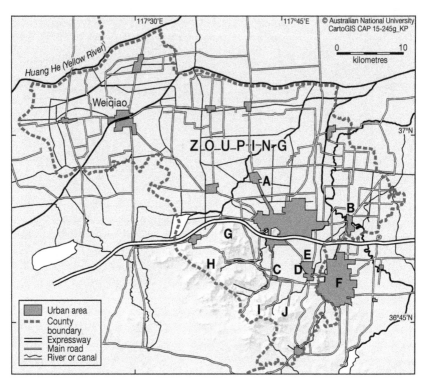

MAP 7. Zouping county in 2012.

Zone, negotiations with various industrial groups resulted in land being developed by private companies. While this process was subject to zoning requirements, large investors would have the leverage to demand amendments to these requirements, though such negotiations would take place in secret, and I could not learn the details of any of them. In other cases, the county government simply auctioned off building sites with various zoning requirements attached and attempted to ensure that the plans and then the actual construction of buildings were congruent with the city's wider urban plan and growing list of building regulations. While such processes are perhaps the norm in most developed countries, even this latter form of planning does not guarantee a purely "rational," "scientific," or "objective" planning process. Practicalities, politics, and subjective judgments continue to intervene.

The image of desirable urban modernity in Zouping has evolved rapidly. Consequently, government planners must deal with a moving target rather than a stable ideal when drawing up regulations. For example, during the 1980s and 1990s detached houses and low-rise buildings were considered

FIGURE 5. Model of the Tianxing development. Photo by author.

most desirable and economically feasible. During the early 2000s, six-story buildings (the tallest permitted without elevators) were encouraged. The twelve-story government headquarters was the only building with elevators during this period. By the late 2000s, however, seventeen-story buildings with elevators became common, and a few taller ones also were built. One result of this construction history is that there are more high-rise buildings on the southern fringes of the New City and the eastern edges of the Development Zone than in the central parts of town.

One exception to this pattern is the large Tianxing project (figure 5). This development occupied a large piece of land in the center of the Old City that had opened up when the the old county government headquarters was demolished. Other portions of this land were built over with low-rise (three-story) commercial buildings. But the Tianxing developers had much more grandiose plans. Their complex included shopping malls, hotels, office towers, and residential skyscrapers. These buildings dwarfed the surrounding sections of the Old City and, at least according to rumor, initially aroused the suspicion and resistance of some government leaders, supposedly because the complex was to be more upscale and majestic than even the government headquarters. When I spoke to an official in the urban planning bureau about the project, he said that plans for several of the buildings were redrawn and reapproved several times, both because the developers had changed their minds about what they wanted to build and because over the years government views on what was considered permissible evolved. The project was under construction for most of the period of my research, but when I last visited in 2012 the entire central part of the project was complete and stores had moved into most of the commercial spaces. It appeared much as the image in figure 5 suggests, though the eight buildings at the upper left were not then complete.

Perhaps the most complicated politics of construction involved the villages-in-the-city and the development of the land they controlled. Much has been written about the politics of appropriating village land in growing cities, the public protests such appropriation can lead to, and the potential for protests to stymie the career ambitions of local cadres. Case studies in other parts of China show considerable variation. In the Pearl River Delta, many extremely privileged and empowered villages-in-the-city have emerged (Chan, Madsen, and Unger 2009; Siu 2007). These villages often refract any attempt of city planners to corral their plans and are often visually quite distinct from the areas around them (Bach 2010; Chung and Unger 2013). Other places, such as Kunming, have become infamous for villagers having their land appropriated without adequate compensation and their protests violently suppressed (Zhu 2014). Zouping is an intermediate case. The Zouping government was not willing to antagonize villages-in-the-city, and since the 1980s some of these units have emerged as important players in the politics of urban land. Yet most villages-in-the-city have not become so powerful, and none appear to be as wealthy or powerful as those in the PRD.

At least since the late 2000s, the city district governments in Zouping (i.e.,governments one or two levels above villages-in-the-city, or jiedao) have tried to encourage the dissolution of village committee governments and the merging of several villages into single communities (*shequ,* which, in urban areas, are supposed to be the lowest level of governance). They have been successful in doing so, however, in only a limited number of cases. In these instances, the city government convinced villages about to give up their land to move to entirely new residential areas (*xiaoqu*) where the households of several villages were given the right to buy apartments at heavily subsidized prices. To entice the villages, these areas were quite upscale. Nevertheless, most villages that were to be incorporated into the city preferred to maintain a separate governmental identity, as they saw separation as the best way to protect their collective interests. Those villages that were individually

FIGURE 6. Anjia entrance arch. Photo by author.

incorporated during the 1980s and 1990s were even more reluctant to give up their separate identities. Those that were economically successful began to assert themselves even more forcefully than in the past. For example, the village of Anjia, originally incorporated into the city during the 1980s, erected a large memorial archway (*paifang*) in 2011 displaying its name over the entrance to the section of urban real estate it controlled (figure 6). The villages of Dongguan and Beiguan also erected public markers of their territory. Such forms of identity assertion resemble those of the villages-in-the-city in the PRD, which often construct new and gaudy lineage halls and other architectural emblems to mark their territory and make claims to place (Chan, Madsen, and Unger 2009; Tomba 2012).[3]

The deals the county government reached with different village governments have varied over time. The county government sometimes delayed incorporating villages that resisted standard terms when convenient and offered slightly better deals to villages in places crucial to the city's plans. The extra value of these deals was compounded by the fact that the villages in the most crucial locations tended to be those that had land that would become especially valuable. The first villages to give up their land for the construction of the New City exemplify some of the better deals. Daizhuang village became the most centrally located and only fully separate village-in-the-city in the New City. It was given subsidies to construct spacious two-story villas on land that would come to be near both the center of Zouping and the new government headquarters. Each household in the village received its own separate villa. The villas were spacious enough to enable households to live upstairs and rent out the downstairs to businesses or individuals. Despite its central location, the village became the most spacious low-rise and least dense residential area in the New City. Since most of the surrounding land was later developed as gated residential areas with six-story buildings and green space between them, the villas and their alleyways make this village-in-the-city stand out like an architectural sore thumb.

Two other villages that controlled land near the center of the New City, Houjia and Huangshanqian, were moved into a standard residential area. But they were allowed to develop a parcel with the commercial buildings that formed the New City's pedestrian mall. Each village controls half of the mall. The village committees manage the development and rental of mall space and divide the income among all village households. As the mall has become one of the main shopping areas of the New City, the rentals has proven quite lucrative. Other villages whose land was taken over to form the outer portions of the New City have received reasonable compensation but not at the same level as that received by Daizhuang, Houjia, and Huangshanqian.

The villages that controlled the land that would become the Development Zone have also met with varying fates. Those that have benefited the most were among the first villages to give up their land and the villages located in places that would become the near edge of the Development Zone. In these latter villages, the agricultural land was taken to build factories, but the original houses and the land around them were left unchanged. After the first factories were built, the villagers discovered that there was a huge demand by the new factory workers for cheap rental housing. The district government attempted to discourage villagers from building rental units, stating that their housing would also eventually be appropriated. Despite this warning, some villagers began to build cheap rental units in their courtyards. Once a few villagers built such units and started to make money, many others followed. The city government then became hesitant to tear down the units for fear of antagonizing the villagers. In Dongfanqian, for example, cheap rental units were already apparent in 2005, when I first visited, and were still there in 2012, the last time I visited, even though the Development Zone as a whole had continuously expanded over this period.

From a planning standpoint most of these villages are a disaster. Because the rental units are quasi-legal and continue to be threatened with demolition, the quality of the construction is poor, the layout haphazard, the infrastructure completely lacking, and the public hygiene shocking. Village households typically built rental rooms of 7 to 10 square meters out of the cheapest available materials. If they built two stories around their existing courtyard-style homes, they could fit about twenty rental rooms on their property, not counting the five to seven rooms of much nicer original housing, which they usually reserved for themselves. As the original courtyard houses had walls around the exterior, the newly constructed rental units became walled-off compounds. While the rooms usually had electricity, no provision was made for running water, toilets, kitchens, waste disposal, or showers. In Dongfangqian a few commercial businesses offering showers sprang up. There were also public, latrine-style toilets in the village, but these were overused and often in disgusting condition. People renting rooms in the compounds obtained their water from a communal pump in their own courtyard if they were lucky; if not, they had to walk to the nearest communal well. Many villagers constructed small concrete trenches to direct wastewater out of their compounds, but these resulted in alleyway ditches outside of the compounds overflowing with wastewater. The parts of the villages with open space became garbage dumps (figure 7). In all, I estimate that between 2002 and 2005 the population of Dongfanqian grew tenfold, from about 1,000 to roughly 10,000. Three or four other villages have developed rental businesses half to two-thirds the scale of those in Dongfanqian, and many more have developed rental businesses on a smaller scale.

The entrenched nature of the problem in Dongfanqian can be seen in the difficulties encountered by the large and excellent primary school at the edge of the village. The school was built on agricultural land that originally belonged to the village and was originally supposed to occupy even an even larger piece of land but ran out of construction funding before the government was able to complete its large outdoor athletic track. The education bureau thus decided to build a temporary school wall around the smaller section of land and open the school without the track in 2005. Within two years the education bureau had the money to complete the track, but by that

FIGURE 7. Garbage in an urban village. Photo by author.

time villagers had constructed more rental units on a small section of uninhabited land. These villagers argued against the government's plans to obtain their land, despite the offer of high-quality subsidized apartments elsewhere in the city. Reluctant to cause a potential uproar while it was preoccupied with taking over land and expanding the city in many other locations, the city government did not force the issue. When I last visited Zouping in 2012, the outdoor track still had not been built and the rental businesses were still operating.

In late 2008 I interviewed a man who had built a two-story, twenty-unit compound on his property in early 2005. He explained that when he saw his neighbors building such units he calculated that the construction would pay for itself in about three years and was thus worth the risk of the city government destroying it. In fact, he gloated, it only took two and a half years to earn back his investment. He paid about 60,000 yuan to build the unit (supplying some of the labor himself) and rented the twenty rooms at 100 yuan each per month. He said that the units were always full and that there were no other expenses involved in running the place as the tenants paid their own electricity. He figured that the city government would one day force him to give up his property and move into a new apartment, but he and his neighbors planned to resist moving for as long as they could. He also said that in the end he hoped to obtain an even better apartment than the ones typically offered, as the government would be desperate for him to move out.

The housing demand that makes such places viable comes from many quarters. The large factories in the Development Zone offer free dorm rooms to single workers and subsidized apartments to married workers, but these options do not satisfy everyone. Some married factory workers, even those with children, need to save money before they can buy a factory apartment or would prefer to save even more money to buy an apartment on the commercial market. While they save their money they look for the cheapest accommodation possible. Some single workers, especially those with a sexual partner, cannot tolerate the social regulation of the free dormitories. Other migrants work in small service businesses rather than factories and do not have access to factory housing. Finally, people wishing to evade governmental regulations, to avoid the birth control policy, or to engage in prostitution, the sale of fake identity papers, gambling, or trade in illicit drugs find the housing in places like Dongfanqian preferable to Zouping's more properly planned spaces.

Villages-in-the-city create a particular type of limit to planning in China. In Zouping, these villages have in some cases been influenced by the planning regulations extant at the time of their incorporation but over time become relatively independent enclaves resistant to upgrades in planning requirements. As their privilege becomes entrenched, some attempt to publicly assert and enshrine their identity. In a few cases, such as Dongfanqian, they grow into planning nightmares. Looking at a place like Dongfanqian from an outsider's perspective, my feelings are mixed. On the one hand, in contrast to the arguments of Scott (1998), I cannot help but feel that especially in the areas of public infrastructure and hygiene city planners have much to offer the majority of people living in a city like Zouping. On the other hand, Zouping's new shantytowns owe their very existence to the popular demand for cheap and socially unregulated housing.

From my tours of the edges of the city, I estimate that there were 20,000 to 35,000 people living in such housing at the end of the first decade of the twenty-first century. Though significant, such numbers represent less than 10 percent of the city's population, so Zouping cannot be considered a place that is dominated by shantytowns. They simply make up one sector of what still feels like a well-planned urban area.

The exercise of city planning requires a proliferation of planners and considerable coordination among them. In Zouping the history of this proliferation can be seen in the multiplication and expansion of the government departments concerned with this regulatory process. Before 2002 Zouping's urban planning took place primarily within a committee of the county government, called the *chengxiang jianshe weiyuanhui*. Though the committee had permanent chairs and vice-chairs, the duties of committee members were somewhat flexible, as they could be reassigned to other areas of the county government when the need arose.[4] In 2002 the committee was formally renamed as a separate bureau, the Zouping County Construction Bureau (Zouping Xian Jianshe Ju); the work of the committee had become too demanding and continuous to allow for easy rotation in and out. In 2007 this bureau moved into a large new office tower in the New City (figure 8). By 2009 the bureau had seventy employees divided into five administrative units, plus two associated units, which acted as profit-making enterprises responsible for their own finances. The five administrative units were the planning office (*guihua gu*), which solicited and approved plans for individual buildings, residential areas, or even new sections of the city; the rural planning office (*xiangcun guihua gu*), which did the same for villages in the county; the planning supervision office (*guihua guanli gu*), which made sure that developers' construction projects actually conformed to the plans they had submitted; the urban projects planning office (*shicheng gongcheng guihua gu*), which planned and supervised public infrastructure projects, including parks, roads, and utilities; and administrative services (*zonghe bangongshi*), which kept files for personnel, contracts, plans, and so on. The two additional units were a planning consulting firm (*zixun fuwu gongsi*), which advised builders where they needed to go for various approvals and how to strategically approach the construction process, and a planning design institute (*guihua shejiyuan*), which drew up plans for builders.

In addition to the planning bureau, related regulatory functions were undertaken by the land bureau (*guotu ziyuan ju*), which, like the planning bureau, was upgraded from committee status in 2002 and occupied its own office building in the New City. The land bureau worked with the planning bureau on issues like measuring and surveying plots, appropriating land from villages for new urban construction, and inspecting sites for violations of land use laws. It was also in charge of regulating private housing construction

FIGURE 8. Zouping County Construction Bureau. Photo by author.

in villages, though, as discussed above, its activities were limited by the need to consider the possibilities of popular protest.

The growth of the land and planning bureaus led to an increase in the number of "planners" outside the government. Developers of residential estates and shopping malls, industrial groups that built new factories, village committees that managed property, and even village households that built rental units on their existing homes—all made plans, both for the architectural specifications of the buildings they erected and for the future financial viability of their properties. Government planners attempted to make all nonofficial planners adhere to the same master plan, but, despite significant successes, planning disjunctures continually occurred.

These disjunctures were in part a matter of conflict of interest, but they were also about divergent visions of the future. The government planners whom I interviewed were remarkably frank about the limits of the planning enterprise in general and the specific powers of their offices. One told me, "City planning is a bit like predicting the future. You have to make educated guesses about the future population size of the city, future levels of wealth, and even the number of automobiles that will be driven in the city in the future." He later gave the following example.

> If we decide that in the next fifteen years demand for electricity will grow and that there will be a need for another generator, then we need to make plans about where that electricity plant will be. Certainly we would put it in the Development Zone near the existing plants. But we would need to appropriate land from the surrounding villages. If we were to cause antagonism in the land appropriation process, that, of course, would be bad. But it would be much worse if we were to appropriate the land, cause antagonism, and then, in the end, find that we do not need the new generator after all and not build anything. Of course, it is also bad if electricity demand far outstrips supply because we have not properly anticipated rising demand. Planning forces us to face dilemmas like this a hundred times over.

Another planner told me that the hardest part of the planning process was to juggle current needs with projected future needs: "People want to live their lives with a minimum of disturbance. Reconstructing the city, whether infrastructure, roads, or new buildings, always creates disturbance. But if you never reconstruct, you limit the potential for growth in the future. In China, the government is pro-growth."

CONCLUSION

The transformation of built space has been one of the most radical aspects of Zouping's urbanization. The New City and the Development Zone were built from scratch, and many sections of the Old City were completely rebuilt. But even such a radical transformation as this is broadly recombinant. The ready availability of the plans, building technologies, and building techniques implemented in Zouping had to do with their already widespread availability in China. Long before the planned revolution of 2000, Zouping's villagers-in-the city were mastering the construction trade. Some of the imaginary forms behind the architecture of these transformations have had a long history in Zouping. The geomantic imagination behind the new government headquarters, Anjia's marking of territory with an archway, and the creation of plazas in a number of locations in Zouping reflect architectural tastes and understandings of power that predate the reform period. Yellow Mountain, long an important landmark in Zouping, became even more important as it moved from the edge to the center of town. The names of streets and parks, though new, reinvent memories of older Zouping landmarks.

The rise of planning agencies in Zouping raises two questions to which I can only provide speculative answers. One concerns the tacit acceptance of villager-in-the-city violation of planning and zoning regulations. Given the expansion of planning power and bureaucracy, why did the county government allow this violation to occur? As indicated above, in some parts of China, like the PRD, villages-in-the-city are even more coddled and empowered than in Zouping, while elsewhere, in places slotted for urbanization, villagers have their rights trampled and their protests brutally quashed. What accounts for this variation? While I have no definitive answer, three factors seem relevant.

The first is the inclinations of leaders at various levels of government. In his analysis of the devastating famine that followed the Great Leap Forward, Frank Dikötter (2010) argues that starvation was far from evenly distributed throughout the countryside. Some provinces suffered more than others; some prefectures within a given province suffered more than others; some counties within a given prefecture suffered more than others. At the village level, some villages saw no cases of death by starvation, while other villages saw more than 50 percent of their population perish. During the Great Leap Forward, the primary question facing leaders was how much grain they would pledge to pass up to the higher levels and what sort of measures they would take to ensure that they collected enough grain to meet their promises. Promising and delivering more grain made them look good to the officials above them (and thus increased chances for promotion); promising and delivering too much, however, could have devastating effects on the populations they governed (and, if discovered by higher-level officials, might negatively affect promotion chances). Some officials more than others bent to the pressure to pledge large amounts of grain and resorted to brutal enforcement methods. Now the major issue for local leaders in China is how to simultaneously promote economic growth and prevent the occurrence of popular protest in their districts. Requisitioning land from villages to expand urban areas can lead to both economic growth and protest. To prevent protest, officials can use both carrots and sticks, and there seem to be tendencies to resort more to one measure than the other in given districts of the country.

The second factor is that it takes money to be able to offer carrots. Thus places like Zouping that are developing successfully and generating increased tax revenues for their governments are more likely to offer carrots than places where development is fleeting. Increasing land values not only generates income for county governments but also creates wealth for villages that retain control over small parcels of urbanizing land.

The third factor is precedent. Once a county or city government offers a good deal to one village, it becomes difficult not to offer similar deals to other villages with similar circumstances. While there has been variation in the benefits Zouping's villages received, this variation relates to concrete differences in circumstances. Being first and having land in valuable locations were seen more as matters of luck than variation in the deals the government offered. In addition, certain aspects of these deals, like the "thirty years of money to replace grain," have been completely standardized. In Zouping deals with urban villages over land requisition began in the 1980s, and the good deals villagers received in that period set a precedent for those that followed. That some villages, like Anjia, received control over parcels of land that turned out to be extremely valuable twenty years later could not have been anticipated at the time those deals were made. All three factors interact to allow distinct patterns of governing villages-in-the-city to emerge in different parts of the country.

The second question regards how the growth of the planning bureaucracy fits more general theories of political modernization. Teleological, development-oriented theories of political modernity typically take the supposedly rational bureaucracies of Western nations as a positive model that other countries should attempt to emulate. Other theories simply emphasize that modernization involves developing a bureaucracy with a specialized role structure or one that is responsive to societal demands.[5] Max Weber argued that bureaucracies would grow in size as countries modernized because "rational" bureaucracies could coordinate the activities of a diverse range of people more effectively than personalized networks (1978: esp. 956–1005). But Weber also clearly saw the negative aspects of bureaucratization and was much less positive about the benefits of this "political modernization" than some others. Foucault (1991) saw modernity in terms of the "governmentalization" of the state, which involved the rise of new forms of knowledge aimed

TABLE 1 Government Employees and Population in Zouping[a]

Year	Number of Government Employees	Population of County
1999	11,389	684,079
2004	14,811	709,570
2011	23,386	729,728

[a] The number of government employees includes those working for both administrative units (*jiguan*) and government institutions (*shiye danwei*), as reported in the county yearbooks. Note that the county government governs both urban and rural areas of Zouping and that though the population of the urban area has increased several times over, the population in the villages has declined significantly; overall, population growth in Zouping county between 1986 and 2011 was only about 12 percent. The sources for the table are Zouping 2005: 224, 266; 2012: 260, 325; 2004: 69, 235.

at governing the population of a given country. However, he did not see this governmentalization as constituting any liberation or enabling much improvement of the human condition (see also Dean 1999). I have not undertaken an ethnography of Zouping's bureaucracy and cannot comment on the extent of corruption, arbitrary decision making, or good governance that has emerged there,[6] but some of the more obvious recent changes in Zouping's bureaucracy fit the more value-neutral depictions of political modernity summarized above.

First, as table 1 indicates, the size of Zouping's government has increased much more rapidly than the population of the county. In total, between 1999 and 2011, while the population of the county as a whole increased less than 7 percent, the size of the bureaucracy more than doubled. Second, the formation of new bureaus from what were formerly committees, as well as the division of the bureaus into many offices, clearly indicates a more highly specialized role structure. Third, at least in the case of the planning and land bureaus, the emergence of the new bureaucratic roles relates to changes in society—namely, the high numbers of new construction projects in a place that is rapidly urbanizing. Fourth, in Zouping as in the rest of China, during the reform era the government successfully increased the education levels of its bureaucrats (Bakken 2000; Kipnis 2011a); Zouping's highly educated bureaucrats increasingly use "modern" forms of technical knowledge, like statistics and detailed maps of urban plans, to govern Zouping.

Although I cannot make any judgments about the efficiency or effectiveness of Zouping's planning bureaucracy, I believe that Zouping's parks and

FIGURE 9. The New City and Yellow Mountain Plaza viewed from Yellow Mountain. Photo by author.

FIGURE 10. The Development Zone viewed from Yellow Mountain. Photo by author.

plazas, its public transportation network and infrastructure, as well as its transportation links to other parts of the country and to the world, have made it a relatively livable city. The relative success of Zouping's planning exercise has been linked to economic growth. The growth of the Weiqiao Group and a few other, smaller companies funded most of Zouping's infrastructure development, through the taxes they paid to the government, the facilities they built themselves (with government input), or the spending of their employees, which has enabled the development of thousands of smaller tax paying businesses. The government anticipated and hoped for this growth and for the period of my research saw it become a reality. The recombinant pathways of this economic growth are the topic of the next chapter.

THREE

Recombinant Production

Understanding industrialization in Zouping over the past three decades requires grappling with many forms of recombination. Foremost among these is the oxymoronic category "local capital." Capital is the most fickle, mobile, and asocial form of power. It moves around the world in search of ever greater rates of return, ready to disinvest in a particular locality at a moment's notice. Capital, in this sense, is a purely abstract force. It is the name we give to the tendencies of a particular dynamic of power, a dynamic that is no doubt powerful in the contemporary world. But being real and powerful neither makes it all-encompassing nor enables it to form the teleological endpoint of a certain phase of history (Kipnis 2008). It is one social force in the world among many. Capital, while always striving for greater profit, must involve itself in localities and be embodied by certain humans. We may call these people capitalists, but like all humans they are many things at once (which is to say, the social pressures on their being come from many sources, not just Capital itself). Some of these pressures relate to their embeddedness in various forms of local society. In addition, Capital often requires land and equipment, which must be physically located in a particular place, and raw materials, which must come from somewhere and be stored somewhere, not to mention a labor source with certain skills, who must live somewhere.

In this sense, Capital everywhere might be said to need to compromise with, to recombine with, to form relationships with various forms of humanity and society (Chakrabarty 2000). The extent and forms of these compromises and relationships vary. In Zouping over the past three decades, these relationships have been localized in many senses. While the forms of relationship between forces of Capital and local society have been evolving, as has local society itself, there appear to be certain forms of path dependency that have evolved from particular initial conditions.

I take the starting point of these initial conditions as the beginning of the reform era, in the late 1970s. While one could point to the roots of current development or rural industrialization in the Maoist era, or perhaps even earlier, at the beginning of the reform era Zouping was an overwhelmingly agricultural society. Over 95 percent of the population lived in villages and belonged to households in which farming was the major economic activity and source of livelihood. During the 1980s, most villages divided their farming between three major crops: on some land they would rotate winter wheat and summer corn; on other parcels they would grow cotton. The wheat was used primarily to pay the grain tax and for household consumption (with mantou, or steamed bread, the preferred staple), and the corn was used as animal feed. In earlier periods of deprivation, corn and other coarse grains were also important sources of human nutrition. Cotton was a cash crop that was sold primarily through the government networks of supply and marketing cooperatives (*gongxiao she*). Most of the first industries that emerged in the county were based on the processing of cotton, wheat, and corn. There were plants that ginned cotton, spun it into yarn, and made cottonseed oil. There were mills that turned cotton yarn into cloth. There were corn starch factories, flour mills, beer factories, and liquor distilleries. At first, the largest of these enterprises were owned by the county government and some of the larger township governments. But as the regulations for starting factories, securing raw materials, and marketing products loosened at the beginning of the reform era, TVEs began sprouting up in villages. When I did research in one Zouping village, Fengjia, during the late 1980s, the village had four factories, the largest of which were a corn starch plant and a cotton mill. There were scores if not hundreds of such small factories scattered across the county's villages and towns. The two largest conglomerates in Zouping today had their roots in these industries, though they did not grow out of the ones in Fengjia. Throughout the 1990s the great majority of these factories, including those in Fengjia, went bankrupt as a few local winners emerged and grew into the larger incorporated business groups of the present.

Zouping's other successful industries of the 1980s, while not tied directly to local agriculture, also emerged from local geography and history. A copper mine attempted to tap local mineral resources; the Hupo Beer factory relied on water from a local spring that was said to be of exceptional quality and on the fact that Shandong was a site of German colonialism and thus had developed local expertise in beer manufacturing; and local wood furniture factories emerged in several villages.

During the 1990s the patterns and strategies of economic growth differed from both the 1980s and the 2000s, especially in the county seat. While the textile and corn-processing industries consolidated and expanded, both inside and outside the county seat, the county government focused on attracting foreign investment. Cadres I met in diverse branches of the local government often complained about how successive Party secretaries (leaders under the Chinese Communist system) had made attracting foreign investment the central focus of the work of all cadres, despite the fact that the missions of most bureaus or agencies had nothing to do with attracting foreign invest-ment per se.[1] Several foreign companies started factories in Zouping, and others invested in or through local companies, but the importance of all this foreign investment, or really simply all the companies that had invested in the county seat before 2000, was dwarfed by the large conglomerates that arrived after the construction of the Development Zone and have dominated the economy since. The two largest of these companies are the Weiqiao Group and the Xiwang Group; the former is a much larger employer than the latter, though Xiwang grew much more quickly in the late 2000s.

A quick description of some of the key county seat enterprises during the 1990s demonstrates the extent of the transformations of the 2000s. For much of the 1980s and 1990s the Hupo Beer factory was one of the most lauded enterprises in the county seat. Important visitors were regularly given tours of the factory, and promotional material issued by the local government gave it a prominent position. Between 1986 and 1995 the beer factory generated 180 million yuan of taxable income. From 1993 to 1995 it was named one of the five hundred most economically efficient enterprises in China, and in 1995 it had 1,200 employees (Zouping 1997: 253). By 2004, however, it was losing money and employed roughly 1,150 people (Zouping 2005: 134–35). By comparison, in 2004 the Weiqiao Group employed over 68,000 workers in Zouping alone (Zouping 2005: 134); at its peak just before the financial crisis in 2008, it employed over 158,000 workers in Zouping (Zouping 2008: 138). In the late 2000s the beer factory was bought out by a private company from northeastern China and began making beer for the Xuehua brand. In 2010 a worker from the factory told me that his wages had stagnated over the past eight years and his work hours had increased. He made 1,200 yuan a month for working 60 hours a week, while workers in the Weiqiao Group averaged over 2,000 yuan for a 45-hour week. Because he had housing with the factory

TABLE 2 Top 5 Earning Corporations in Zouping, 2011

Company Name	2011 Gross Income	2011 Pretax Profits
Weiqiao Pioneering Group	151 billion yuan	13.6 billion yuan
Xiwang Group	21.2 billion yuan	2.0 billion yuan
Changxing Group	13.7 billion yuan	2.2 billion yuan
Chuangxin Group	13.7 billion yuan	0.31 billion yuan
Qixing Group	12.4 billion yuan	0.69 billion yuan

SOURCE: Zouping 2012: 129–31.

and because the company had laid off some of the workers, he dared not resign or even complain to his managers. The Xuehua company lost money in 2010 but turned a profit of 16 million yuan in 2011. In that same year the Weiqiao Group had a profit of nearly 10 billion yuan (Zouping 2012: 130). (See table 2.)

Another important enterprise during the 1990s was the copper mine. Early in the decade it employed over 600 people and generated over 10 million yuan in pretax profits a year (Zouping 1997: 258). While it maintained this level of employment until at least 2004 (Zouping 2005: 136), when I spoke to a former worker at the mine in 2007 he said the company was going bankrupt. I could find no mention of the company in the economic and statistical literature produced by the county after 2005.

In 2000 considerable excitement was generated when a Japanese company (known in Chinese as the Shandong Riqing Shipin Youxian Gongsi) agreed to establish a food processing company in the county seat. It made dried food for the export market, including the dried vegetables that go into instant noodle packages. The county Party secretary held a major news conference and a ribbon cutting ceremony for the opening of the new plant in November of that year, and local press coverage was extensive (Zouping 2004: 35). While this company has continued to make products in Zouping as far as I know, in 2004 it employed only 300 people (Zouping 2005: 140), a drop in the bucket compared to the major conglomerates. It has lost all visibility in local media and business yearbooks.

In short, the rise of the Development Zone corresponded with two major shifts in Zouping's economic structure. Before 2001 the major businesses in the county seat employed between 500 and 1,500 workers. Though there was a mixture of local, national, and international companies, the county government appeared to be focusing on foreign investment as its major strategy for economic growth. Since the establishment of the Development Zone, the local economy has been dominated by a few major conglomerates, especially the Weiqiao Group, which since 2005 has employed between 100,000 and 160,000 workers. Two other conglomerates, the Changxing Group and the Xiwang Group, have been growing rapidly, each employing between 5,000 and 15,000 workers. A few other conglomerates employ in the range of 2,000 to 5,000 workers, and all of them have outpaced the important businesses of the 1990s. Local businessmen control the shares of most of these large groups, including Weiqiao, Changxing, and Xiwang. Moreover, the Weiqiao and Xiwang Groups began and continue to work in the most traditional industrial sectors in Zouping—cotton spinning and corn processing. While both of these groups existed in the county before 2000, they arrived in the county seat only after that date. Weiqiao moved much of its production from the town of Weiqiao to the county seat in the early 2000s, while the expansion of the county seat north brought the Xiwang Group into the county seat's urban area. Both groups continued to expand after their production began contributing to the growth of the county seat. Let us consider their histories in greater detail.

SHANDONG WEIQIAO PIONEERING GROUP COMPANY, LTD.

Reconstructing the history of this large business is a difficult task. From the outside, I have personally witnessed aspects of its growth and interviewed many people who have worked there, including a session with the CEO in 1999. It has a number of websites, and it received considerable coverage in the official press, much of which I collected. It is possible to construct a history of the company from these sources, even a history that seems plausible given the physical growth I witnessed, but it is a self-congratulatory history, particularly regarding the role of Zhang Shiping, the company's founder and CEO for the entire period of my research. I also had access to less flattering sources of information. First, there is the rumor and gossip that circulates in Zouping; while I heard few negative comments about Zhang Shiping himself, many sarcastic and cynical stories circulated about his children, particularly his son, and other relatives, all of whom have significant managerial roles in the company. Second, there is the business reporting in Hong Kong and South China, which gives various descriptions of the company's restructuring and reshuffling of key personnel during the 2000s. And finally, there is the newspaper reporting, Internet coverage, and gossip that followed a major industrial accident at one of the company's aluminum plants in 2007. For a brief period, this accident generated negative reporting even in the official Chinese press and for a longer period enabled critical discussion in Internet forums and among concerned individuals in Zouping regarding safety measures and working conditions in the company.

I will not endeavor to unify these sources into a single narrative but rather present several aspects of the company as a way of discussing the tensions between pressures generated by Capital and those that result from various forms of local social embeddedness. The multiplicity of the narrative also reflects the fact that in a company as large as the Weiqiao Group it is doubtful that even Zhang Shiping himself understands a tenth of what goes on. As Margery Wolf (1992) demonstrates in her threefold exploration of a case of spirit possession that occurred over a much smaller spatial, social, and temporal scale, multiple perspectives can enrich almost any ethnography. I begin with an overview of the company's growth and development from the early 1980s to the late 2000s. This overview gives a positive view of the company, and necessarily so. Its spectacular growth as well as its contributions to the local economy and the families of tens of thousands of workers are undeniable. For a company that started out in a small rural township and has fostered a large group of loyal employees, it is not possible to attribute this success to either political connections or the simple exploitation of workers. It is the result of producing superior products at a competitive price and the continual upgrading of its production processes, marketing strategies and networks, and business models. Below I examine ownership shifts and restructurings over the 2000s as the company went from being a public enterprise under the control of the local Supply and Marketing Cooperative to a complex business group under the control of Zhang Shiping and his extended family. I consider the question of whether this privatization will curtail the company's local social embeddedness. The final section examines the industrial accident of 2007 and the compromises the company makes in its attempts to pursue profit.

The Growth of Weiqiao

Depending on the source of information, Zhang Shiping was born in the town of Weiqiao in 1946 or 1947. In 1964, at the age of 17 or 18, he began working and in 1966 was sent "down to the countryside,"[2] though in his case, coming from a township rather than a large city, the contrast to his previous experience may not have been great. Nevertheless, he credits this experience with "forging his iron will."[3] During the 1970s he returned to Weiqiao and began working in the Weiqiao Town Supply and Marketing Cooperative, rising to the position of factory head of the cooperative's cotton ginning and seed oil factory (*youmian chang*) in 1981.[4] At the time, the Supply and Marketing Cooperative's main function was to collect agricultural products and do some basic processing, such as separating cotton seeds from fibers using cotton gins. From here it supplied the fibers to cotton spinning mills, but as a sideline it also pressed oil from the seeds. In 1981 the cotton ginning and seed oil factory had 150 workers but made very little profit and paid quite low wages. According to my interview with Zhang, it was a typical late socialist era factory with a bloated and unmotivated workforce. One of Zhang's first innovations was to apply the household contract responsibility system (*chengbao zerenzhi*), then being instituted in rural China to decollectivize farming communities, to the factory production line. Each worker or group of workers was given specific production quotas and offered bonuses for meeting and exceeding quotas (see also Zouping 1997: 306). The reform proved successful, and over the next several years the factory's profits grew. Zhang then turned his attention to breaking out of the traditional supply and cooperative business of raw cotton processing and moving into cotton spinning and cloth manufacture. He reasoned that Zouping county had a large reservoir of peasants who would be willing to work very hard if given the opportunity of a factory job and an ample supply of high-quality cotton. He thought these conditions afforded a competitive advantage and an opportunity to move into more profitable aspects of the cotton yarn, cloth, clothing, and high-quality cotton goods production sequence. For a couple of years he investigated machinery and markets, and in 1984 he had the factory invest in its first cotton spinning machinery (Zouping 1997: 306). In 1986 the company invested 1.3 million yuan in 52 machines to make cotton towels, one of the simpler forms of cloth (Xu 2007; Zouping 1997: 306). In 1989, as the Chinese textile market softened, Zhang spotted an opportunity and began buying up more yarn spinning and cloth production machinery from factories that were doing poorly. By the end of 1989 the factory's spinning capacity exceeded 10,000 spindles and it owned 336 cloth weaving machines (Fen 2007: 148). Almost all of the money for these investments came from the factory's profits. In the late 1980s the factory changed its official name from Zouping Number 5 Cotton Gin and Seed Oil Factory (Zouping Di Wu

Youmian Chang) to Weiqiao Cotton Textile Factory (Weiqiao Mian Fangzhi Chang), known locally as Wei Mian, an appellation that many people still use. The company was still owned and controlled by the County Supply and Marketing Cooperative, but the cooperative gave great leeway to Zhang in terms of investment strategy and personnel.

At this point, Zhang had set some of the basic strategies he would follow throughout the 1990s. The business was to expand in the direction of the relatively high-tech, high-quality, high-profit end of cotton-based products. Profits were to be poured into expansion of the business whenever possible. Careful research was to precede aggressive strategies of machinery purchase. With regard to the workforce, a twofold strategy was employed. On the one hand, strict systems were implemented to push employees to work hard and efficiently. On the other hand, because Zhang saw Zouping's own peasantry as the source of his workforce, it was important for him to maintain a positive reputation as a fair employer. Because of the level of its wages and the timely way in which it paid them, many rural people in Zouping I spoke to at the end of the 1980s saw Wei Mian as a good employer. Over the course of the 1980s, the factory's profits, tax revenues, and levels of employment increased roughly tenfold (Ding, Zhang, and Li 2005).

The 1990s followed the patterns of the 1980s but with a significant trend toward internationalization. In the early 1990s Zhang organized groups of managers at his factories to investigate markets, machinery, and expertise outside China. He began to replace the machinery he had purchased from other Chinese manufacturers with the latest cotton spinning and cloth weaving machinery from Hong Kong, South Korea, and Japan (Zouping 1997: 304–6). In my interview with Zhang, he explained that he did not hesitate to bring in highly qualified technical advisers from these countries to teach his technicians how to use and maintain the machinery, even if he had to pay them a hundred times the wages of local technicians. Greater and greater percentages of the cloth and yarn produced by Wei Mian were deemed to be of "export quality," and the factory sent its products to manufacturers in Hong Kong, Japan, South Korea, and the United States. Zhang also expanded the company's product line into the dyeing of cloth and the manufacture of clothing and high-quality bed linens. By 1995 Wei Mian had 4,500 workers and a gross production output of 500 million yuan and generated a pretax profit level of 90 million yuan. These figures represented a thirty-fold, hundred-fold, and three-hundred-fold expansion over the 1981 numbers (Zouping 1997: 306). In 1995 Zhang was named a national model worker (*quanguo laodong mofan*) (37), a recognition that reflected the fact that he was considered a government cadre as well as a business leader. From the 1980s to the privatization of the company in 2001, Zhang held the political position of Chinese Communist Party (CCP) secretary of the factory or business group, in addition to being its CEO.

The second half of the 1990s brought continued expansion. One important break came in 1998, when the company obtained the legal right to export directly to its foreign customers. Up to the mid-1990s China had a special form of currency, foreign exchange certificates, that mediated trade between foreign currencies and the Chinese yuan. Local companies had to go through state-owned import-export companies to sell their products abroad and convert the profits back into Chinese yuan, as well as to purchase equipment overseas. The import-export companies always took a cut. In 1994 foreign exchange certificates were abolished, and in 1998 the provincial government grated Wei Mian the right to trade directly with foreign suppliers and customers. During the late 1990s the company also began sourcing some of its cotton from Xinjiang rather than Zouping, as its demand for raw cotton exceeded local supply. When I interviewed Zhang in 1999 he said that the company had grown to employ 13,000 workers and that in 1998 it earned 181 million yuan in pretaxprofits (both figures roughly double those of 1995). They were using all their profits, plus an equivalent amount raised from selling bonds and bank loans, to invest 310 million yuan in building their sixth cloth factory in Weiqiao town and a heat and power plant. Since Chinese utilities charge relatively high prices and Wei Mian had grown so large that it used massive amounts of electricity and heating, Zhang had discovered that there were even greater profits to be made in supplying his own company with heat and power rather than simply producing textiles. Zhang further explained that with cheap electricity, top-notch equipment, the technological knowledge to keep the equipment smoothly working, and a hardworking labor force that kept the machinery running 24 hours a day, 365 days a year, Wei Mian was already four times more efficient than the average Chinese textile mill and would soon become the most efficient cloth producer in the world. Because of the number of different production lines and factories it was operating, during the late 1990s Wei Mian changed its official name to Weiqiao Textile Group (Weiqiao Fangzhi Jituan).

By the end of the 1990s the Weiqiao Textile Group had become by far the largest employer in Zouping county. It was, however, still located in the relatively small town of Weiqiao. This placed limits on both the development of the county seat and the continued growth of the company. The 2000 decision to build a development zone in the county seat fit with Wei Mian's plans for continued expansion. The county seat offered more convenient transportation connections than Weiqiao town, and a development zone could be designed with Wei Mian's needs in mind.

Wei Mian's explosive growth in the early 2000s outstripped everyone's expectations. When I interviewed Zhang in 1999, he said that he hoped to grow the business to the point where it employed 35,000 workers by 2005 (from 13,000 in 1999). However, according to the county's statistical year-books, Wei Mian already employed over 68,000 workers in 2004 (Zouping 2005: 134) and over 137,000 workers in 2006 (Zouping 2007: 126). The increase in the number of workers in the early 2000s relied in part on a shift in the source of the company's workforce. During the 1990s and earlier, almost all its workers came from villages within Zouping county or surrounding areas. The company's growth in the early 2000s required recruiting workers from farther afield. This was accomplished by word of mouth, the Internet, and conducting recruiting trips to technical schools in Hebei, Gansu, Sichuan, and Shaanxi provinces.

The move to the county seat in 2001 supported the company's growth in several ways. It provided properly zoned land on which the company could quickly build new factories and workers' facilities without going through lengthy approval processes. The company also took over several smaller textile plants from the county government and started up large electricity generation and aluminum refining and foundry plants. Though these businesses did not employ as many workers as textiles, they generated relatively large profits. The electricity generation business is an extremely important part of the aluminum refining business because the process used (the Hall-Héroult, or electrolysis, method [*dianjie lü*]), consumes large quantities of electricity. The profits from the aluminum business fed the growth of the textile business and enabled Wei Mian to become, by 2004, the largest cloth producer in the world. Local rumor had it that the world market price for several types of cloth was determined by Wei Mian. In addition to the company headquarters in the county seat, the company maintained some of its original production facilities in Weiqiao town and, in 2001, also developed new plants in Binzhou, the capital of the prefecture in which Zouping is located, and Weihai, another Shandong city and prefectural capital. The rapid expansion of the business in the early 2000s was accompanied by at least two restructurings and reorganizations. In 2001 the overarching business group that directed the various enterprises in the four different locations took the name Shandong Weiqiao Pioneering Group Company, Ltd. (Shandong Weiqiao Chuangye Jituan Youxian Gongsi).

Work-Unit Culture

In addition to understanding the growth of Wei Mian as a business enterprise, we must consider its role as a social enterprise, or what in Chinese is known as a work unit, or danwei. Work units were one of the primary institutions organizing society in Mao-era China. They were places of employment, such as factories, but also places that provided housing and sometimes education, health care, shopping, and government services to their employees. Often work units constructed walls around their compounds with gates and security guards who checked all comings and goings. Some large work units provided their employees with so many services and benefits that it was possible to live one's entire life without leaving the work unit's walled territory. During the Mao era, one's quality of life was closely tied to the level of services and facilities one's work unit could provide; there was considerable inequality between work units, but there was a fair amount of social equality within them. Though work units could be excellent welfare providers, because they controlled many aspects of employee life, they also could be sites of considerable political pressure and control (Bray 2005; Henderson and Cohen 1984; Walder 1986).

The post-Mao era has brought considerable changes to the work-unit system. Housing and other forms of social provision in most places have been privatized and separated from work units. Intra-work-unit inequality has grown sharply, and some employees now have much better salaries and benefits than others. But work units did not disappear entirely. Many well-off government units and enterprises have continued policies of providing multiple forms of benefits to their employees, and some have even continued to provide housing benefits long after they were supposedly banned.[5] Thomas Cliff (2012) uses the term *neo-danwei* to describe the work units that exist in the twenty-first century. Such work units provide extensive benefits, including housing, to at least some portion of their employees. In the particular case that Cliff describes, the work-unit benefits are quite extensive. But rather than promote intra-work-unit equality, the managers enable inequality by categorizing employees into different types and affording different types of employees different types of benefits. There are segregated housing sections in the work unit, as well as sharp divisions between "permanent" and "casual" employees. Wei Mian today can be considered such a neo-danwei.

Understanding how Wei Mian's structure as a neo-danwei affects the social experience of working at the company requires an analysis of the historical legacy of the work unit as a category of desire. At the start of the reform era, from the point of view of Zouping's rural masses, almost any social position was superior to that of being a peasant, or nongmin. Working at a factory, almost any factory, was considered a step up from being a farmer and living in a town a step up from living in a village. When I did research in Fengjia village in the late 1980s, I was shocked by working conditions in its factories and could not understand why young people preferred positions there to farming in the open fields. If I asked them, the young people would describe the factory jobs as more "modern" and "advanced" than farmwork, which they associated with the outmoded lifestyles of their parents. Though the government technically labeled villages "work units" too, to most villagers only urban factories with extensive benefits were real work units.

Over the 1990s the prestige of a being a factory worker declined (though it was still considered better than farming), but this did not signal a decline in the prestige of work-unit employment. During the 2000s, as secure work-unit jobs with good benefits became more and more scarce, people in Zouping and throughout China began considering permanent employment in a proper work unit a type of elite status. In 2009 one angry woman who sold wares from a small cart told me loudly about all the forms of discrimination she faced. She concluded that "peasants" in China were still oppressed. When I asked why she, an urban dweller who sold trinkets from a pushcart, should be considered a peasant, she replied that China had two types of people: peasants, a category that included everyone who did not have steady employment in a proper work unit; and work-unit people (*danwei ren*), a category that in her mind comprised mainly government officials, bankers, teachers, and doctors. In the late 2000s I heard many other less privileged Zoupingites use similar terms, with work-unit people being contrasted to everyday people (*laobaixing*), the masses (*qunzhong*), and peasants. In short, over the past three decades, working in a factory or a work unit has occupied a privileged position in Zouping's social imaginary. At present, at least for some Zouping farmers, Wei Mian positions are desirable precisely because they represent stable danwei-like work in an urban environment. For others, however, Wei Mian confuses the entire basis of the division of the social world into work-unit and non-work-unit people. On the one hand, most Wei Mian workers are relatively poorly educated manual laborers of rural origin. On the other hand, the benefits they receive, the permanence of their employment, and, in many cases, their salaries place them solidly in the category of work-unit people.

This sort of social imaginary structured Zhang Shiping's industrial strategy from the beginning. In Zouping he saw a large population that would take factory work and work-unit membership as social progress, as an advantage in the competitive arena of textile manufacturing. In addition, as a Communist cadre, model worker, and political as well as industrial leader, he saw providing Zouping's peasantry with industrial, work-unit-style jobs as a moral cause. In both the public front that Zhang presents to the world and the company's treatment of its permanent employees, this strategy and moral position remained apparent through 2012, when I completed the research for this book. In 2009, when Hu Jintao (then general secretary of the CCP) toured the company, newspapers reproduced a huge bulletin board hanging in several of Wei Mian's plants that declares, "150,000 peasants transformed into factory workers."[6] At the end of 2010 the company announced it was rapidly expanding the availability and quality of housing for its Zouping workers, with 15,000 new apartments to be completed over the next four years (Zuo 2010). In 2012 I photographed the first of these apartment complexes (figure 11). Finally, I should point out that the very name of the company, officially Weiqiao Pioneering Group, could be translated as Weiqiao Employment Creation Group by taking a more literal reading of the Chinese compound *chuang ye* (创业). Public officials often play with this pun when discussing the company (see, e.g., the headline in Zuo 2010).

In both the county seat and the town of Weiqiao, the company has set up multiple compounds that resemble work units. In the county seat the company has built two types of walled-in spaces: production districts (*shengchan qu*) and living districts (*shenghuo qu*). (Note that in figure 11 the sign at the lower right is not yet complete; there is space for the final two characters of *shenghuo qu* to be added). Some of the production and living areas are linked by bridges, so it is possible to walk from one to another without passing through the gates and security checks. To get into the living districts to conduct my interviews, I usually had to arrange to meet someone who lived there at the gate. The living districts include blocks of worker apartments for married workers and blocks of dormitory rooms for single workers or married workers who do not wish to purchase an apartment. Dormitory beds (eight beds to the room) are provided for free. During the mid- and late 2000s,

FIGURE 11. New Wei Mian worker apartments, 2012. Photo by author.

worker apartments were being sold at a cost of 70,000 to 120,000 yuan for 70 to 110 square meters, roughly one-third the market price for apartments of similar size and quality in that area. By purchasing a company apartment, Weiqiao workers secured the right to live there until they quit the company or, if they worked until retirement, until they died. When it reclaims an apartment, the company is supposed to return the purchase price to the family who lived there. As the apartments were all relatively new and the workers relatively young during the period of my fieldwork, I did not run into or even hear about a single case of the company reclaiming an apartment. Among the families who purchased such apartments, both husband and wife often worked at the company, so one of them could afford to quit without losing their apartment. The company had built several large living districts by the mid-2000s and continued to build new ones, with a rapid acceleration of this construction occurring in 2011. One of the areas, the "number one living district," was reserved for managerial-level employees and had slightly larger apartments and considerably tighter security at the entrance to the compound. All Weiqiao apartments came with free heat and below-market-price electricity, courtesy of the company's power generation facilities. They were wired for cable TV and high-speed broadband Internet. Through 2011 the apartments were in six-story walk-ups, though the post-2011 apartment buildings shown in figure 11 were even more modern 17-story buildings with elevators. All living districts had recreational facilities such as basketball courts and playgrounds and ample space for parking. The dormitories were not so luxurious, but in 2008 the company installed air conditioners in all the rooms (figure 12). The dormitories were used mainly by single workers and married locals who chose to live in their village homes, commute to work, and occasionally spend a night in the company quarters.

The company also provided worker cafeterias with subsidized food in all of its dormitory living districts and helped build several supermarkets and shopping areas near its compounds, which, being outside of the walled-in areas, were open to the general public. The company also built two large, extremely well-equipped primary schools in the Development Zone.[7] Though these were run by the county education bureau, and open to all children living in the Development Zone (including the children of workers in other smaller companies and the children of the villagers-in-the-city whose land had been confiscated to make way for the Development Zone), by 2011 over half the children in these schools were those of Wei Mian workers. One of the school's walls abutted the walls of one of Wei Mian's largest living districts, and Wei Mian built a gate that was open only for the half hour before and after school for the convenience of its families whose children attended that primary school. The company's management demanded that all of its workers' children be offered a place at one of the schools, even those who arrived partway through the school year or who were particularly trouble-some. This policy was not popular with the principals and teachers at the schools and did not apply to the children of workers in other enterprises. The company also built a large preschool exclusively for the children of its work-ers. The preschool's schedule was arranged to coincide with the company's factory shifts, and the cost for places at the preschool was roughly two-thirds that of other preschools in Zouping. Finally, like many other work units, Wei Mian provided its workers with a vast array of irregular benefits: special deals on vacation packages (especially if workers used them in a period encouraged by the factory to complement its work cycles), fruit and other gifts of food on holidays, and discounts on various consumer goods, from home computers to electric bicycles.

Workers at the company were divided into two main categories: contract (i.e., relatively permanent) and temporary. Everyone began as a temporary

FIGURE 12. Wei Mian dormitories. The street is empty during shifts; before and after shifts, the street is packed with an impromptu market. Photo by author.

worker but had the right to apply to become a contract worker after a year or two of employment if he or she met certain conditions, including age restrictions and educational level. The company adjusted the conditions according to its perceived need for relatively permanent workers. Though I could not collect figures on the ratio of permanent to temporary workers, from the number of apartments available and my interviews with permanent workers who chose not to live in company apartments I estimate that the company employed roughly 50,000 contract workers (out of a total of 100,000–150,000) in the county seat. There were two main benefits of being a contract worker: contract workers were not laid off when demand for the company's products declined, and married contract workers had the right to purchase a company apartment.

Many younger workers, especially those from outside Zouping, were quite satisfied to remain temporary workers. They could not imagine spending their entire lives working for Wei Mian and did not want to purchase a company apartment. Some calculated that they would not profit if the value of their apartment increased over time. As in most of China, real estate values were increasing rapidly in Zouping during the 2000s, and selling one's home at the same price for which one purchased it did not seem like a good deal. Others simply did not trust that the company would return the purchase price when it reclaimed the apartment. One such worker said, "If I get into a fight with my boss and quit or the company faces an economic catastrophe and fires me, will it really just give me the money back? They don't even give you the deed [*fangchan zheng*] to the apartment." For many, becoming a contract worker was a matter of committing one's life to the company. It indicated one's trust and commitment to Wei Mian as much as it indicated the company's commitment to the worker, and these employees were not willing to take that step.

In addition to representing a step up in social prestige from rural village life, the structure of life in a work-unit-like company replicates in an uncanny way certain features of rural life. For many social theorists, what separates "industrial/capitalist" societies from "agricultural/traditional" societies is the way in which the former creates a divide between public and private, home and work, between a place where one's time belongs to one's employer and a place where the employer has no say and for which the employer takes no responsibility (Graeber 2001). In agricultural societies, and indeed all preindustrial forms of human society known to anthropologists, such a separation is unknown. People live where they work, and while there are almost always gendered divisions of labor, the labor of reproducing the household and maintaining the home and the labor of procuring food and sustenance belong to the same conceptual category. While work units do pay wages, in their provision of homes and the institutional bases of reproducing the household and in their lack of separation of home from work, they reproduce an important feature of village life. The prevalence of work-unit-like employment in Wei Mian, but also most of the other large employers in Zouping, is perhaps indicative of the historical proximity of village/agricultural lives to capitalist industrialization in Zouping.

Privatization and Rumor

In China, the privatization of state-owned enterprises (SOEs; the act of privatization itself is typically referred to in Chinese as *gaizhi*, or transformation of the system) has been a continual process across the reform era (in contrast to the "shock therapy" of mass privatization that rapidly occurred in Eastern Europe during the late 1980s). Much of China's restructuring occurred between 1995 and 2005, but it is an ongoing process and has taken several forms, including the divvying up of shares and formation of private shareholding companies, management buyouts, bankruptcies, auctions, liquidations, listings, and de-listings (Garnaut et al. 2005: 1–5). In Zouping, most of the initial privatizations of county and township SOEs occurred between 1999 and 2003 (many collectively owned enterprises at the village level were privatized during the 1990s).

In the case of Wei Mian, the first step toward privatization took place at the end of 1999, but, at least according to *New Fortune Magazine* (*Xin Fuhao,* a business magazine licensed in Guangdong province and run from Shenzhen, www.xcf.cn), the restructuring continued through 2010, in ever more complex forms, enabling Zhang Shiping to become the richest person in all of Shandong province by 2011. The official county yearbook reports that Wei Mian was first divvied up into shares at the end of 1999, that additional shares were issued twice in 2002, and that the shares in the textile portion of the company were listed on the Hong Kong stock exchange in 2003. According to the yearbook, after the second time shares were issued in 2002, the "responsible enterprise" (*zeren gongsi,* presumably the Supply and Marketing Cooperative) controlled 77 percent of the shares, Zhang, his son Zhang Bo, and twelve other managerial personnel controlled 20 percent, and three private parties controlled 3 percent (Zouping 2004: 175). Also according to *New Fortune Magazine,* until late 2007 Zhang and his family members only controlled 6 percent of the company's shares; over 90 percent was controlled by Zouping's Supply and Marketing Cooperative. A 2007 restructuring allowed the Zhang family share to rise to 36 percent and shrank the cooperative's share to 51 percent. Then, in 2010, the Supply and Marketing Cooperative itself was restructured, with Zhang ending up with 25 percent of its shares, as well as purchasing other shares and splitting off the most profitable portion of the aluminum refining business into a separate enterprise that he fully owned. As a consequence, Zhang and his family controlled more than 50 percent of the stock and had the final say on all management decisions.[8] According to *Forbes Magazine*'s list of billionaires, as of March 2013 Zhang Shiping was worth US$3 billion, making him the twenty-fifth richest man in China.[9]

Determining which of these accounts is the most truthful is beyond the scope of my research. The Supply and Marketing Cooperative as well as the Weiqiao Pioneering Group have acted as shell companies with eleven or more production enterprises under them, each of which has also been divvied up into shares; deciphering exactly who owns what and how this has shifted over various restructurings is a task for a forensic accountant. More interesting here is the local gossip that surrounds the privatization of the Weiqiao Pioneering Group and what it tells us about the social tensions surrounding the company. During the late 2000s, I often heard the statement, spoken with a sly smile, that Wei Mian was a family-controlled stock corporation (*jiazu konggu youxian gongsi*). The sarcasm arose because in Zouping "stock corporation" sounds like an extremely modern form of economic enterprise, the term arriving in the area only after 1999, while "family business" sounds like a premodern and hence defective entity. That Wei Mian had become a family-controlled stock corporation made it a prime target for gossip. The phrase "family-controlled stock corporation" was often the start of a juicy story that sounded like the plot of a television soap opera.

The most common gossip surrounded Zhang Shiping's son, Zhang Bo. According to one friend, Zhang Bo graduated from senior middle school in the late 1980s but did not make it to university. In the early 2000s, after a few years of working for companies in Binzhou (positions secured only through his father's connections), he was appointed head of the Binzhou group of Wei Mian factories. He was brought back to the central company in Zouping in 2006 and appointed chair of the company's board of directors. Stories circulate about his sexual appetites, about how many girlfriends he has had, which of them he had gotten pregnant, and how much the family had paid for the pregnant girlfriends to go away, have an abortion, and never bother Zhang Bo again. The constant affairs supposedly led to his wife divorcing him in 2006. Another story has him going on a gambling spree in Macao, losing a significant chunk of Wei Mian assets, refusing to pay up, being kidnapped by Macanese casino thugs, and needing his father to fly to Macao, buy his freedom, and take him back to Zouping.

In addition to his son, Zhang Shiping has two daughters, both of whom have risen to important positions in the company. The eldest daughter, Zhang Hongxia, went to a two-year technical middle school (*zhongzhuan*) before going to work at the factory in 1987 at the age of sixteen. She was rapidly promoted up the ranks and has played an important role in training textile workers and supervising the acquisition of textile machinery. She became a Party member, a provincial model worker, and the lead manager in the textile division of the corporation (Zouping 2004: 579). The second daughter, Zhang Yanhong, graduated from the Weihai branch of Shandong University and was appointed head of the Weihai branch of the company. According to gossip, the Weihai branch company was formed by Zhang as a dowry (*jiazhuang*) for the second daughter on her marriage to the son of an important Weihai official and also to pay off the Weihai government for arranging for her to be admitted to the Weihai branch of Shandong University in the first place. This gossip also suggests that despite her impressive dowry, Zhang

Yanhong's husband wants to divorce her, either because she refuses to have sex with him or because she has affairs with other men, depending on the version being told. The eldest daughter is more respected, and some suggest that if ultimate control of Wei Mian could be passed on to her rather than Zhang Bo the company would be better off.

Another type of gossip surrounds the relative lack of education of Zhang's children and the other relatives Zhang has appointed to Wei Mian's managerial elite. One man discussed with me in great detail the numerous relatives of Zhang who now own stock in the company and have been appointed to high-level management positions, even writing a list of over fifteen names on a piece of paper. In addition to his three children, these relatives include his first younger brother, Zhang Shide, supposedly a junior middle school graduate whose only previous work experience involved driving a tractor before he entered Wei Mian's managerial ranks; his second younger brother, Zhang Shijun, who only graduated from primary school and is said to spend all day chasing women and ignoring his managerial responsibilities; and ten nieces and nephews (mostly children of Zhang's younger sister, his *waisheng*) and their spouses, not a single one of which, according to this man's account, attended university. To make room for these appointments, a large number of more qualified and experienced managers with proven track records of success were moved aside throughout the 2000s.

Though I cannot say which of the above statements might contain a grain of truth, I can point to some broader social facts such gossip evinces. First, this gossip is typical of the discourse that circulates around the children of the rich and the children of high officials in China (*fu erdai, guan erdai*), who both in general and in the example of Zhang Shiping are one and the same. Such discourse articulates the corrupting influence of power, especially as it plays out across generational divides. As a genre of talk, it directly challenges the Party's propaganda about the necessity and beneficence of continued Party leadership. It suggests that over time the CCP will necessarily sink into a morass of ever-expanding corruption and degeneracy. In Zouping these stories also serve to domesticate Wei Mian and raise questions about its long-term viability. As the most powerful actor in Zouping, and one that in many senses is responsible for the economic prosperity of the county as a whole, Wei Mian is simultaneously feared and desired and is thus an actor that many Zouping residents feel the need to tame with gossip. That is to say, many in Zouping both envy the wealth of Zhang and his family and realize that their own fortune is in some way tied to the continuing economic success of the company. Gossip provides an outlet to grapple with such ambiguous feelings. The gossip also embeds the abstract power of Capital in the all-too-human foibles of a group of local human beings.

The gossip further points to a widespread belief in the importance of university degrees and qualifications in Zouping and Chinese society more broadly and the fact that Wei Mian, in many respects, defies this belief. My earlier work analyzed the feverish desire for university degrees in Zouping, a desire that causes many parents to represent the pursuit of academic success as a moral cause for their children and the Party to require higher degrees from almost all of its aspiring members (Kipnis 2011a). Wei Mian contradicts this moral code in three ways. First, as the rumors above suggest, when appointing managers Zhang does not seem to value higher degrees. None of his own children attended prestigious universities straight out of senior middle school, and we can surmise that they did not score well on the university entrance exam (*gaokao*); moreover, if the above rumor about his other relatives is true, lack of education among Wei Mian higher management may be commonplace. Second, the company offers relatively high salaries and secure employment to uneducated, blue-collar workers who commit to the company and have physically demanding jobs. It links salaries to the physical difficulty and discomfort of particular jobs. While there are some relatively comfortable low-level office positions in the company, these pay only about half as much as production line positions on the shop floor. The highest paid blue-collar jobs go to shop floor workers with technical savvy in machine repair. University degrees count for little. Finally, as a neo-danwei, Wei Mian defies stereotypes about the relationship between higher degrees and steady danwei-like employment in contemporary China. Though I do not have systematic data on this topic, in my experience it was relatively educated Zouping residents who most enjoyed sharing gossip about Wei Mian.

The stories also point to the stereotype of the newly rich but unsophisticated country bumpkin (*baofa hu*), a contemporary Chinese figure that closely corresponds to that of new money tycoons in the United States in the early twentieth century, as expressed in novels like *The Great Gatsby*. According to this stereotype, conniving, lucky, and relatively uneducated individuals suddenly amass great wealth but do not know how to use it in an elegant and morally constructive way. They succumb to corruption and flamboyance in an attempt to compensate for their lack of acceptance into the more sophisticated sectors of society. Such a social dynamic suggests at least one side of the local social embeddedness of the Zhang's company. Though the privatization of the company would seem to enable Zhang and his family to take their money and leave Zouping, if they were to do so it is hard to imagine what sort of social position they could take up. Their social personae are tightly linked to the company itself, and given their lack of formal quali-fications, it is hard to imagine them securing similar positions outside of Wei Mian. If they were to move to other places, it is likely that the stereotype of new money would attach even more closely to their social being. More important, gossip suggests that Zhang and his family members could be accused of corruption. If they were to attempt to take their money and leave, high-ranking people in Zouping's government would have incentives to make such accusations and, given the anticorruption political climate insti-tuted under Xi Jinping, such accusations could have serious consequences.

Industrial Safety and Post–Financial Crisis Decline

On the evening of August 19, 2007, an explosion occurred in one of the com-pany's aluminium casting plants. According to official news accounts of the incident, 16 workers were killed and 59 were injured, but unofficial accounts on the Internet often put the number of workers killed at 55, and in some of the oral depictions of the incident I have heard, the number of deaths is over 100 and in one case 200.[10] As Fred Chiu (2003) points out in his analysis of a strike in Hong Kong, the production of numbers in accounts of incidents and accidents, whether in newspapers, official reports, or rumor, is never transparent; no number should be taken at face value. The immediate cause of the accident was molten aluminum (heated to 900 degrees Celsius in the casting process) leaking out of the pouring line and coming into contact with cool water, generating a steam explosion that literally blew the roof off the factory building and caused it to collapse.

According to the Sichuan News Net analysis (see note 10), based on the official reports of the Bureau of Industrial Safety Inspection (Anquan Shengchan Jiandu Guanli Ju), six types of human error caused or exacerbated the accident, most of which relate to the company's too rapid entry into and expansion of its aluminum business. First, the design of the industrial process for casting aluminum at the plant was done by a person without formal qualifications in the relevant areas of industrial design. Second, the blueprint for the industrial process did not have proper systems for the draining away of the recycled water used in the process. Third, the building itself was not constructed according to the blueprints; some of the ventilation pathways were blocked, causing the buildup of pressure from the steam to reach higher levels than it would have otherwise. Fourth, the foreman at the scene did not close down the plant quickly enough when he first discovered a leakage of molten aluminum. He had noticed the leakage twenty minutes before the explosion but neither closed down the industrial process nor ordered the evacuation of the building. Fifth, the safety regulations and guidelines at the plant were not sufficiently detailed and were not up to standard. Sixth and finally, the emergency response plans and procedures at the company did not meet the appropriate industrial standards.

Blogs and Internet forums provide another window on the accident. There were both pro- and anti-company comments. The pro-company comments stressed the contriteness of the leaders, the rapidity of the response of Zouping's emergency services, the first-class medical treatment the injured were receiving at company expense, and the large amount of compensation to be given to the families of severely injured and killed workers (310,000 yuan). Anti-company comments raised a wide variety of issues, some of which did not relate directly to the accident. In addition to questioning the official numbers of the dead and injured, some emphasized that most of the fatalities were young men between the ages of 19 and 25 and that the compensation was paltry for people of that age. Others accused the company and the Zouping government of a cover-up, saying that reporters were blocked from the accident scene and were harassed in their hotels by police and that the hospitals where the injured were being treated were surrounded by police to prevent reporters from interviewing doctors and family members. Others claimed that the explosion occurred nearly an hour earlier than the time given in the official reports (8:10 P.M.) in order to make it appear that the emergency response was faster than it in fact was. Finally, some claimed that foremen at the company pushed emotionally shocked but not physically injured workers to go back to work less than 48 hours after the accident.

Other accusations were more general in nature. They suggested that Wei Mian commonly cut corners in the pursuit of profit, that workers were often forced to work overtime when they were extremely tired, and that as the company moved into new production areas it gave workers new responsibilities without properly training them. Under such circumstances, these accusations suggested, a serious accident was all but inevitable. Finally, there were accusations that went far beyond the accident itself. People complained that they or their friends had been fired from the company without cause, that certain foremen or managers were unreasonably harsh; that the company was a major polluter and its profits from electric generation and alumnium production came at the expense of the environment.

Coming rapidly on the heels of this accident was the 2008 financial crisis. In late 2008 and early 2009 I heard many rumors that Wei Mian was about to go bankrupt. According to these rumors, the accident had caused the company to lose state backing and the financial crisis had cost it many orders, leading to mass layoffs. While I heard from local officials that total employment numbers at the company had dropped from roughly 150,000 to 100,000, one man on the street told me, "Never trust government statistics or the claims of government officials. I guess there are less than 30,000 people working at Wei Mian now. The place is doomed and good riddance. All they do is exploit female textile workers. My wife used to work there, and she hated it." In 2008 the official county yearbooks stopped reporting employment numbers for individual companies, but they do show that total employment in Zouping dropped from a peak of 214,000 in 2007 to a low of 160,000 in 2009, recovering to 190,000 by 2011; and that the number of textile workers in the county seat went from 170,000 in 2007 to 106,000 in 2009, recovering to 120,000 by 2011.[11]

Ultimately, the predictions of Wei Mian's demise proved false. As mentioned above, in 2010 and 2011 the company was still building new apartments for its workers (mostly in textiles) and salaries were continuing to go up even if the total number of employed workers went down. The Development Zone continued to expand, and I interviewed many relatively satisfied company employees. Nevertheless, the Internet reporting and criticism after the accident and the street rumor of 2009 demonstrate both that the company has its detractors and that corner cutting likely did occur during the rapid expansion of the early and mid-2000s. The tensions between the pursuit of profit and the provision of desirable danwei-like employment continue.

XIWANG GROUP CO., LTD.

For most of the late 2000s, the Xiwang Group was the second largest employer in Zouping (though since 2010 Changxing has caught up). When I interviewed the Group's director of human resources in 2009, she said that the company had just grown to over 10,000 employees (figure 13). To give this chapter some comparative perspective, as well as to demonstrate that many aspects of Wei Mian's history were hardly unique, a short history of Xiwang is helpful.

FIGURE 13. The headquarters of the Xiwang Group, 2009. Photo by author.

Several parallels to Wei Mian emerge. Xiwang's most important business, corn oil production, derives from the processing of local agricultural products. The Group's business expansion was driven by an ambitious entrepreneurial patriarch, Wang Yong. Like Zhang Shiping, Wang Yong began as a Party secretary in charge of a small factory, grew the business into a large conglomerate, became a national model worker, and amassed a personal fortune during the privatization of the 2000s. The Xiwang Group is also a neo-danwei that provides housing and extensive benefits for its employees. Two differences to Wei Mian are that Xiwang started out as a village-owned enterprise rather than a factory under the township Supply and Marketing Cooperative and that Xiwang, at least in the image it presents of itself and the broad reputation it has in Zouping, places greater emphasis on hiring highly educated people.

The Xiwang Group takes its name from Xiwang (Western Wang) village. In the early 1980s, the village was on the edge of the town of Handian, which was the first town directly north of the county seat. During the 1990s the village became part of the town, and during the 2000s the town physically merged with the county seat (see chapter 2). Though it is now part of the urban area of the county seat, to this day the bulk of the Group's facilities are located on land that used to belong to the village. In 1986 Wang Yong

(b. 1950) was running a flour mill as a family enterprise. He became a Party member, took a position on the village committee (*cunwei*), and came to an agreement with the village leadership that he would give the family enterprise to the village if it backed his vision of expanding industry there. The village then invested 400,000 yuan in a cotton ginning plant. The investment was successful, and in 1988 Wang was appointed Party secretary of the village and put in charge of its collective enterprises. In the same year the village attracted a 600,000 yuan investment from a Jinan animal feed factory. In 1990 the village invested 2 million yuan in a new corn starch plant. The processing of corn products became the focal point of the village businesses. At this point all of the employees of the various enterprises came from the village and the village collective owned the factories. In 1994 the village paid a 520,000 yuan royalty fee to purchase the right to use a patented process for making corn syrup. By 1995 average village income was 3,000 yuan (roughly double that of other villages in the county), and the village owned 70 million yuan of productive capital and had hired over 1,000 employees from throughout the township (Wang 2006: 86–95; Zouping 1992: 499).

In 1996, after another year of rapid expansion, the village enterprises began to lose money. Wang Yong concluded that the business had expanded beyond the size that the relatively inexperienced and uneducated management team at Xiwang could handle. In 1997 he brought in an experienced outsider to run the corn starch factory. The new factory head fired 190 Xiwang villagers in the first year, and a conflict arose. Wang sided with the outsider and managed to convince his fellow villagers that they should focus on the benefits they received as the collective owners of the factory rather than on the role of the factory in providing employment to otherwise unemployable villagers. By late 1997 the corn starch factory began turning large profits again (Wang 2006: 96–97). From that point on, Wang Yong emphasized recruiting highly educated outside expertise and encouraging talented young villagers to attend university and then return to the Xiwang Group. One locally famous hire was a Ugandan man who had earned a PhD in biochemistry from a Chinese university. The biochemist's wife was also African, and they had two daughters who had grown up in China. The company offered the man a high salary, an apartment, and placement for his daughters in the local primary school, where they quickly rose to the top of their classes. The success of this African family in Zouping received considerable local press coverage (Wang 2006: 229–30).

Over the late 1990s and 2000s the Xiwang Group continually upgraded its product line and expanded into a few new business sectors. In 2000 it constructed its own heat and electricity plant, for the same reasons that Wei Mian had done so. In that year it also secured the right to directly export its products and acquired a liquor and mineral water factory in county seat. From the corn starch and syrup business, various sugar products, including glucose drips for hospitals, were developed. The Group also developed sidelines in construction, real estate, and steel girders.

During the same period the Xiwang Group and the village became a sort of doubly nested neo-danwei. Some types of living benefits were created for Xiwang villagers, others were created for company employees, and some were shared between the two groups. Housing for the two groups were laid out in separate but adjacent walled compounds. Both groups enjoyed services related to infrastructure built by the company such as free heat and electricity from the company power plant and free access to the excellent company-built primary and junior middle schools. The township government agreed that employees of the Xiwang Group did not have to move their household registrations to Handian to attend these schools. Consequently, employees from other parts of rural Zouping can move to Handian but leave their household registrations in their home villages and maintain land rights there.

In 2001 the village gave up all of its land to the company for industrial expansion. In exchange for the land, villagers received luxury housing in apartment buildings for free or housing in villas (*bieshu*) if they were willing to pay for it, as well as a free supply of wheat flour (the company still had a mill) for at least thirty years or longer if the company still exists. In addition, since 2005 villagers have received the following benefits: scholarships for all youth who attend university; preschool at no cost; free comprehensive medical coverage; a free place in the newly built old age home for all those over the age of 65; and retirement benefits for all women over the age of 55 and men over the age of 60 (Wang 2006: 230). When I toured the company in 2009, the village choir, with over 40 members between the ages of 50 and 75, was using the company's stage to rehearse for an upcoming revolutionary song (*hong ge*) competition (figure 14). In part because of the genre of the competition but perhaps also reflecting the good fortune of their village, the songs they sang glorified the Party for creating a beautiful and harmonious society.

In our 2009 interview, the human resource manager explained that the benefits employees receive depend on their category. The company distinguishes between unskilled workers and workers with higher or technical degrees. Those in the former category received salaries in the 1,500- to 2,500-yuan per-month range in 2009, while the skilled workers and managers all

earned over 3,500 month, sometimes much more. Skilled workers and managers were recruited from all over the country and also included a few managerial personnel from the village, but these villagers had all graduated from prestigious universities. While villagers with appropriate degrees received preference in hiring, they were let go just as quickly as anyone else if they did not meet standards. Unskilled workers generally came from Zouping county but not from Xiwang village itself, as these villagers had come to feel that such work was beneath them. In 2009 there were over 500 families living in company apartments. As in Wei Mian, these were sold to the families of workers at construction cost but must be sold back to the company at the same price if the employee leaves. The Group also has smaller apartments that it rents at below-market rates to skilled employees only and (in 2009) over 3,000 dormitory beds, which were free to unskilled workers (though they charged a nominal fee for water). All employees received health, retirement, and life insurance policies. In addition, the Group provided a cafeteria for workers and a fancier restaurant for skilled workers and management, both of which sold food at subsidized prices. High-level managers had breakfast in the restaurant every morning to encourage informal interaction and information exchange among managers and skilled workers. Irregular benefits, such as vacation packages, food gifts at holiday periods, or company-sponsored wedding ceremonies, were also commonplace.

Like Wei Mian, the Xiwang Group was privatized during the first decade of the twenty-first century. Wang Yong became a national model worker in 2000 (Zouping 2004: 577), but this collective, political honor did not inhibit him from pursuing personal wealth. The Group was first divvied up into stocks in 1999, but a 2002 reorganization saw Wang Yong and several other leading managers gain a larger proportion of the stock, though the village collective also retained control of a significant share (Wang 2006: 125–27). Though I have not been able to locate any reports of subsequent reorganizations, I suspect there must have been some, as in 2013 *Forbes* declared that Wang Yong had become China's latest billionaire, with a net worth of US$1.3 billion. The magazine also stated that Wang and his family owned 66 percent of the Xiwang Group and that his son, Wang Di, had become the Group's vice-chairman.[12]

CONCLUSION

Zouping's economic growth over the past three decades (especially since the construction of its Development Zone in 2001) has been spectacular. With the rise of Wei Mian and other large business groups, growth during the twenty-first century has taken a slightly different form from that of earlier periods. The fortunate coincidence of Wei Mian's spectacular growth with the establishment of the Development Zone has been the most important driver of Zouping's urbanization. While the growth of many businesses in Zouping has been rapid and the growth Wei Mian was rapid and steady from the early 1980s to the 2008 financial crisis, the scale of Wei Mian's growth, which occurred after the move to the Development Zone (from 13,000 employees in 1999 to over 150,000 in 2007), was large enough to single-handedly make the Development Zone and urban area as a whole prosper.

While the industrial transformation of the county seat has been rapid, many forms of social memory, some of which bridge the entire twentieth century, are evident. The names of conglomerates like Weiqiao and Xiwang, for example, speak to their places of origin. The main focal points of their industrial production still reflect the agricultural products of the area. The neo-danwei form of their workplace organization both speaks to social desires that existed even before the 1980s and allows the continuation of a form of life in which a worker's home and the social reproduction of his or her family are not entirely separate from his or her employment as a wage laborer.

While privatization has been an important aspect of industrial transformation in Zouping during the past decade, the leading capitalists of Zouping are locals, not outsiders. The social embeddedness of Capital in Zouping thus remains important to its organization of production.

In their depictions of the political economy of Zouping county during the 1980s and early 1990s, Andrew Walder (1998) and Jean Oi (1998) used the term *local state corporatism* to describe the close links between capitalist production and local government. Walder even called the county government itself an industrial corporation. While these terms can no longer be used today, what I am calling the social embeddedness of local capital links historically to the Zouping they described. The main capitalists depicted in this chapter are nationally recognized Party members who once held positions in the local government. Even after formal privatization, links between their corporations and the local government remain tight. Cooperation on issues like the construction and management of schools, infrastructure, and public transportation in the urban area and the management of the household registrations of workers is evident. More important, the continuation of danwei-like industrial growth demonstrates a degree of embeddedness of both the government itself and the major business groups in local society. Both groups conceive of the population of Zouping as a constituent whose economic well-being should be developed.

George Hobor (2007, 2012) has done extensive research on cities that have deindustrialized in the U.S. Rust Belt. While all have suffered, some have done much better than others, retaining high enough levels of employment to survive and in a few cases even to thrive. One significant factor in the ability of these cities to avoid devastating declines is whether the firms that were originally located there develop new business lines in the same place when their businesses in one sector decline. The desire and ability of capitalist firms to do this relates to the extent to which they locate their product research and development in particular cities, which often reflects the extent to which they are socially embedded in certain communities. Corporate actors who remain loyal to particular locales can enable these locales to survive waves of industrial decline. From this perspective, that so much of Zouping's capital has grown locally and is owned locally would suggest a relatively stable future for Zouping. As Hobor (pers. comm.) puts it, how a locality comes up (i.e., develops during waves of economic growth) often determines the way and the extent to which it goes down in periods of economic decline.

FOUR

Recombinant Consumption

Consider the types of social transformations linked to what is commonly called the consumer revolution. First, as Walter Benjamin (1999) writes, the spread of shops, malls, and arcades creates new forms of public space and hence new dreamscapes or phantasmagoria.[1] In Zouping these new types of public space have grown rapidly as the county seat has urbanized. Second, advertising rises as an industry and assumes a prominent position both in public space and in various media (Horkheimer and Adorno 1972). In Zouping commercial advertising and marketing activities have come to dominate the streetscapes of the commercial districts as well as to fund and permeate the ever-expanding domains of online, film, radio, television, and print media. Third, the consumption of new technologies changes everyday practice in concrete fashion. As the quotation from Proust in the opening chapter suggests, our memory is tied up with the objects that we use in everyday life. When technology changes rapidly we tend to forget both the practical skills necessary to operate the outmoded machines and the more social and emotional relationships we had with both the objects themselves and the people with whom we used the objects. As a result, technological changes can mark generational divides. Finally, as David Graeber (2011) points out, the origins of the category of consumption and its use to group under one signifier activities as diverse as purchasing medicinal foods for one's elderly parents, wearing clothes of a particular style, or socializing with friends at a roller-skating rink is itself a hallmark of modernity.[2]

Yet all of these transformations enable forms of social and psychic continuity as well. New public spaces can be modeled on old ones; advertising can draw from images and associations long extant in a given society; updated technologies recycle bits from old ones, as in the case of computers deriving the layout of their keyboards from the typewriter. The renowned anthropologist of consumption Daniel Miller portrays even stronger forms of social continuity across the temporal divides of rising consumption. In *A Theory of Shopping* (1998), he makes an extended analogy between the ancient practice of ritual sacrifice and the modern one of shopping. Both activities, he notes, are ways of expending the surplus generated by "productive" activities. Both activities may be analyzed in the frame of the same three-phase structure. Sacrifice begins with an emphasis on the destructive consumption of the goods to be sacrificed. Next comes a sacralization of the destruction by channeling the offering into devotion to the gods. Sacrifice ends with a profane reordering of the social relationships among the people in the community or family who make the sacrifice. For shoppers the process begins with an embrace of the wastefulness of materialist consumption. This "excessive" consumption is then sacralized by focusing on the value of thrift in concrete practices of consumption. Thrift is a virtue that is closely tied to the reproduction of the household or the community group on whose behalf the shopping is done; the practice of this virtue is itself seen as a form of sacrifice to the family, house, or community. Finally, the products procured in shopping are used to reproduce or reorder the relationships between the shopper and the people on whose behalf the shopping is done (Miller 1998: 151). While I do not intend to follow Miller's analysis too closely here, his premises point to an important aspect of consumption in Zouping. Especially when one focuses on the relationships that are created, reproduced, or manipulated in the purchase and dispersal of consumer goods, it is often the case that these relationships are similar to those that were created, reproduced, or manipulated before the growth of consumption. In fact, the visibility of consumption makes these relationships easier to analyze.

Dismissive or overly critical views of consumption tend to focus on the first stage of Miller's three-stage process (the wastefulness of materialist consumption), refusing to acknowledge either the sacralization of thrift or the final use to which consumption is put. The connotations of the word *consume* reinforce dismissive social perspectives on consumption. As Nick Tapp (2000) and Susan Sontag (1979) note, consumption is also an old name for tuberculosis—a "wasting" disease that "consumes" its host. What positive might be produced of that? The use of the word *consumption* to mean "eating" is slightly more positive but also often deprecating. In consumer societies, obesity is ugly. As food enters individual bodies, both eating and obesity become metaphors for selfishness. "All he does is eat" implies "What a useless person" in almost any language.

Particular state bureaucratic or managerial capitalist accounting perspectives likewise attempt to distinguish consumption from production in ways that are not always useful for anthropological analysis. For example, entertaining in order to build relationships with useful government officials or business partners is considered an investment; entertaining in order to solidify relationships with distant relatives is categorized as consumption. Electricity used to manufacture aluminum is part of the production process; electricity used to cook for one's child is simply consumption.

Consumption is also often linked—experientially, historically, and metaphorically—to sexuality, especially male sexuality. Advertising joins desire and consumption, as sex, everywhere it seems, sells. Prostitution, the "oldest profession," involves the male consumption of female sexuality. After the man ejaculates, he is "spent" in more ways than one. He has dissipated his sexual energy, his semen, and his funds while metaphorically eating (consuming) the prostitute's body. One moral debate about prostitution hinges on whether this "spending" involves the man consuming the prostitute or himself. That this debate involves such a venerable profession should give us pause in asserting the modernity of the moral dilemmas that consumption poses.

The imaginative and linguistic links between consuming, desire, eating, wasting, and sexuality work as well in Chinese as they do in English. This might be because of commonalities among the sex industries, the advertising industries, and the physiologies of sex and eating in China and "the West" but also comes across in semantic structures of the terms. The character *xiao* 消 is used in compounds that mean "to spend money" (*xiaofei* 消费), "to consume or deplete one's resources and energy" (*xiaohao* 消耗), "to waste or wither away" (*xiaowang* 消亡), and "to digest food" (*xiaohua* 消化). *Hao* 耗, the other character in the base term for "consume," is also used in the ancient Chinese medical term for depleting seminal essence through excessive ejaculation (*haojing* 耗精).[3]

In this chapter I explore recombinant transformations by simultaneously depicting the radical changes that rising consumption has brought while emphasizing the forms of dialectical continuity and social memory that continue to link the present with the past. I focus primarily on changes in the objects and technologies consumed and their implications for social relations and everyday practice, saving discussions of the phantasmagoria of advertising and public space for the next chapter. I reject overly dismissive vantages on consumption by turning the production/consumption dichotomy on its head. That is to say, I view acts of "consumption" as *producing* something positive—relationships, sociality, families, social status, human hierarchies, even subjectivities.

TIME-SPACE COMPRESSION . . . AND REEXPANSION

In Zouping as in much of China, leaps in transportation and communications technology have rapidly shrunk the time it takes to travel and get messages to places and people both within and outside the county. As discussed in chapter 2, paved roads now link almost every village in the county to the county seat, and the combination of the Zouping city public bus system and the local intracounty long-distance buses provide relatively convenient links between the county seat and the villages. Buses, airplanes, and high-speed trains provide rapid and increasingly affordable connections between Zouping and other cities in China and, for a few, the rest of the world. High-speed Internet access and cell phone coverage allow quick communication both within the county and between Zouping and other parts of the country. From a consumer point of view, especially retail, the most important aspects of these developments are the products and services that people buy to make use of the infrastructure: travel agencies and Internet cafés, mobile phones, computers, tablets, motorcycles, electric bicycles, and automobiles.

Let me begin with Internet access. I first went to an Internet café (*wangba*) in Zouping in the mid-1990s. These sites proliferated in the Old City into the late 1990s but faded out of existence for a couple of years as many residents gained access to the Internet from their homes on personal computers and the cafés were banned from areas near schools. Since 2002 almost all of the hotels in which I stayed offered Internet access in their rooms. But also in 2002 Internet cafés reappeared in the Development Zone to serve the large numbers of migrant workers who did not have their own computers. From the late 1990s on, local specialty stores, electronics shops, and department stores began selling a wide range of computers and offering support to customers setting up Internet connections. In 2009, when doing fieldwork in a primary school in which almost all the students were of rural origin (either Wei Mian workers or villagers-in-the-city), I was shocked to learn that one of the Chinese teachers required students to do homework assignments on the class blog. Access to the blog required a computer linked to the Internet. "Do all of the students in your class really have Internet access?," I asked? "Yes," he replied, "and even if one or two don't they have no trouble getting their homework done by using a friend's computer." Almost all of the families I interviewed since then did have a home computer with Internet access, and the very few who did not had easy access to a computer through a friend or neighbor.

While this teacher made extensive use of blogging, others were reluctant to do so. They worried about the effects doing homework on a computer would have on the students' handwriting, reflecting wider debates about the importance of handwriting and calligraphy in Chinese society (see Kipnis 2011a: 96–103). Though it is too early to say whether computer technology will lead to a decline in handwriting competence and though the rapid rise in the number of years spent in educational institutions guarantees that overall levels of literacy are increasing, the issue nicely illustrates the ways in which new technologies can disrupt traditions of embodied training. As the Jia Pingwa novel discussed in the introduction suggests, the differences between social memories of communication by letter writing and those of communicating by text message mark generational divides.

Mobile phone use is so ubiquitous that it is easy to overlook. When I first came to Zouping during the late 1980s, there was only one (landline) telephone in the entire village where I did my fieldwork. Connection to that phone had to go through a county operator and was tightly controlled. Most people in the village had never made or received a phone call. Mobile phones began to become commonplace in Zouping during the late 1990s. By the mid-2000s every adult I met owned a mobile phone. For many in Zouping, as in most of China, India, and the developing world, mobile phones did not follow from landline phones but were the first type of telephonic device ever used. Stores selling phones emerged all over the city, and the phone networks themselves became more and more versatile, offering weather, news, and information services; greeting cards, jokes, and games; photos, images, and movies; and, with the introduction of smart phones in the late 2000s, a seemingly endless range of practical and entertainment applications. In bus and train station waiting rooms, sometimes more than half of the people were playing with their phones. In 2008 I was exchanging text messages with a twenty-year-old and was amazed at the rate with which he could compose messages: in less than 30 seconds he would reply to my 4- or 5-character text messages with 2- or 3-sentence, 30-character paragraphs. Thus new technologies lead to new competencies at the same time that they displace old ones. As Assa Doron and Robin Jeffrey (2013) have observed for India, mobile phones grant their users considerable communication autonomy. For young people, talking to someone their parents would not want them to communicate with about a topic their parents would not want them to discuss becomes easier. This autonomy is the target of regulation at many levels: the Chinese state attempts to control the spread of politically damaging "rumor" by requiring tight control and registration when purchasing SIM (subscriber identification module) cards, and parents and teachers set rules on student cell phone use that they enforce with varying degrees of success. Yet, though the communication autonomy that cell phone use enables can be used to combat patriarchal relations within the family, cell phones are usually used to increase communication within already existing networks of relatives and friends. Moreover, cell phones can be used by parents to nag and check up on their children. The "revolution" of cell phone technology thus does not necessarily entail a revolution in social relations.

The explosion in communication and information technology has been matched by changes in transportation technology. During my time in Zouping, many urbanites I knew went from commuting by bicycle to traveling by electric bicycle and then to motorcycle and finally automobile. It is the last step in this progression that shocked me (and changed Zouping) the most. Before 2009 only the very wealthy in Zouping owned automobiles. But that year the first car dealers began to spring up along the road between Zouping and Handian, and between 2009 and 2012 this 2-kilometer stretch of road went from being surrounded by fields to being lined by car dealerships. All of the middle-class families I knew purchased cars, as did many of the Wei Mian factory worker households I met. They used them not only for trips around the city but also for vacations or to make the hourlong drive to the provincial capital, Jinan, for some weekend shopping. All these cars, however, have not necessarily increased the speed and convenience of transportation in Zouping; their arrival has led to a rapid increase in the number and severity of traffic jams. In 2011 and 2012 I had to learn to avoid trips during rush hours (before and after work and before and after lunch), as even the city buses could encounter long delays. Traffic jams were caused not just by the increased number of automobiles but also by the fact that so many drivers were inexperienced and traffic laws were only sporadically enforced. Over these years, driving schools became a common new type of service and a lucrative business. Parking, in the central shopping area of the Old City especially, also became a problem.[4]

The selection of shops and services located in and around Fortune Plaza (Xiangyun Guangchang), which is near the largest Wei Mian dormitories in the Development Zone, reveals much about the particular consumption habits of young, single migrant workers (mostly between the ages of 17 and 23). The primary items for sale are mobile phones, shoes, birthday cakes and other forms of fast or premade food, and inexpensive clothing. The primary services on offer include Internet cafés, hairdressers, roller-skating rinks, pool halls, and a few private trade schools specializing in courses like computer skills and accounting.

Three or four factors structure this world of consumption. First, living mostly in dormitories, young migrant workers have very limited space in which to store their possessions. The space they do have is often insecure, and items of value are vulnerable to theft. Migrant workers keep their mobile phones and shoes with them at all times, so these two items constitute the only forms of consumption through which they can express their identities. Second, as Leslie Chang (2009: 95–97) describes for the "factory girls" of South China, in a world in which one does not have a permanent address and in which one changes jobs frequently, the mobile phone becomes the anchor of one's social network, the only means by which friends and family can contact you and through which acquaintances can remember your name. Switching mobile phones often results in or accompanies a conscious attempt to change one's identity.

In the view of many conservative Chinese parents, the purpose of working in a factory while young is to accumulate the resources necessary to purchase an apartment or a house and then to get married. Though some migrant youths rebel against this ideal, many I spoke to, both women and men, did save a large percentage of their salaries and dream of starting families. With salaries (in the late 2000s) of over 2,000 yuan per month and free dorm rooms, the young migrant workers certainly did have the resources to spend freely, but the rather limited range of services on which to spend money and their low prices indicated that thrift was common.[5] Many simple food items, such as ice cream bars and bottles of mineral water, were 30 to 40 percent less expensive in the Development Zone than in the Old or New City district.

The particular services on offer to young workers allowed a modicum of personal expression and reflected the consumer fads of the era. Hairdressing salons enabled both men and women to dye their hair in a variety of colors and emulate the hairstyles of East Asian film and pop stars, as displayed in the magazines and posters in the shops. Some of these shops also offered tattooing, but this aspect of the business declined after Wei Mian enacted a ban against hiring workers with tattoos, on the grounds that tattoos sometimes indicated gang membership.

Birthday cake shops in part reflected the popularity of birthday parties among young workers. Workers would act as hosts for their own birthday parties, treating all their friends to cakes, alcoholic drinks, and other goodies. Some would drink to excess on these occasions. The costs of these parties could amount to half a month's salary, and they were the only occasions when I witnessed young migrant workers spending lavishly. Internet cafés were used predominantly by young male workers for gaming. Mobile phones and text messaging especially were used for communication, but while gaming at the Internet cafés male workers would also use instant messaging to contact friends from afar. Roller skating was popular among both young men and young women,[6] but the rinks sometimes competed with one another on price by letting women or first comers in for free (figure 15). There were three or four rinks in close proximity, but on the nights I went there were only enough skaters to fill one or two of them. The workers preferred to skate in places that were relatively crowded, as socializing and showing off skills to a crowd counted for more than room to maneuver. Some skaters moved fast and aggressively, weaving in and out of the slower skaters and doing plenty of spins as they sped along, forward and backward. One young woman told me, "I got so many scrapes and bruises learning to skate, I fell a hundred times, but it was worth it. It is the only thrilling thing we can do. Now I skate fast and never fall."

A final venue in this area worthy of mention was a popular milk tea bar, which was open every evening from about 5:00 P.M. to midnight. Milk teas (*naicha*) are sweet drinks that have become popular among young people throughout China. This bar featured a bulletin board on which young workers would leave Post-it note messages; these could be about anything—buying and selling personal items, for example—but were usually about the search for romance. Like a newspaper personal ad, the messages included a brief description of the individual (gender, age, height, distinguishing characteristics) along with the desiderata one sought and one's QQ (instant messaging) number. Words indicating sincerity (*chengxin, chengyi, chengzhi*) were commonly used.

FIGURE 15. Entrance to roller-skating rink before opening time. The sign reads "Free for Women and First Ten Men." Photo by author.

In sum, I would argue that there is something both quite new and quite old in this consumption. As I argue in chapter 10, the entire category of youth is linked to that of modernity. It appears and expands alongside such institutions as schools, nonarranged marriage, and job markets that enable and require finding a job outside of working for one's parents on the family land. Arguably, Fortune Plaza is the first public space in Zouping devoted primarily to the consumer needs of this social group (figure 16). Yet much of the consumption that goes on there, as well as the practices of thrift that limit this consumption, relate to the search for a future spouse and the reproduction of the household.

CONSUMPTION AND THE PRODUCTION OF FAMILIAL RELATIONS

It is not just young people who consume for their families. Perhaps most of the services on sale in Zouping could in some sense be related to familial relations. These included services for children (after-school care, enrichment

classes, braces, and books), restaurants and supermarkets (food was often consumed in family groups), health and beauty products and services (usually for married women), home products (furnishings, linen, and decorative items), and businesses specializing in family rituals, especially weddings. That such services are used to construct, alter, or reproduce familial relations does not imply that they necessarily produce happy or harmonious kin relations. One family member might attempt to use them to steer another family member in a direction the latter resists, as was often the case when parents shopped for children.

Businesses offering services for children were among the most common type of enterprise and were scattered across the three districts of the city. A few such services had been available since the late 1990s, but their numbers grew in the 2000s and mushroomed in 2008 after restrictions on the length of the school day at public schools began to be enforced. Most prominent were forms of educational enrichment, including private tutors, after-school homework classes (*buxi ban*), and oral English classes. Art, music, and dance classes were also prevalent. A small number of businesses offered sports classes, such as tae kwon do (*taiquandao*) and, in summer, swimming.[7] There were also some toy stores in Zouping, but these were not nearly as common as stores that offered products that encouraged learning, such as books, tools for drawing, painting, and calligraphy, and musical instruments. In 1999 I discovered an orthodontic clinic in the Old City. Since that time I have seen an increasing number of children with braces on their teeth, and by the late

2000s braces were common among children even in schools catering to migrant worker families and villagers-in-the-city. Throughout Zouping parents were clearly willing to spend money on products and services that they see as improving their children's "quality" (*suzhi*), especially those that increase their chances of attending university.[8]

Fast-food restaurants especially are places for family meals or buying children a treat. A wide range of such restaurants exist and are especially numerous in the shopping districts of the Old City and the pedestrian mall of the New City. Kentucky Fried Chicken (KFC) is the only international chain. There are three or four Taiwanese chains, such as Yonghe Soy Milk and Mingdao Coffee, but the great majority of chain restaurants are of Chinese origins such as Guoqiaoyuan Mixian (a Yunnanese rice noodle chain) and Luxi Feiniu (a beef hot pot chain). Many of the foods sold in supermarkets are also targeted to children, some claiming to boost children's intelligence or memory or another school-related "quality." Many children told me that they loved Western fast foods like fried chicken and chicken burgers, a taste that did not usually please their parents and teachers but was sometimes tolerated as a treat. These foods were available at a number of Chinese fast-food chain stores, in addition to KFC.[9] Fast food did not exist in Zouping before 1999.

Other shifts in the food sector accompanied the rise of large supermarket chains in the 2000s. Previously almost all food shopping was done at one of two large open-air markets, where mostly local vendors sold a great variety of consumable goods (figure 17). The nonlocals who sold at these markets came from within a 200-kilometer range, as they depended on hauling produce by truck for their businesses. During the 2000s, large, provincewide chains set up roughly a dozen supermarkets throughout the city. These were crowded whenever I visited, and everyone I asked said that they shopped at these supermarkets at least some of the time. The supermarkets were seen as more sanitary and convenient than the open markets, though some people believed the open-air markets had fresher food. One of the open-air markets shut down in the early 2000s, though the other remained open at least through 2012.

Several shifts in diet resulted from the new food distribution system. Before 2000 steamed bread, or mantou, was the staple food. Most people ate it three times a day, almost every day of the year. While steamed bread is still a staple for many, rice, noodles, dumplings, bread, and a range of other starches are now also consumed with far greater regularity. Dairy products are also much more widely eaten than before, with many varieties of milk and

Outdoor market in 2012. Photo by author.

yogurt available in the supermarkets. New technologies of food production have also expanded dietary ranges. During the late 2000s, soy milk machines (*doujiang ji*) became popular, enabling customers to make a wide variety of hot drinks from various beans and grains.

Parents spend money on their adult children as well, especially for weddings. The larger hotels all have grand rooms for holding wedding banquets. The ritual itself, which is increasingly handled by commercial wedding companies (*hunqing gongsi*), is usually staged at the beginning of the banquet. These companies provide an emcee to direct the ritual and also record the event on video and with still cameras. While the manner of organizing these rituals might seem new, their structure often invokes the traditional. For example, one common theme is that of the rural wedding in the city (*nongcun hunli chengli ban*), which mimics the structure of a patrilineal, virilocal wedding by emphasizing the incorporation of the "daughter-in-law" into the husband's family rather than the mutual blending of families; at one such wedding I witnessed, none of the bride's relatives attended as such events are staged primarily for the husband's family. Another common wedding motif is that of a match between a "scholar" and a "beauty" (*caizi jia ren pei*).

Themes are announced in wedding invitations and decorations at the wedding venue. Some companies specialize in wedding photographs (the bride wears a fancy wedding dress and the groom is in a tuxedo). Some couples spend close to a month's salary to have these pictures made years after their weddings occurred.[10]

Home decor businesses are also common in this "apartment proud" city. As Miller (1998) points out, products for the dwelling space of the family take on a "sacred" dimension in cultures where "house," "home," and "family" overlap conceptually and the reproduction of the family is a paramount value.[11] Such is often the case in Zouping, especially among those families who have managed to purchase apartments in one of the new residential areas. As such new apartments are most common in the New City, the pedestrian mall has become one of the centers for such products. Stores specializing in artwork, bed linens, curtains, and furnishings have concentrated in this area, as well as in some of the larger department stores of the Old City.

Beauty and spa services have also proliferated. Clinics specializing in weight loss and skin whitening and products promising these same results were especially common. Jie Yang (2011) has written about the rise of the "beauty economy" in China in general and the ways in which this economy normalizes certain forms of gender relations and links beauty to class and discourses of human quality, or suzhi (see also Notar 1994). But Yang also emphasizes that middle-aged and older women consume these products and services just as frequently as do young women and that their motives are much more complex than simply "pleasing" their husbands. One woman Yang interviewed depicts her attempts to look younger and more beautiful as a form of revenge on her husband for his affairs, while another claimed that improving her appearance was central to success at work. In Zouping too these industries primarily target already married, middle-aged women in their advertising.[12]

CONSUMPTION, MALE BONDING, AND (THE SEX) BUSINESS

Consumer services for wheeling and dealing among businessmen (occasionally businesswomen) and government officials expanded during most of the period I was in Zouping, though official newspapers suggested at least a temporary downturn in cadre entertainment spending after Xi Jinping came to power in late 2012 and enacted strict regulations on cadre banqueting. Restaurants and hotels that cater to this sector, in Zouping as in most of China, feature private dining rooms of varying sizes. As the 1990s and 2000s progressed, both these rooms and the meals served in them became more extravagant. By the mid-2000s, the private dining rooms featured expensive furniture and table linen, private bathrooms, air conditioning, and perhaps karaoke equipment. Banquets could include all manner of imported seafood, local specialties, and rare, exotic, and medicinal dishes (Farquhar 2002). High-end restaurants were available in the major hotels in all parts of the city, with another concentration in the all-night district of the New City. This latter concentration was not accidental: the New City houses the government headquarters and most of the government departments. Some departments, such as the education bureau, had fancy restaurants in their office towers. In addition to restaurants, karaoke bars became common venues for business entertaining, and several of these appeared in both the Old and New City Districts. Like the restaurants, the karaoke bars offer private rooms rather than public seating. They also sell drinks and snacks, and it is even possible to arrange the delivery of full meals to one's room.

John Osburg (2013) describes how during the 2000s sexual services became more and more central to business entertaining among wealthy entrepreneurs in the city of Chengdu. The privacy of the karaoke bar or banquet room allows for the hiding away of both outrageous degrees of drunkenness and the transgression of conservative sexual norms. While I cannot speak to the exact place of sexual services in Zouping's entertainment industry, I can say that the sex trade became increasingly visible in Zouping in the twenty-first century. Especially in the mid- and late 2000s, no matter what hotel I stayed in, I would receive nightly calls on my room phone from women asking me if I needed "special services" (*teshu fuwu*). Most of the hotels also had in-house massage businesses. Condoms were available for sale in hotel rooms, as well as at the check-out counters of most supermarkets.

While family groups would also use both the karaoke establishments and the upscale restaurants and while some groups of cadres included women, all-male groups were the most common customers at these places. The hotels were also mostly, but certainly not exclusively, male spaces, with the majority of customers being businessmen from other parts of China. Over the 2000s the number of hotels grew rapidly in Zouping; in total, I stayed in seven different hotels during my visits there and learned of at least six others. During the mid-1990s I knew of only three. In sum, consumption related to wheeling and dealing, both among businesspeople and between businesspeople and government cadres, expanded alongside the economy throughout the period of my research. While both the volume and the types of services consumed shifted over time, the social and emotional spirit of this consumption seemed quite stable to me, enacting forms of (mostly) male bonding necessary for economic (and political) cooperation.

CONSUMPTION AND DISTINCTION, CONSUMPTION AND CLASS

The place of class in practices of consumption in Zouping seems to be both everywhere and nowhere. As is the case perhaps everywhere in China and most of the world, products, especially high-end luxury products, are marketed as distinguishing the consumer. Geng Song and Tracy Li (2010) argue that upper-class masculinity in China is constructed through the concept of *pinwei* and explain: "Although *pinwei* is often translated as 'good taste,' the English phrase fails to convey the semantic content of hierarchy and élitism of the original word. *Pinwei* is a compound, *pin* meaning 'grade' or 'quality' (the character was also used for the ranks of court officials in ancient China) and *wei* indicating 'position' or 'rank'" (163). Thus when marketers tell (usually male) consumers that their product is a mark of pinwei, they are suggesting that users of their product have a form of good taste that demonstrates their superior position in a ranked social hierarchy. Such a position is naturally assumed to enable the man who holds it to attract women. Clothes and accessories are often marketed in this way in Zouping.

Over the course of the 1990s and 2000s, high-end products in Zouping's department stores went from items I could afford even as a graduate student to those I would not consider purchasing as a well-paid professor (e.g., US$1,000 suits and US$150 shirts) (figure 18). During the 2000s, the quality of dress worn by Zoupingites in white-collar jobs surpassed my own, and some high-level government officials and upper-level managers did wear high-end department store clothing. However, I also heard rumors that officials never purchased such items for themselves but were given them as "gifts" by those seeking to curry favor. According to at least one salesman, the purchasers simply sought out the most expensive items in a given product category and left the price tag on the item when giving it to an official (or teacher or doctor), perhaps wrapping the product in attractive packaging.

FIGURE 18. Advertising billboard in the Old City for expensive clothes. Photo by author.

Although advertisers used the concept of pinwei in marketing and some residents wore expensive clothes, Zouping was generally a rather unpretentious place. After all, Zouping is not Shanghai or Beijing. While there are a few very successful businessmen, the most ambitious and successful Zoupingites generally leave Zouping for larger cities like Jinan, Qingdao, or Beijing. Moreover, in Zouping there are plentiful, relatively well-paying manufacturing jobs. Thus, compared to the large Chinese metropolises, class differences in Zouping are less pronounced. To use an American analogy, Zouping is more like Akron, Ohio, during the manufacturing heyday of the mid-twentieth century than a city of class extremes like contemporary New York or Los Angeles. While some companies used the same sort of advertising materials in Zouping and in larger cities, I am not certain that they were received in the same way.

Li Zhang (2010) suggests that in the larger Chinese metropolises, many wealthy people attempt to distinguish themselves through consumption because their wealth was accumulated in a dubious manner. Such people cannot distinguish themselves by discussing career accomplishments as they are embarrassed to discuss their careers at all. In Zouping, while some people did attempt to distinguish themselves through their dress and while rumors of officials receiving gifts in shady transactions do corroborate Zhang's suggestion of shady accumulation, in this case the shady accumulation occurs through consumption rather than production. More important, I am not certain that the people in Zouping who wore expensive clothes and fancy watches were really that much wealthier than those who did not.

Perhaps the only arena of consumption in which I heard a discourse of distinction explicitly articulated by Zoupingers themselves was housing. Even here, the discourse did not seem to fit the economic facts. Several proud apartment owners in the New City asserted that the apartment complexes in the New City were vastly superior to those in the Development Zone. But in my visits to apartments in various sections of the city, I found both the construction of the complexes and the amenities in individual apartments quite similar. The biggest differences stemmed from the evolution of quality during the 1990s and 2000s. Given that the overall age of the Development Zone was exactly the same as that of the New City, age was not a distinguishing factor in the quality of the apartments in the two parts of the city. Even the Old City has seen a large number of new buildings constructed. Though the proud New City apartment owners found my observations hard to believe, they countered that even if there were new buildings in other parts of the city, the superior environment in the New City, with its greater distance from polluting industries and more numerous parks and cultural amenities, made it a much more livable space. While I did like the parks of the New City, I doubted that a few kilometers made that much difference in terms of air pollution. More important, each time I inquired about apartment prices in the three districts of Zouping, they were remarkably similar. At most, commercial apartments in the New City were 5 to 10 percent more expensive than those in the Development Zone, with prices for the best apartments reaching a peak of roughly 5,000 yuan per square meter in 2011 and 2012. Many relatively well-off families who worked in the Development Zone purchased apartments there simply for the convenience of living close to their workplace, so all parts of the city experienced a strong demand for housing.

In an analysis of consumer desire for new apartments by migrant workers and laid-off workers in the northeastern city of Harbin, Mun Young Cho (2013: 46–67) invokes and critiques Pierre Bourdieu's (1984, 2005) classic work on social class and taste. Bourdieu argues that the pro-housing policies of the French state (in the areas of subsidized loans and tax policy) encouraged the lower middle classes to aspire to home ownership even when they could not afford it, causing a fair amount of suffering and anxiety. In contrast, the working classes shut themselves out of the lower middle classes by refusing to participate in this desire. They dismissed home ownership as a pipe dream inappropriate to people of their status. In contrast, in Harbin Cho finds that many working-class people, even those who had been laid off, strongly desire new apartments. They too suffer from not having the means to fulfill their desire. Cho argues that this desire is in part a legacy of the Maoist years when workers were entitled to good housing (by the standards of that time) because of their status as members of work units.

In Zouping too both blue-collar and white-collar workers desire new apartments, but the class situation differs from that in both France and Harbin. In Zouping the lack of a large upper and upper middle class and the presence of a large, relatively well-paid working class make housing prices relatively uniform and make housing affordable to dual-income households of most occupations. Subsidized work-unit apartments are even affordable for single-income households. In contrast to Harbin, there are hardly any laid-off workers in Zouping. Most people are from rural backgrounds, and I hesitate to describe their desire for housing as a direct reflection of any recent state policy. Rather, at least since the 1980s, housing has been more closely related to gender and kinship mores. During the 1980s in Zouping's rural villages, the provision of a house by a man or his family was seen as a prerequisite for attracting a wife (Kipnis 1997). In Zouping today, apartments are sometimes purchased by a man or his family and sometimes purchased with contributions from husbands, wives, or perhaps both of their families, but rarely are they purchased by either a woman or her family for the benefit of a woman and her husband.

CONCLUSION

In Zouping, as in most places in urban and eastern China, rapid economic growth and technological innovation over the past two decades have enabled a true revolution in the range of products consumed. While those residing in relatively wealthy countries have also experienced the technological revolution associated with computers, the Internet, and mobile phones, they may find it difficult to imagine a place where this transformation has occurred alongside shifts from bicycles to automobiles, from local outdoor markets to supermarkets, from no phones (rather than landlines) to smart phones, and from a few run-down stores and restaurants to high-end shopping malls, vibrant, people-packed shopping streets, and seemingly endless culinary options.

These shifts have effected a variety of changes in the lives of Zoupingites. Faster communication has often translated into a faster pace of life. The world and China have become smaller places, easier to navigate both in the imagination and through travel. The sex industry has thrived as advertising uses sexual imagery to sell products and links masculinity to consumption and femininity to beauty. From a more global perspective, one might also argue that the world's environment may become warmer and more polluted as the level of consumption in rapidly developing places like Zouping catches up to that in wealthier countries (Gerth 2010).

But Zouping's revolution in consumer products should not be taken as demonstrating a sharp historic break with the past. The types of social relationships consumption mediates and the way in which consumption mediates these relationships continue to involve kinship relations imagined in patrilineal fashion and extrafamilial relationships among men. The search for distinction and status in these relationships is not new, even if the place of consumption in this search has grown. The extension of childhood and the continued decline of arranged marriage have made more space for social relationships among unrelated young people. This shift, though reflected in some forms of consumption and marketing, has not been caused by Zouping's consumer revolution. Moreover, the idealization of romantic relationships has a long history in China (Jankowiak 1993, 1995).

Continuity in Zouping's social life is both a matter of the endurance of long-standing tastes embedded in habitual practices (what Bourdieu calls habitus) and a matter of a more dialectical, conscious form of revival or reappraisal in which a long stride in one direction brings about a critical reaction and a desire to take at least one step back toward the place that is imagined as the starting point. To illustrate this dual movement with a concrete example, consider that one may eat the foods of one's childhood out of habit or because one has decided that shifts in diet have become both politically undesirable and unhealthy and that a return to the culinary practices envisioned in idealized memories of one's childhood would be beneficial. Continuity can involve one or the other of these processes or both at the same time.

FIVE

Recombinant Phantasmagoria

In his book *Real Cities: Modernity, Space, and the Phantasmagorias of City Life* (2005), Steve Pile argues that what is "real" about cities is their psychic effects on the people who inhabit them—the "structures of feeling" evoked by their ever-changing spaces, the fleeting and sometimes secretive emotion that well up in those who wander its streets.[1] Pile takes the term *phantasmagoria* from the work of Walter Benjamin and explains:

> What is key is that phantasmagoria both consisted of a procession of images that blended into one another, as if in a dream, and also concealed the means of its production. Benjamin was simultaneously evoking both aspects of the experience of phantasmagoria: both the spectacle of movement and the requirement to look beyond surface appearances to the means of their production. Thus, by using the term phantasmagoria to describe modern city life, Benjamin is highlighting both the new forms of experience visible in modern cities, such as Paris, and also the invisibility of the social processes that create the city's many spectacles. (Pile 2005: 20)

Benjamin saw this phantasmagoria as what I would call a recombinant modernity. That is to say, he saw classic urban modernity—a world of arcades, crowds of strangers, advertising, shifting modes of fashion, and constantly rebuilt urban space—as constitutive of the fleeting images that form a phantasmagoria at the same time that he saw tradition and history as constantly haunting these images, as always being dialectically intertwined with this modernity.[2]

Pile explores contemporary urban phantasmagoria through streetscapes, urban spectacles, ghost stories, the architectural magic used in geomancy, and dreamscapes. In this chapter I examine some of the fleeting images that make up the phantasmagoria of Zouping, with emphasis on the interrelation of the traditional and the modern. While I do not analyze the social processes behind these spectacles in great detail, I point out from the beginning that almost all of them relate to advertising, marketing, or state efforts to conjure legitimacy for the leadership of the Party.

THE CREATION OF PUBLIC URBAN SPACE

Urbanization in Zouping, especially since 2000, has involved the construction of many new spaces of leisure and consumption. Some of these spaces are more commercial than others, but they all might be considered, in varying degrees, "public." Spaces like parks and plazas and sidewalks in shopping districts are open to all. Places like shopping malls are controlled by private entrepreneurs but also open to all, even window-shoppers. Fast-food restaurants are limited to paying customers but seat people in large, open spaces where they may interact with one another if they wish. Finally there are some spaces of consumption, including many formal restaurants, that offer their services in relatively private rooms. Despite the importance of this latter category, one of the most interesting contrasts between Zouping of the late 1980s and Zouping of 2012 was the emergence of many different types of "public" space where one could gaze upon others while being gazed at and interact with friends and family as well as strangers and new acquaintances.[3] Such spaces are a joy for ethnographic field-workers like me and anyone else who wishes to meet people and engage in conversation.

Since the late 2000s, especially on Friday and Saturday nights, several sections of the city have grown into bustling, hot and noisy (*renao*) spaces of possible interaction. The main shopping streets of the Old City District are crowded with shoppers and people gazers, sometimes making it difficult to navigate them. The malls and restaurants are full. The most upscale of these are located in the Tianxing development discussed in chapter 2. Less expensive are the vendors and fortune tellers who set up temporary stalls on the sidewalks. Some stores blare Chinese pop music into the street to attract attention. Others go further, setting up temporary stages on the sidewalk in front of their stores and holding either product giveaways or some sort competition that usually involves pretty young women dancing or singing or modeling clothes. On a weekend in 2010, for the first time in Zouping, I saw a beggar on the main shopping street. Since then I have seen them often, evi-

FIGURE 19. Pedestrian mall in the New City. Photo by author.

dence of the growing prosperity of the place and the degree of concentration of relatively well-off people in the types of public places in which beggars might hope to receive money. The beggars often write out their hard luck stories on poster-sized paper that they display in front of their (sometimes crippled) bodies while sitting or kneeling on the sidewalk. In the New City District, the walking street fills up with lunchtime traffic every day. In addition to the shops and restaurants that line the mall, food vendors set up temporary stalls in the middle of the pedestrian strip (figure 19). In nice weather, especially on weekends, the parks also fill up with people walking, fishing, playing croquet, and roller skating. In the parks people are especially open to interaction with strangers. They observe each other's activities close up, and those who are friendly and outgoing often strike up conversations. As a foreigner, if I went to a park and stood or sat around in a leisurely manner, I could almost always count on someone coming up to me and asking me where I was from and what I was doing in Zouping and maybe even asking to take a picture with me. In the Development Zone, especially on weekend evenings, the area around Fortune Plaza fills with clothing stalls and carnival like game stalls aimed at entertaining young migrant workers. Nearby roller-skating rinks, pool halls and internet bars become hot and noisy. On most evenings, the more private spaces of consumption—the banquet halls of the larger

hotels and restaurants and the private rooms of the karaoke clubs also fill up, as evidenced by the cars which fill the parking lots and sidewalks near the hotels, and in the all-night district (*buye cheng*) of the New City (figure 20).

As Piper Gaubatz (2008) points out, parks, plazas, sidewalks (including walking streets lined with arcades), and shopping malls have become important urban spaces throughout China. They are sites of various types of public performance and practice, including collective dancing, roller skating, street art, martial arts, begging, photography, people watching, and public events. These spaces are often actively policed, and it is quite rare that active political protest occurs. What Gaubatz finds striking compared to previous eras is the extent to which these spaces are not walled in and the extent to which they are open to the wider public. While in some large older urban areas, parks have walls around them and charge entry fees, in places like Zouping all parks and plazas lack walls and are free of charge.

Many in Zouping feel pride in their relatively new sites of entertainment and excitement. Once, in 2011, at lunchtime on a Saturday, I was dining alone in one of Zouping's better fast-food restaurants on the main shopping street of the Old City. The street and the restaurant were both crowded and, in my search for table space, I bumped into an old acquaintance—a driver from one of the government units. We had first met in the late 1980s when both of us were single, and on that day in 2011 he was dining out with his wife and daughter, a 19-year-old who had just returned to Zouping after her first semester at college in the large city of Qingdao. While we ate together he asked me with a broad smile, "When you first came, could you have ever imagined that Zouping would have restaurants as nice as this?" His daughter then added, "Zouping is getting more and more *renao*, even in the part of Qingdao where my university is there is nothing like this. Zouping is even more fun than Qingdao!"

A SEXUAL MODERNITY?

Pile (2005) emphasizes the sexual tensions and overtones (and sometimes explicit sexuality) of the many urban legends, ghost stories, and vampire tales he collects from around the world. He relates this sexuality to the urban mingling of strangers in public space: "In the modern city, where strangers, races, and sexes find themselves in close proximity, desire and anxiety sit side by side in the driving seat" (117). Certainly in Zouping's streets and parks, one is likely to see a stranger to whom one is attracted, but, most likely, a relationship with this stranger would not receive the approval of one's parents or the wider society. Moreover, as the use of pretty young women in product giveaways suggests, marketing in Zouping often relies on sexualized images of women. In addition to actual women selling products, these include large billboards of women in lingerie on the streets and in stores (figure 21), pictures of nearly naked women on magazine and book covers, often displayed prominently to attract customers to newsstands and bookstores, and advertisements and programming on television and the Internet. Sexual imagery is subject to the constraints of censors, but advertisers and shop owners often push the limits. I rarely saw such imagery in Zouping before the mid-1990s, but by 2005 it had become ubiquitous.

One evening in Zouping in 2007, while searching through the TV channels back in my hotel room, I came across an infomercial on a local channel that shocked me for its levels of sexual explicitness and racism. It ran every evening for at least a few days but then stopped. As I had never seen anything like it on Chinese television either before or after those few days, I assume that the television censors finally noticed and banned it. The infomercial sold a drug called Jin Han Ma (金悍玛), which was supposed to cure impotence and premature ejaculation, as well as increase male sexual endurance and penis size. The infomercial began with a picture showing packages of the product and a voiceover that asked, "Do you want to do it like those Western

FIGURE 21. Advertising billboard. Photo by author.

[*oumei*] men do?" It then cut to a cartoon of (what I assumed to be) an African American man (dark-skinned, with a large Afro) and a blonde and buxom woman purchasing condoms in a pharmacy. First the blonde holds up a condom package marked "M" and the man shakes his head no, while uttering "uh-uh" in a deep Barry White-ish voice. Then she holds up a package marked "L" and he again says no. Finally she holds up a package marked "XXXXL," which is as large as the man's chest, and he nods his head yes. The cartoon then cuts to a bedroom where they are naked and having sex. She is lying on her back with her legs high in the air while he is standing with his back toward the camera. Though his XXXXL-sized penis remains hidden, we sense its power, as her large breasts and blonde hair, the bed, the bedside dresser, and a digital clock on the dresser all shake in reaction to his thrusts. She calls out with rhythmic, high-pitched cries of pleasure. At the start of the bedroom scene the digital clock reads 11:00 P.M., and there is one condom wrapper on the dresser; then it cuts to 1:00 A.M., and there are four wrappers on the dresser; at 3:00 a.m. there are six or seven wrappers; and at 5:00 A.M. the dresser is covered with an uncountable number of wrappers. Her cries of pleasure never stop and provide the only sound track throughout this sequence. The infomercial then shifts to a video of male Chinese scientists in

white lab coats busily producing the drug. The blonde's cries of pleasure are still audible but quieter so that a male Chinese voiceover can be understood. The voiceover describes the combination of Western science and ancient Chinese medicine behind the drug, the years of research that went into its discovery, and the high-tech production methods that ensure quality standards. Finally, the infomercial shifts to a series of interviews with very proper-looking Chinese women who discuss sex in euphemistic terms and only refer to postmarital sex with their husbands. With the blonde's never ceasing cries of pleasure still audible in the background, they say things like, "Since he started taking Jin Han Ma, *that place* on my husband's body has grown so big and strong"; and "We were married for six years, but before my husband used Jin Han Ma, I didn't understand what the word *orgasm* meant."

Many aspects of the infomercial could be analyzed. I would guess that the cartoon was not created for the infomercial but rather was lifted from some campy American production. In the American context, the over-the-top use of exaggerated racial and sexual stereotypes might be considered by some to be more humorous than racist (it enacts what Alexei Yurchak [2006; Boyer and Yurchak 2010] calls a stiob type of humor). But in the Zouping of 2007, where these stereotypes would have been barely legible (and their critiques totally unknown), I fear that some may have read it literally. The infomercial also fits with Dru Gladney's (2004) argument that public portrayals of sex in China must associate female lasciviousness with foreign or Chinese minority women, in order to discipline ethnic majority Han Chinese women into a proper sexual demeanor.[4]

Everett Zhang (2007) analyzes the rise of men's clinics (*nan ke*) in post-Mao China. The term *men's clinic* is a euphemism for a center for treating impotence, and Zhang notes that while traditional Chinese medicine has long offered both cures for impotence and various aphrodisiacs, before the post-Mao era there were no clinics that specialized in this problem. In Zouping during the late 2000s I discovered at least one hospital claiming to house a men's clinic (Zouping Huakang Yiyuan). Zhang concludes that the cultivation of individual male sexual desire has become a signpost of modernity in contemporary China (504). Certainly the Jin Han Ma infomercial could be read as further evidence for Zhang's conclusion.

Of course, in an area like sexuality nothing can be considered completely new. As Zhang points out, there have long been treatments for impotence and aphrodisiacs, and old Chinese books such as the sixteenth-century novel, *The Plum in the Golden Vase* (Jin Ping Mei), depict not just about every imaginable sexual practice but also an enormous range of moral attitudes and emotional reactions to human sexuality.[5] In addition to such novels, there have also long been ghost stories with sexual overtones in China, usually involving some form of female ghost, demon, or "fox fairy" (*huli jing*) seducing a man and leading him to a troubled fate. Such stories resemble very much the ghost stories described by Pile, and they still circulate in various forms in Zouping. One of the most famous Chinese authors of such tales, Pu Songling, lived in Shandong province during the Qing dynasty less than 50 kilometers from Zouping. But, despite these continuities, subtle shifts in cultural emphases regarding sexuality and majority attitudes toward sexuality can be detected (Farquhar 2002).

The infomercial seems indicative of two such shifts. First, contemporary narratives of sexuality often associate hypersexuality with some sort of human figure rather than a ghost or demon. Whether it is African American men and buxom blondes or the children of the rich and powerful, as suggested by the rumors discussed in chapter 3, or movie stars and celebrities, as insinuated in many popular magazines, such depictions assert that someone out there is enjoying all the sex they want, regardless of the consequences for others and themselves. Second, male desire to gain control over women is expressed not just through the assertion of physical force, or through access to money, but also through a masculinity that measures manhood quite literally and seeks the ability to provide women with ceaseless sexual pleasure. These emphases fit well with at least two aspects of urban modernity in Zouping. First, since arranged marriages are banned and the period of youth (as a sexually mature but single individual) is extended, men desire to cultivate a persona (and a body) that they imagine will be attractive to women. Second, as public space is filled with both attractive strangers and sexy images, the possibilities for sexual encounters seem to expand and the existence of hypersexed others becomes easier to imagine.

CONSUMING THE LOCAL, THE NATIONAL, AND THE GLOBAL

Chapter 4 described how supermarkets enable Zouping residents to consume a wider range of foods than previously possible, with a great number of them selling products of nonlocal origins. These supermarkets are just one aspect of Zouping's increasing involvement in widespread, nonlocal economies of exchange. While entanglement in the global or national economy is usually examined as an economic phenomenon, it also feeds phantasmagoric images of the local, the national, and the international and the use of such images in marketing. These images sometimes represent factual depictions of product origins but are also used to dupe customers about the geographic origins of products. While such marketing often sells the exotic, it also panders to nativist reactions against the exotic through the use of tokens of the local.

The wide and expanding variety of restaurants in Zouping illustrates both the sale of the exotic and the marketing of the local. Against a tendency to simply call such expansion globalization, I insist, at least in places like Zouping, that it is more national than global. During the 2000s I found two or three restaurants that claimed to offer non-Chinese cuisine (a Brazilian barbecue venue was the most popular), but there were scores of restaurants that claimed to sell styles of food from other parts of China. These included the Yunnanese noodle shop described in the previous chapter, Sichuan restaurants, Sichuan hot pot restaurants, beef hot pot restaurants, a dim sum restaurant, a Cantonese restaurant, Manchurian restaurants (*dongbei guanzi*), Korean restaurants (where "Korean" refers to the food of Korean Chinese minorities rather than from the nation of Korea), Mongolian (again Mongolian Chinese) hot pot restaurants, Xinjiang-style barbecue restaurants, Peking duck restaurants, donkey meat restaurants, a Hunanese restaurant, Chinese Muslim (*qingzhen*) restaurants, Chinese Buddhist vegetarian restaurants, Shanghai-style restaurants, and Jiangxi-style bakeries, as well as a few recognizably Taiwanese food chains. Other places claimed to sell local, rural, and Shandong-style foods such as dumpling (*jiaozi*) restaurants and jujube date candy stalls. Many hotels had pages on their menus devoted to local specialties (*techan* or *tuchan*), such as Chinese yam dishes (*shanyao*) and various forms of stewed chicken. Except for one or two of the hotel restaurants, none of these existed during the 1980s.

The particular variety of foods available at these restaurants reflected not just the desire to symbolically consume the nation but also the ongoing tastes and habitus of local food consumption in Zouping. Many locals told me that the reason there were so few Cantonese restaurants in Zouping (only one plus a dim sum restaurant) was that Cantonese food was too light and sweet and that Shandong people preferred rich, salty, and meaty flavors. The Yunnanese noodle shops were branches of chain restaurants (there were actually two or three different such chains copycatting each other) that were of Shandong origin, and I cannot testify to the extent to which restaurants claiming a stylistic fidelity to food from another province actually had any ties to that place. Nevertheless, at least during the 2000s, I heard no complaints about the lack of authenticity of these foods from other parts of China. Zoupingers were more concerned with taste and cleanliness.

The symbolic consumption of the provincial, the national, and, occasionally, the international was evident in other arenas of consumption as well. Opportunities for travel and family vacations expanded rapidly during the 2000s. Shandong has several famous beach resorts within a two- to three-hour drive from Zouping (buses and trains also provide transportation to these places). In 2005 I once asked a group of primary school teachers whether they had ever taken a vacation to the seashore, with or without their families. None of them had, and they teased that only a rich Australian like me could imagine such a thing. By 2009, however, most families I asked, including those of teachers and Wei Mian workers, reported having taken a beach vacation within the past two years. In 2011 and 2012 many reported driving their own automobiles. Most families had also taken trips to the major Shandong cities of Jinan and Qingdao. Trips to Beijing and Shanghai were far from rare. In geography classes schoolchildren were given lessons about the famous attractions in these cities, and many parents told me that they thought it important to let their children experience what they had learned in class. A few families reported taking vacations to other famous cities or natural wonders across China, including Yellow Mountain (in Anhui Province), Mount Tai (Shandong), Jiuzhaigou (Sichuan), Dali (Yunnan), Hangzhou, Suzhou, Shenzhen, Xian, Nanjing, and Chengdu.

Entertainment venues offered other opportunities for consuming the global and the national. Karaoke bars were the most numerous. Though they could be sites where businessmen consumed sexual services, they were also sites where families and mixed-sex groups of friends came to sing and relax. The bars offered a great variety of music. At one such venue in 2010, I saw over 400 songs listed in nine different genres. One of the smallest genres was "foreign songs." The rest were popular Chinese songs (though one genre included songs of Taiwanese and Hong Kong origins). The same songs could be found on karaoke menus almost anywhere in China. Marc Moskowitz (2010) describes how "mandopop" (Mandarin-language popular music) derives most of its stylistic characteristics (including simple melodic structures but nuanced and poetic lyrics) from being a genre composed to be sung at karaoke venues. Mandopop songs are easy to sing, but their subtle and emotive lyrics allow a wide range of performative expression by amateur singers.

New and relatively expensive cinemas also came to Zouping in the late 2000s. Before this there was a government-owned theater in the Old City that showed cheap Chinese videotapes on small screens. The first multiplex cinema with surround sound, large screens, and 3-D capacity opened in the New City in 2007. It cost more than triple what the old theater charged. In addition to the top Chinese films, it screened Hollywood blockbusters, such as the Harry Potter movies. After 2010 two more multiplexes opened in Zouping. Most of the movies shown at these venues were targeted to children and teenagers.

While cinema and karaoke provided Zoupingers with increasingly cosmopolitan fare, television was an arena in which there was a shift back toward the local during the 2000s. During the 1990s the number of television channels available in Zouping rose to over 40 and included those from most of the provinces, in addition to the 12 CCTV (national) stations. But during the 2000s some of the most interesting expansion took place in local channels. The prefectural city (Binzhou) opened two stations, and Zouping itself developed four. The Xiwang Group also launched four stations. In addition to local news, sports, and government propaganda, programming space was devoted to local tourist destinations, cooking shows, infomercials (including the one described above), and demonstrations of lifestyle or hobby skills (e.g., knitting and fishing). One of the most interesting programs was called "Zouping Stories" (Zouping Gushi). At the same time that standard Mandarin was gaining ground over local dialect in many contexts (Zouping children were beginning to speak standard Mandarin even when playing with each other), this show reasserted local dialect by voicing over scenes from popular national and international shows and movies with new dialogue spoken entirely in Zoupingese. The show's comedy relied on the irony derived from this juxtaposition. On days after each evening show aired, friends often discussed its content with me and attempted to teach me a joke or a humorous phrase that turned on a bit of local dialect from the show. This show was the first to purposely use local dialect on Zouping's television stations.

CONSUMING THE URBAN, THE RURAL, MODERNITY, AND TRADITION

In an essay on the "romantic reappraisal" in China, Michael Griffiths, Malcom Chapman, and Flemming Christiansen (2010) suggest that in contemporary China a contradictory revaluation of the rural is progressing (see also Tapp 2000). Such a revaluation had been noted much earlier in the West, in the late eighteenth and early nineteenth century, and was analyzed in relation to consumerism by Colin Campbell (1987). In both places the basic oppositions between self and other, rule and unruliness, order and disorder, culture and nature, human and animal, and clean and dirty were mapped onto the opposition between urban and rural. In China during the 1980s, this mapping tended to idealize the urban by associating it with rule, law, order, culture, cleanliness, and the human. This idealization necessarily denigrated the rural, and, by association, disorder, lawlessness, dirt, animals, and nature. But dissatisfaction with the urban experience led to an inversion of this valuation. Rule became constraint and unruliness freedom; the human became the artificial and the animal the natural; law became convention, while lawlessness became creativity; cleanliness became sterility, while dirt became fertility. In China as well as in most of the world, both the original idealization of the urban and the cultural reappraisal of the rural are central to the marketing strategies of a wide range of products and perhaps even consumption itself.

In China this reappraisal is most apparent in the rise of peasant food and restaurants and rural inns or resorts (*nongjiale, nongjiayuan*). Such establishments grew in popularity in China throughout the 2000s, especially in the rural fringes around large cities. Griffiths, Chapman, and Christiansen (2010) point out that many (male) customers in these places enjoy freedom from rules; they can take their shirts off, spit on the ground, drink to excess, and speak loudly. Some customers were urban youth sent down to the countryside during the 1960s and 1970s, and their consumption has a nostalgic air. For residents of large cities, however, the desire for such consumption arose only after decades of urban living. In Zouping as early as 2009, a large flock of peasant restaurants (*nongjiale*) appeared first on the eastern edge of the Old City and then in several other parts of town (figure 22). The restaurants usually included outdoor seating in parklike settings, sometimes with canvas ceilings and mosquito net walls to keep out rain as well as bugs. They made hearty, simple, rural dishes in an earthy (*tu*) atmosphere. They were often small establishments run by villagers-in-the-city from their original homes, which were now located on the urban fringe. Though I had seen many such establishments on the outskirts of large cities before, their sudden appearance in Zouping shocked me and ran against the grain of the above analysis. Could Zouping urban residents, almost all of whom are of recent rural origins, really

FIGURE 22. Nongjiale restaurant in Yellow Mountain Park, in the morning, before opening. Photo by author.

feel nostalgia for their village homes so soon? I concluded that perhaps some could, but I also sensed that one source of the popularity of such places was not so much a matter of a dialectical *re*appraisal of a once despised and discarded rural lifestyle as it was an indication of a persisting rural habitus. Just as Judith Farquhar (2002) has shown how a Maoist habitus lasted well into the 1990s in some social contexts, I believe that some newly urban Zouping residents have never really parted with "rural" ways of living.

Another aspect of this seeming romanticism was the small but growing market for outdoor activities in Zouping. In 2010 I noticed the first camping gear store, just off the pedestrian mall in the New City. It sold hiking boots, tents, sleeping bags, camp stoves, and other gear for backpackers. The owner of the shop told me that the new hiking trails groomed for local tourists in the mountains south of the county seat had encouraged a growing number of day hikers to take the next step and go on extended expeditions. I met one such hiking enthusiast at a clothing stall in the Old City. The stall's walls displayed pictures of the stall owner on top of various mountains. When I asked him about them, the owner told me of five hiking expeditions he and his buddies had taken to mountainous areas in various parts of China. While

I had expected such hikers to be educated white-collar workers, this man was a relatively uneducated villager-in-the-city who had no employment other than running his small stall. His hiking buddies were likewise villagers-in-the-city. In the New City in 2009, I met the owner of a bicycle shop, which was quite unlike the older bicycle shops I had known in Zouping, which specialized in utilitarian bikes. This one instead sold expensive road bikes and mountain bikes. The owner showed me pictures of a group of more than twenty cyclists, both men and women, dressed in racing gear astride their fancy racing bikes. He said that this group of Zoupingites (which included himself) regularly went on rides of more than 100 kilometers and that they had even taken biking trips around the province.

In tension with this form of the urban idealization/rural romantic reappraisal dialectic is the discourse, perhaps most powerfully articulated in the popular TV series of the 1980s, *Death Song of the River* (He Shang), that associates the rural with an overly rule-bound and orderly Confucian tradition and the urban with modernity, freedom, and creativity.[6] This discourse also has its own form of romantic reversal, in which Confucian tradition is reified as a source of familial happiness and traditional virtue. Both the original discourse and its reversal commonly appear in the motifs for weddings, including those created in photographs and those performed in ceremonies. Young couples in Zouping can go to considerable lengths to portray themselves as both traditional and modern, as simultaneously filial children and romantic lovers. They have photos taken in both traditional Chinese and Western outfits (red for the bride in the former and white in the latter) and sometimes hold several wedding ceremonies with different ceremonial emphases for different audiences. Locally made and marketed products, such as liquor and furniture, also invoked tradition in their marketing campaigns, either through the clothing worn by the people pictured in the ads or by reference to the person of Fan Zhongyan, the Song dynasty scholar-official who is said to have grown up in Zouping. Many other products invoked a spirited modernity through notions of individuality (*gexing*). Products targeted at unmarried young people in particular tended to use this strategy. Youth, this marketing suggested, saw "traditional virtue" as little more than listening to their parents.

Finally, the material characteristics of certain products also invoked nostalgia by acting as mnemonic devices. One day a teacher introduced me to her mother, who had a small business selling handmade bedsheets. She made them on a handloom and sold them as "old-style coarse cloth" (*lao cubu*). She explained, "The thick thread of this style of sheet is especially comfortable and warm in winter. It reminds me of my own mother back in the countryside and how kind she was. Because of this feel, many people want my sheets, but I can only make one set at a time. That is why I have a backlog of orders and can sell them at over 200 yuan even though machine-made sheets cost only a quarter of that."

ERASURES OF MEMORY AND INVOCATIONS OF TRADITION

Marketers and consumers are not the only actors in Zouping who reinvent tradition (Hobsbawn and Ranger 1983). The local government also plays an important role in both erasing the past and re-presenting it. To a large extent, state and market acts of "past presencing" (Macdonald 2013) reinforce one another. This mutuality exists because companies desire state support and generally would not dare to create an image that the state would disapprove of and because the local government desires to support the marketing efforts of local companies in order to shore up its own tax revenues. Moreover, as chapter 3 demonstrates, many local firms started off as state-owned enterprises and began their marketing campaigns when they were still controlled by branches of the local government.

The local government has reiterated Zouping's imagined past in the names of streets, parks, and landmarks (see chapter 2). They also use the image of Fan Zhongyan. A large government-sponsored billboard facing eastbound traffic just before the Zouping exit on the Jinan-Qingdao superhighway presents an eight-character couplet: "The ancient home of Minister Fan (Zhongyan); Scenic Zouping" (Fangong Guli; Shanshui Zouping) (figure 23).

This couplet is not a mere slogan but represents the material reality created by the government in the form of parks, both in the city of Zouping and in the mountains south of the city, as well as the placement of a statue of Fan in Daixi Park. In these summations of the past, Minister Fan is tied to the scenery of Zouping's parks to invoke pastoral wisdom and tranquillity in the midst of Zouping's booming industrialization. Officials responsible for the naming, design, and building of Zouping's streets and parks told me of the historical origin of various names and insisted on the importance of educating Zouping residents about their past. Politically, as Michael Herzfeld (1991; [1997] 2005) points out, such "structural nostalgia" may be used by differently positioned people in different ways. As discussed in chapter 2, the

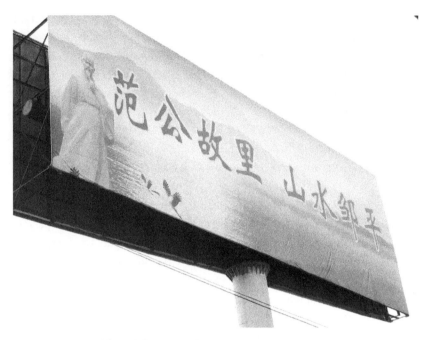

FIGURE 23. Highway billboard. Photo by author.

village of Anjia invoked the past when it built a "traditional" memorial arch-way at the entrance to its collective property. The claim to territory nostalgi-cally made by Anjia, however, was one that the county government tolerated but did not support. These invocations of the past often mask the modernity of the places they label. Until the late twentieth century, Zouping had no public parks and the territory marked by the Anjia archway was not the terri-tory controlled by Anjia village before it was relocated in 1988.

In addition to various forms of selective remembering, Zouping's struc-tural nostalgia involved forms of purposeful forgetting, as occurred in the move away from revolutionary memory in the renaming of the March 8 Reservoir as Black Creek (Daixi) Lake. The dynamics of state erasure and reinvention are particularly evident in the politics of religion and religious buildings. For the twenty-five-year period of my research, the county seat was completely bereft of any form of traditional Chinese temple, a fact that often shocks researchers who work in other parts of China. From the late 1980s until the mid-2000s, despite several searches, I could not find a single tradi-tional temple that was actively being used anywhere in the county, though I did find two abandoned temple buildings that were used as storage depots.

During the late 2000s the county government rebuilt a few temples outside the county seat as support to tourism and refurbished the Ming dynasty Tangli An, located in a village about 10 kilometers west of the county seat. The only religious building I discovered in the county seat itself was a Protestant church that was built by Baptist missionaries in the 1920s, was put to nonreligious uses during the Maoist decades, and was reopened as a church during the 1980s. Though Christianity is thriving in Zouping and the church is actively used (Kipnis 2002), the building itself has a low profile. Its door opens away from the street, the street-facing windows are blocked off, and it is hard to identify the building as a church or find the entrance to it if you do not know what it is and where to go. The destruction of temples in Zouping occurred throughout the first six decades of the twentieth century, as the town endured a series of wars and then the Cultural Revolution. While the Communist government was not responsible for all of this destruction, it was responsible for some of it and was complicit in the lack of temple rebuilding.

In her analysis of state practices of forgetting in Mongolia, Manduhai Buyandelger (2013) identifies three stages. First comes the physical destruction of the people, buildings, and artifacts that are to be erased from social memory. Next comes the suppression of the memories of the acts of destruction themselves, which she calls "the forgetting of forgetting" (67). Finally is the creation of a new history or new memories to cover up the gaps created by the acts of erasure.

In the case of religion in Zouping, Buyandelger's scheme fits but must be adjusted to the fact of the legitimacy of the recent revival of tourism-related religion. When I visited the newly built tourist temples in the hilly areas south and west of the county seat, I never encountered large crowds, and I wondered if the location of the temples in remote places was a purposeful strategy to prevent temple activity from becoming part of people's daily routines. Various plaques in the temples and the official pamphlets written about them were strong on presenting the ancient history and legends associated with the temples but very weak on the temples' twentieth-century history, at best briefly mentioning the destruction of the original temple during the war with Japan and never mentioning the destruction or abandonment that occurred during the Maoist decades. In one of the new tourist temples, a hall devoted to the worship of Fan Zhongyan was added to underscore "the love of Zouping's people" for Minister Fan and the respect of the people for Fan's devotion to study and the quest for knowledge.

Despite the government's manipulation of religious sites and history, Zouping was far from being completely secularized. In addition to Christianity, Zouping was home to various fortune tellers and geomancers, healing cults and Mao worshippers, as well as places in the mountains and fields where people went to burn incense for whatever ancestor or spirit they believed dwelled there. One older woman I knew liked to walk a rarely used path on Yellow Mountain to a rock crag where she would burn incense and bow deeply. She told me that during the Cultural Revolution, a young female Red Guard member had been raped and murdered there. Because of the violent manner of her death and becauset she was not originally from Zouping, the young woman had become a ghost but not necessarily a malevolent one. She came to the aid of other women who were away from home. The older woman's two daughters had both left home—one was working in Jinan and the other attending university—and she came to this spot to ask the ghost to protect them. This woman's practice, with its invocation of ghosts from the Cultural Revolution, demonstrates precisely those forms of memory that the Chinese government hopes to erase. Other cases of religious practitioners are introduced in part 2.

OFFICIAL SPECTACLES

Zouping's streets and plazas were sites of official spectacles sponsored by the government. These spectacles were by far the largest public events in Zouping and included activities like military parades on National Day, performances by students on Teachers' Day, dance contests on Children's Day, and an "Olympic Spirit" singing contest just before the 2008 Olympics in Beijing. Predictably, these events were opened by the highest-ranking Party official present in Zouping at the time, followed by speeches by other officials in hierarchical order, ending with whatever performances the occasion called for.

One of the largest of these spectacles was the Red Song contest, organized to congratulate the Chinese Communist Party on the ninetieth anniversary of its birth. Taking place in Physical Education Plaza on June 30, 2011, the event was officially titled "Follow the Party Forever: Sing Red Songs and Extol the Party's Benevolence" (永远跟党走: 唱红歌; 颂党恩). Red Songs are anthems that depict or have origins in the Party's revolutionary history, including the Maoist decades of postrevolutionary rule. They were particularly favored by the now-fallen, former contender for national leadership, Bo Xilai, whose enthusiasm led to such events being held throughout the country. In Zouping twenty-five choruses, whose members wore elaborate uniforms, organized by different government units and local business groups, rehearsed for months to enter the contest. Counting the choruses (many with over 50 members), their family members, and those who just came for the show, an audience of well over 1,500 packed the plaza (figures 24, 25). Folding chairs were laid out in neat rows on most of the plaza, with the front two rows reserved for the local Party leaders. The event was enhanced by superb sound and lighting systems and stagecraft. The performances were quite professional, and all the performers I spoke to were delighted to have taken part. At the very least, they had had time off from their regular jobs for rehearsal. The songs and speeches heaped endless praise on the Party, portraying past national and local leaders as a seamless parade of unified patriots and do-gooders (while neglecting the conflicts among them), as well as portraying Zouping as a wonderful place to live and work, where all strive in unison, where the people are always well treated and love the Party, and where there is no corruption and unending development (figures 26, 27). But even at an event like this there was some room for subversive opinion. A few of the performances involved songs about how the working classes (*gongren*) had built the new China, and a friend who viewed the contest with me noted that it was okay to celebrate factory workers' sacrifices from the past but that if we wrote a song about the factory workers who died in Wei Mian's 2007 accident we would be arrested. Regardless of the political overtones, and despite the fact that the event dragged on for over three hours on a hot and muggy summer evening, all those whom I spoke to enjoyed it. They said that the performance standard was high and the costumes were authentic.

Every official event I have witnessed in Zouping, like the Red Song contest, manifested an extreme degree of Party-defined political correctness. Arguably the performance of such political correctness is not only meant to subjectify the local population, but is also staged by Zouping officials to impress those higher in the Party hierarchy than themselves. Provincial and prefectural officials are invited to and occasionally attend such events, and also can see them on television and other media. The local Party elite must impress their superiors if they are to have any chance of promotion, and they also strive to encourage policies that favor Zouping as a locality. But regardless of the intended audience, this political correctness intimately mixed modernity and tradition. It both drew on China's socialist past (and a much longer tradition of authoritarian governing) and displayed Zouping's recent urbanization. The county seat of the early 1980s would not have had the

FIGURES 24 AND 25. Preparing for the Red Song contest. Both photos by author.

public space, the resources, or the population to put on an event like the Red Song contest. Part of what made the event enjoyable for locals was the fact that the level of its performances represented the wealth and cultural talent of Zouping as much as its "love" for the Party. Perhaps more important, the striving for political legitimacy evinced by such events reflects a mass-mediated era of modern politics in which the public performance of legitimacy becomes a social necessity.

FIGURES 26 AND 27. Red Song contest performances. Both photos by author.

CONCLUSION

In *Society of the Spectacle* (1977), Guy Debord sharply criticizes the role of spectacle in both the form of the commodity and the ideology of Communist governments. He insists on the link between modernity and spectacle, going so far as to open his book with the claim, "In societies where modern conditions of production prevail, all of life presents itself as an immense accumulation of *spectacles*. Everything that was directly lived has moved away into a representation" (1; emphasis in original). While Debord's dual focus on

Communist ideology and commodities is useful for understanding the phantasmagoria of Zouping, the sharp line he draws between modernity and tradition as well as his overwhelmingly negative view of spectacle as a source of alienation run against the grain of my presentation of spectacle in Zouping. Benjamin's and Pile's much more recombinant understanding of modernity, in which tradition and modernity intertwine and dialectically interact with one another, better summarizes the experience of phantasmagoria of Zouping. Moreover, Zouping's spectacles cannot be reduced to occasions for alienation. Even an event like the Red Song contest brings joy and pride of place to some while also allowing at least a little room for subversive interpretation.

To give a final example, consider Georg Simmel's (1971) often and perhaps justifiably criticized analysis of the psychosocial changes brought about by urbanization. Simmel suggests that the density of social relationships in urban environments leads to a psychically destructive overstimulation of the senses. This fear has proven for the most part unfounded (see Smith 1979 for a critique) and resembles the fears some old fogeys like me have about the effects that the constantly wired social environment might have on the psyches of today's youth. But one aspect of the growth of consumption in Zouping allows us to add another dimension to this by now classic critique of Simmel. The thrill young Zoupingites take from congregating in renao, overstimulating social environments, like those that occur at Zouping's shopping malls on weekends, in the New City's pedestrian mall on Sunday afternoons, and in the shopping streets of the Old City and around the Development Zone's Lucky Plaza on Friday and Saturday nights, represents not so much a new form of sociality as the continuation of an old rural tradition—the love of the social heat of crowds that demonstrate the potency of the community, as can be experienced in family rituals like weddings or community events like temple fairs.[7] In other words, in Zouping social "overstimulation" is positively valued, and this valuing itself is evidence of some of the continuities of life extant between rural and urban society.

PART TWO

Transformers Transformed

INTRODUCTION

The second part of this book examines the lives of the people who have come to live in Zouping and constitute its nearly sevenfold population growth since 2000. I divide them into five groups: married migrant blue-collar workers from nearby locales (inside the county or from nearby parts of neighboring counties); married migrant blue-collar workers from distant locales; villagers-in-the-city; middle-class families; and youth. Though there are people living in Zouping who straddle two or more of these categories or do not fit well into any of them, the majority of Zouping residents and households do fit the schema. My decision to classify people in this way reflects both my own analysis as a social scientist and local understandings of social difference. The structural dimensions that organize the groups—place of origin, educational/occupational distinction, and social age—are common sociological foci but are also shaped by the specific historical context of Zouping.

Youth is not simply a matter of the number of years one has spent on the planet but rather a culturally constructed category that includes unmarried people who have left home and no longer attend academically oriented schools. They have come to Zouping to work in the factories or in the service sector, or perhaps to attend one of the vocational schools that are closely linked to factory or service sector jobs. I do not include students in the academic high schools, as their lives are considered to be on hold until they complete the university entrance exam. Vocational school students, though a borderline group, are firmly on the path to blue- or pink-collar jobs. Everyone I have included in the youth category was between the ages of 15 and 24. The social pressure to get married in Zouping is extremely high, and while older unmarried people surely existed, they were stigmatized enough that they did not announce their status to me. What makes the category of youth important for the purposes of this book is the relative openness of their futures, the significant life choices that remain in front of them. Marriage curtails this openness.

While "youth" is an important category in Zouping, notions of the "second generation of migrant workers," that is, the now adult, unmarried children of migrant workers who have grown up in urban areas in which they do not have household registrations (Pun and Lu 2010), is not as significant to Zouping as it is to the long-standing, larger urban areas of China. Migrant workers have not come to Zouping for a long enough period to have raised a second generation there. More important, household registration regimes in Zouping are relaxed enough that most migrant workers could easily attain local household registrations if they so desired.

The category I designate as "middle class" relates but is not reducible to educational attainment. I include here the somewhat overlapping groups of people who came to Zouping for white-collar work and some of the long-term residents of the county seat. White-collar jobs in Zouping include teaching, medicine, working for the government, and management positions in the large business groups. Those who attain such positions are well educated, though the standard of what counts as well educated has evolved over the years. Those who secured government jobs in the early 1980s may have had only a high school or technical college diploma, while those who secure such positions today have four-year university degrees at least. During the Maoist decades, government-assigned "class statuses" counted for as much as educational attainment in securing government positions (Billiter 1985). Thus long-term residents of the county seat were not all highly educated, but they tended to have relatively high levels of education and were usually privileged in other ways.

The government, hospitals, and schools were among the largest employers in the county seat before the industrialization of the past twenty years. Thus many long-term county seat residents come from white-collar backgrounds, and even those who reached these positions before high levels of educational attainment were important to government recruitment built strong connections to local sources of political power. Before the 1990s, even county seat factory jobs were considered relatively privileged positions, and those recruited to take such jobs tended to have more education and political connections than average. In addition, the county seat has historically offered more educational opportunity than the surrounding villages, so those who have grown up in the county seat generally received more education than did those from the surrounding countryside. While not all long-term county seat residents are highly educated, there is a strong correlation between education and long-term residence.

What makes the category "middle class" important for this book is the tendency for those who constitute that class to distinguish themselves from Zoupingites in humbler positions. Because of the importance of education to social discourses of distinction in China, and the ways in which this importance is reinforced through discourses of "human quality," or suzhi, members of the middle class sometimes pretend to be more educated than they actually are. As discussed in chapter 4, local discourses of distinction sometimes involved practices of consumption as well.

Villagers-in-the-city, nearby blue-collar migrants, and more distant blue-collar migrants were less educated than those I have designated as middle class. They came primarily from the countryside. Almost all those in the latter two groups worked in factories. They were less interested in distinguishing themselves from others in terms of educational attainment or "quality" and more often identified as members of the masses (minzhong), peasants (nongmin), or common folk (laobaixing). But the distinct places of origin of each of these groups resulted in different structures of opportunity and constraint; consequently, they experienced their move to Zouping and the process of urbanization differently. Wealthy villagers-in-the-city often identified themselves in terms of their village of origin.

Other analysts may reasonably have chosen to create a chapter on the category "entrepreneurs" or small-scale businesspeople. Such people are common in Zouping, but socially Zouping natives often saw them as belonging to one of the other five categories. Anyone can attempt to start his or her own business, but the constraints and opportunities that influence the types of business one is likely to enter relate to place of origin and educational attainment. I present examples of entrepreneurs in each of the five groupings.

Finally, in each of the five chapters of part 2 I introduce a theoretical focus: transformation in kinship practice for the nearby migrants, hope and alienation for the distant migrants, the construction of community for the villagers-in-the-city, class reproduction and distinction for the middle classes, and fantasy and habituation for youth. All of the themes could be used to illuminate aspects of the lives of each of the groups, but each theme came out in a particularly strong fashion during interviews with members of the group I associate with that theme. The chapters also alternate between using numerous (roughly ten) short case studies or three or four longer ones. This approach in part reflects the theme chosen for each chapter and the stories each group of people were able to tell me. The purpose of using so many case studies is to illustrate organically both the points of commonality and the variety within each group, as well as something of the personality and singularities of particular households.

———

SIX

Between Farm and Factory

MIGRANT WORKERS FROM NEARBY

One important thread of the literature on modernization suggests that kinship ties simplify and become less important when social environments evolve from rural agricultural societies to urban industrial ones. "Traditional" Chinese kinship practice includes patrilineal reasoning (thinking kinship primarily in terms of agnatically related men and tracing kin relations over time through agnatically related descendants), virilocal patterns of residence and care (married couples residing with the husband's family rather than the wife's and, consequently, enacting closer and denser material, labor, and emotional exchanges with members of the husband's family than with the wife's), and patriarchal power (a pattern of familial relations in which men dominate women and the elderly dominate youth).[1] The transformation away from tradition involves the reduction of household size, the emergence of free choice or love-based marriages rather than arranged ones, and the relative independence of young people in relation to their parents (Yan 2003b). Some call the relative independence of young people from their families a trend toward "individualism," a term I reject because the independence from familial domination is typically paired with various forms of social dependence on state and market institutions (Kipnis 2012b). Nonetheless, at a gross or macro level, I would agree that there is an overall trend toward a reduction in familial domination in urbanizing Zouping. However, this reduction is both more partial than a straightforward modernization theory would suggest and, more important, not nearly as linear. Rather than a straightforward decline of patriarchy, patrilineal thinking, and virilocal familial relations, what occurs is a continual struggle over their terms and a reinvention of their practices in new contexts. As the practical circumstances of the five groups of people I examine in this book differ, the extent and manner in which patriarchy, patrilineal thinking, and virilocal familial relations reemerge is likewise variable.

Migrants to the county seat from the same county or nearby bordering regions often maintain close relationships with their families in their home villages, living lives that are split between village homes, on the one hand, and apartments, rented rooms, or dormitory beds in the city, on the other. The majority of such workers come from rural villages, live in the Development Zone, and work in Zouping's factories, though there are also cases of people who have migrated from nearby towns or who have started their own businesses in the county seat. The construction of paved roads throughout the county means that almost all villages are less than a 45-minute drive or motorcycle ride from the county seat, and as factory workers have gotten richer (most salaries were over 2,000 yuan [US$330] per month in 2011), almost all of them could afford at least a motorbike. For those who do not like to drive their own vehicles, there are regular buses from the county seat to all the townships with stops within a kilometer or two of all but the most isolated villages. Many possibilities for concrete living arrangements exist. Workers, married or single, can live in village homes and commute daily to jobs in the county seat. Youth regularly shuffle back and forth between dormitory beds (which are free) and their parents' homes in villages. Those wishing to have some privacy, perhaps because they have a lover, can rent a room for 100 yuan (US$16) per month in one of the villages bordering the Development Zone and shuttle between their rented room and village home. Many married Wei Mian workers purchase one of the company apartments but also regularly return to their village homes on days off and host family visitors from their village homes.

Because buying a house in one of Wei Mian's compounds requires contract worker status and because the act of buying the apartment itself indicates a relatively high degree of commitment to and trust in Wei Mian, the workers in this housing tend to have worked at Wei Mian for a number of years, to have come from villages within Zouping county, and to plan on spending the rest of their lives working for the company. They are largely satisfied with their jobs and either scoff at reports of young people who complain that work in the factory is too bitter or say that they are used to it. I have also interviewed long-term contract workers who have chosen to either purchase housing on the open market or live in their village homes and commute daily rather than purchase the subsidized Wei Miao housing (which must be sold back to Wei Mian at the purchase price when the worker dies or leaves

Zouping). But regardless of whether or not they chose to purchase company apartments, or even of whether they work at Wei Mian or elsewhere, most migrant families from nearby locales live lives that complicate the rural/urban divide and notions that urbanization gives rise to individualism, the demise of extended families, and disembedding from local communities.

WEI MIAN APARTMENT DWELLERS OF RURAL ORIGINS

I interviewed enough married worker couples who purchased apartments from the Weiqiao Group to give some simple quantitative data about their life circumstances. I was able to interview these couples by establishing research projects in the primary schools their children attended. I divided my time between a second-grade class and a fifth-grade class, with the result that the couples I interviewed were of two, overlapping age cohorts. The parents of the second-graders were mostly born during the late 1970s and early 1980s and, because of the birth control policy enacted in 1980, averaged many fewer siblings than the parents of the fifth-graders who were, on average, a few years older. In all, I interviewed 30 such couples for this project.

Though they lived in apartments in the city, most of these couples still had land rights in the villages where the husband was born. As is commonly the case throughout rural China, on marriage, women in rural Zouping lose land rights with the family and in the village where they were born and gain them in the family and village of the husband. This virilocal pattern of land allocation influenced the kinship practices of these couples. In the majority of these households (24 of 30), the couple's land was farmed by the husband's parents, with help from the husband during busy periods (such as the wheat harvest) and on weekends. Eighteen of the husbands said that they went back to their home villages most Saturdays or Sundays to visit their parents and help with farming. Of the six households in which the husband did not help out with farming, in four cases the husband had a brother who lived in the village and had taken charge of farming the family's land. In one case, the husband's parents had died and the couple chose to rent out their land to neighbors; and in the final case the couple's family had lost their land rights when the husband's parents agreed to take factory jobs in a township-run enterprise in exchange for those land rights. In none of these 30 households did either the husband or the wife regularly help out with the farm chores of the wife's parents.

In part as a result of their farmwork, the husbands in these households tended to work fewer hours in Wei Mian's factories and, consequently, to receive lower salaries. The shift and salary structure in Wei Mian was complex, as the Group produced a variety of products and paid more for work that was tiring, required night shifts, or required relatively rare technical skills. But one basic difference was between a standard day shift workweek (*changbaiban*—five or six 8-hour daytime shifts a week) and a rotating shift workweek (*lunban*—six or seven 8-hour shifts a week including day, evening, and night shifts). Rotating shifts paid about 25 percent more than standard day shifts because they involved 15 to 20 percent more hours and because of bonuses paid for night shifts. In the 18 households where the husband regularly did farmwork, he always worked the standard day shift, but in 10 of these households the wife took a rotating shift. This situation corroborates the findings of Alan de Brauw et al. (2008), who debunk the myth that farming is becoming feminized in China. It also runs against the stereotype that in most households husbands work longer hours outside the home and earn more than wives.

Clearly couples who own an apartment in the city and live there with their children but not their parents can be labeled as exhibiting "neolocal" residence patterns in standard anthropological kinship terminology. But such a label masks not only the ongoing labor exchanges these households enact with their parents but also the fact that relationships with the husband's parents and those with the wife's parents are not equivalent. Perhaps because of the standard way land is allocated in Zouping, these exchanges exhibit a virilocal character, and I label the households that enact them "viricentric."

Viricentricity was also apparent in patterns of child care. In the families of the second-graders especially, the parents desired after-school care for the children. In 12 of the 15 second-grader Wei Mian apartment households that I interviewed, one or both of the paternal grandparents regularly came to the household to provide child care for their grandchildren. In most cases, the child care provider was the paternal grandmother. Often the paternal grandmother lived with the couple during the week and sometimes returned to the village on weekends with the father when he went to farm. In such households the paternal grandfather would spend most of his time in his village home. In some households both paternal grandparents would move back and forth between their village homes and their son's apartment, usually traveling by bus. Only in one of the 15 households did the couple rely on the wife's parents for child care. In this household, the parents had a daughter in the second grade and a one-year-old son who lived with his maternal grandparents in their village home. But the husband in this household had several brothers, one of whom lived with his parents in their village home, so the paternal grandparents had less need for and less time for a close relationship with this household.

Sometimes these viricentric arrangements were justified with reference to patrilineal norms of calculating relatedness. That is to say, when I asked why the paternal rather than the maternal grandparents provided child care, the response was that it was because the children and paternal grandparents were of the same lineage or clan (*jiazu*). The logic of viricentric child care was also apparent during summer vacations, when many children spent weeks or sometimes the entire vacation back in their paternal grandparents' village homes but only occasionally visited the homes of their maternal grandparents.

The birth control policy made multi-son families illegal, exacerbating the logic of viricentricity among Weiqiao apartment dwellers. While couples with a firstborn daughter usually also had a younger child, couples with a firstborn son were not allowed a second child. As with maternal grandparents providing child care, the apartment dwellers were more likely to have limited relationships with the husband's parents when the husband had brothers. Sometimes limitations on relationships with the husband's parents led to increased interaction with the wife's parents. In other cases, there was less interaction with both sets of parents. As the birth control policy was strictly implemented in Zouping, the younger male contract employees overwhelmingly came from households in which they were the only son. For this reason, the households with fifth-graders exhibited slightly less viricentricity than the households with second-graders, a trend that might become stronger over time if birth rates remain low despite the 2015 relaxation of the birth control policy.

A third aspect of viricentricity among Wei Mian apartment dwellers was apparent in their patterns of elder care. Of the 30 couples, 10 said that the husband's parents lived with them during the winter months. The Wei Mian apartments had free heat during the winter, but village homes, for the most part, were without heat. In addition, there was little farmwork to be done during the winter. Couples told me that by letting the paternal grandparents live in their apartments during the winter, they could protect their health. None of the couples, however, reported having the wife's parents live with them during the winter. The couples' parents were generally too young (mostly in their fifties) to require significant care, but the pattern of inviting the husbands' parents to live in the apartment during the winter seems a harbinger of more viricentric elder care in the future. Researchers looking at old age care in other parts of China told me that sometimes wives control the household budget and send money to their parents (both with and without their husband's knowledge) in lieu of viricentric care, though I cannot confirm the extent of this practice in Zouping.

A series of case studies illustrates the life patterns typical of Wei Mian apartment dwellers, the intersection of kinship practice and household economy, and their overwhelmingly positive attitudes toward Wei Mian.

Wei Mian Apartment Household A

Both parents are from villages in Matou (a township adjacent to Weiqiao town) and were born in the late 1970s. The mother began working in cotton spinning in 1992, when the company was located in Weiqiao town, after she graduated from junior middle school. The father joined the army in 1994 but came back to his village and began working at Wei Mian in cloth manufacturing in 1998. They knew each other in junior middle school and were reintroduced at a factory dance and married in 2000. Their only son was 9 years old at the time of my interview in 2011. The company told them to move to Zouping city in 2005; they had been reluctant to do so because company housing was more expensive in the county seat than in Weiqiao town. Though they did lose a bit of money when they returned their first company apartment and secured a new one in the county seat, they soon became thankful for the move because the schools were better in Zouping.

In 2011 the mother worked the rotating shifts and earned 2,800 yuan per month, while the father worked five day shifts a week and earned 2,400 yuan per month. The father often went to his village home on weekends to help with the farming. The paternal grandparents took turns living with them and taking care of their son. The grandparent not with them lived back in the Matou village, enjoying time with other relatives and doing some farming. The mother visited her natal family in another Matou village at least once every two months, but socialized or helped her mother with housework rather than farming. It was a 50-minute drive to either the father's or the mother's village. When I suggested that working rotating shifts would be tiring, the mother said that she was used to it, and the father commented that she could "eat bitterness" (*chiku*).

The couple owned a car and a motorbike and had taken vacations to the ocean in Qingdao. The father said, "A few years ago we wouldn't have imagined owning a car or taking a vacation to the ocean. Work at Weiqiao is hard, but we are used to it now and it has been good to us. What else could we do? We will stay here until we retire."

Wei Mian Apartment Household B

The parents were born in different townships in northern Zouping county in 1980. Each graduated from his or her township's junior middle school and started working at the factory in 1998. They met at the factory and were married in 2002. They were told by the company to move from Weiqiao town to the county seat in 2005 and bought their apartment in the company compound in 2006 for 70,000 yuan. They have two daughters (ages 9 and 2 in 2011). The mother's and oldest daughter's household registrations were at the factory so that the daughter could go to school in the county seat, but the father's and younger daughter's household registrations remained in his village home to maximize their family's land allocation. The youngest daughter lived in the village with the paternal grandparents, but the grandparents often brought her over on weekends. They planned to move the youngest daughter and her household registration to the county seat when she became old enough to begin primary school. The father, who worked only four shifts a week in 2011, went back to the village once or twice a week to help with farming. When the mother was too busy, the paternal grandmother also came to the apartment to help with cooking and with the eldest daughter. The mother said she visits her parents two or three times a year. They owned a motorcycle and an electric bike. It was about a 40-minute ride to the father's village. They had taken vacations to Qingdao on tours organized by the factory. They said that they will stay at Wei Mian at least until their children finish school.

Wei Mian Apartment Household C

The parents in household C were from different townships near Weiqiao town. They were born in the early 1970s and, after junior high school, began working at Wei Mian in 1989. They moved with the company from Weiqiao to the county seat in 2005, purchasing the largest company apartment they could (110 square meters) for 80,000 yuan in 2007, even though they only had one son (10 years old at the time of my interview in 2010). They also owned a car and had taken vacations to Qingdao, Shanghai, Beijing, Jinan, and Penglai. The father explained, "Our entire family lives and works at Wei

Mian. I have an elder sister and a younger brother, and they both work at Wei Mian and own apartments; my wife has four siblings, all of whom work and live at Wei Mian; even my wife's father and my father worked at Wei Mian until they retired. My parents now live with my younger brother in his Wei Mian apartment, and my wife's parents live with her younger brother in their Wei Mian apartment. Since our entire family is here, we do whatever we can with the company: take tours with them, buy apartments with them, we even got a discount on our car because of them. We will stay here as long as the company is viable."

. . .

Two final points might be made in terms of a comparison between Development Zone viricentricity and practices observed in (fully virilocal) Chinese rural settings. First a point of contrast: Ellen Judd, who also did research in rural villages in this part of Shandong during the late 1980s, has pointed out the importance of agnatic kinship in the subordination of women in village settings (Judd 1994). After virilocal marriages, village men are surrounded by close relatives with whom they grew up, while women were isolated. Such settings can place women at a profound disadvantage in cases of spousal conflict or divorce (Sargeson 2012; Sargeson and Song 2010). In the Development Zone, women living in viricentric apartments do not suffer this particular source of disadvantage. As case C illustrates, sometimes entire families work and live in Wei Mian and, as far as I could tell, husbands and wives were equally likely to have siblings working at the company.

The second point, however, suggests some continuity. Margery Wolf (1968, 1972) describes how women attempted to form close emotional bonds with their sons to counter their lack of place and power in the patrilineal, virilocal villages of Taiwan. She called the unit consisting of a mother and her sons the uterine family. In both the Wei Mian apartment families and Taiwanese villages, it seems that women responded to their lack of position within an extended (patrilineal) kinship grouping by focusing their labor on more narrowly defined kin groups. For the women from rural Taiwan, this required investing extra affective care in their relationships with their sons. For those in Wei Mian apartments, it meant earning money that could be streamed into the budget of the narrowly defined household rather than exerting labor on farming, which would benefit the more broadly defined patrilineal extended family.

I interviewed people from half a dozen blue-collar households of local origins who lived in the Development Zone but either did not live in Wei Mian apartments or were not of rural origin. These households were all organized viricentrically, and several included paternal grandparents who lived permanently with their children and grandchildren. I discovered no three-generation households involving the wife's parents.

Local Migrant Household D

The six members of this family (paternal grandfather, paternal grandmother, father, mother, elder sister, younger brother) lived in a village about a 15-minute motorcycle ride from the county seat. The father was a long-term contract worker in cotton spinning at Wei Mian. Because he was adept in machine repair and worked rotating shifts, he earned over 3,000 yuan per month. He had reserved a room in one of the company dorms for free, which required him to move his household registration to the county seat. He only slept in the dorm room when time between shifts was really tight or if he had business that kept him in town. Otherwise he went back to his village home every night. Mother and grandmother farmed the land and the kids went to primary school (and kindergarten) in their township. Grandfather sometimes farmed and sometimes did some business (*maimai*). They owned a car and a motorcycle.

Local Migrant Household E

This family of six (including paternal grandparents and two daughters) moved to Zouping from Changshan township, the part of the county that was most urbanized during the 1980s but that had since fallen behind economically. The grandparents had given up their land for factory employment during the 1980s but lost their jobs in the late 1990s. After several years during which all adult members of the family bounced around various temporary urban jobs, the parents found more stable work at Wei Mian. The father started there in 2003 and the mother in 2004. The father worked day shifts in cotton spinning and earned 2,200 yuan per month; the mother worked rotating shifts and earned 3,000 yuan per month. The grandfather made

1,800 yuan per month as a temporary employee doing maintenance in the Wei Mian dormitories (there were age restrictions on becoming a contract worker). He also ran a fortune-telling, naming, and geomancy business on the side.[2] The grandmother did the housework and looked after the kids. They bought their 90-square-meter apartment in the Wei Mian housing compound in 2006 for 80,000 yuan. All six lived in the apartment permanently and had no other housing.

The grandfather liked to talk, and, though all six members of the household were present during my interview, he dominated the conversation the entire time, correcting or interrupting others when they tried to speak. He told me, "Our family is doing well now thanks to the two 'Pings.' Deng Xiao*ping*[3] started the era of reform and opening, and Zhang Shi*ping* founded Wei Mian. This has given our family a way out [*chulu*]. We now own two motorcycles and two electric bicycles and will soon buy our own car. The good fortune given us by the two Pings demonstrates the power of naming. This is the root of my business. Giving people or businesses good names can bring a family prosperity."

Local Migrant Household F

The final case in this section is slightly unusual in many respects, but its idiosyncrasies illustrate much about patterns of work at Wei Mian, kinship in Zouping, and the comparison between life in villages and life in the Development Zone. The household comprised four people at the time of my interview in 2011: father, mother, 8-year-old daughter, and paternal grandmother. They lived in a rented four-room house in a village-in-the-city at the edge of the Development Zone. This was the only household I interviewed that was renting an entire four-room house for themselves (most renters took only one or two rooms) and the only local migrant household that had chosen to rent. They paid 4,500 yuan for the year (slightly less than the 100-yuan-per-room-per-month standard rate) and had been there for two years while they were saving to purchase their own apartment. At the time of the interview they had just purchased a 90-square-meter commercial apartment in the Development Zone for 280,000 yuan (putting 100,000 yuan down and taking a 20-year mortgage on the remaining 180,000). They were paying another 20,000 yuan for interior finishing (apartments in China generally come unfinished) and planned to move in in 2012.

Both parents came from villages in Matou township and had been living in the husband's village, where the mother farmed the land with her parents-in-law and the father had a business transporting produce in his own truck. In 2007, as Wei Mian was expanding employment, the mother heard from her sisters (who worked at Wei Mian) about new employment policies that would enable her to begin work there as a contract worker despite her relatively advanced age of 34 at the time (the company had previously given preference to younger workers). She jumped at the opportunity both for the money and for the opportunity to enroll her daughter in county seat schools. However, the daughter had remained in the village school at first because they did not want to move their household registration to the county seat and lose rights to some of their farmland in the village. By purchasing the apartment in the Development Zone, they were able to enroll the daughter in local schools without moving their household registration. So the parents moved to the Development Zone in 2008 and brought the daughter and grandmother over in late 2010, when the daughter was in first grade, just after signing the paperwork on the apartment. Because the mother found Wei Mian work very tiring at her age, she asked her mother-in-law to live with them and take care of the child and do housework. In 2011 the grandfather lived alone in the Matou village, farming the land of all five household members by himself, with occasional help from the father.

The mother was born in 1973, the father in 1975. For unknown reasons, they were not able to have their own children and adopted their daughter as a newborn when the mother was 30 years old in 2003. Thirty is considered late for a first child in Zouping, and the couple told me that they were too old to adopt or attempt to give birth to another. The pattern of the husband being two years younger than the wife was typical of rural households in much of Shandong until the reform era. The pattern has been gradually fading since then, though it still occurs more often than one might think in a country where both marriage law and urban norms make husbands who are a few years older than their wives typical.[4] In Shandong, marriages in which the wife is two years older often indicate that the couple is of rural origin and that the marriage was arranged by a village matchmaker. The logic behind this pattern developed in the era of arranged marriages. Before 1949, when couples were often married in their early teens, it was assumed both that the wife needed to be older as her adjustment during marriage was greater than that of the husband (she must move to the husband's home) and that (especially in the case of early teenage marriages) a slightly older wife would ensure more rapid pregnancy and childbirth.

ENTREPRENEURIAL LOCAL MIGRANTS

Working at Wei Mian offered stability and a decent income and provided a good platform for raising a family. That so many people who grew up in the villages near Weiqiao town took this path made Wei Mian a safe, conservative choice by local standards. The lives of entrepreneurial households tended to be less regular than those of the factory workers. Entrepreneurial work is necessarily more risky (and occasionally much more lucrative), and the family patterns of those who made this choice seemed slightly less conventional, though I did not interview enough such households to make numeric arguments about this. In my small sample of 5 such households, there were 2 cases of divorce, though I came across none among the 30 Wei Mian apartment dwellers I interviewed. For various reasons, affinal relations were also more prominent in these households, especially in the following case. Like their factory working counterparts, however, the entrepreneurial households did maintain links to village homes.

Entrepreneurial Household G

The parents in this family were born in villages in Jiuhu township, and the mother was two years older than the father. Both went to technical high schools (*zhongzhuan*) after graduation from junior middle school and attempted to start careers in Jinan but failed. They briefly returned to their villages and were introduced by a matchmaker and wed at the relatively late age of 26 for the woman and 24 for the man. They did not have their son until the mother was 28, in 2002.

The father studied cooking at a technical school, so they decided to start a restaurant in the Development Zone in 2003. They were successful and in 2008 purchased a 90-square-meter Development Zone apartment on the open market for 180,000 yuan, cash. The father's parents and only brother died in an automobile accident in 2009, so the father only went back to his village occasionally, but they regularly visited the wife's parents and siblings. The wife's brother and sister both worked for Wei Mian. The wife's parents farmed their land back in Jiuhu township. The son stayed in the wife's par-

152 · TRANSFORMERS TRANSFORMED

ent's village home until he finished kindergarten, and during this period the mother returned to visit her parents and son two days every week.

Entrepreneurial Household H

The parents were the same age and from villages near Weiqiao town. The mother went to work at Wei Mian when it was still located in Weiqiao in 1998 when she was 20. While working there she met her husband, who had worked there briefly before quitting to drive a taxi. For a while they lived with the husband's parents in his village, though they both worked outside the village. After their son was born in 2002, the wife developed arthritis from the repetitive motion in the factory, so she quit Wei Mian and began selling clothes in Weiqiao town. In 2009 she rented a shop front in the Development Zone in order to expand her business. Her son initially stayed in the village home with the father and paternal grandparents, but she moved him to the Development Zone in 2010 when he started first grade because of the better schools. The son and the mother usually slept in a room in the back of the shop. They cooked on a hotplate and had to use the public toilets in the shopping arcade. The father sometimes stayed with them and sometimes at the village home, depending on where his taxi fares left him at the end of the day. The clothing business was going well at the time of my interview, averaging around 4,000 yuan a month in profits. The mother said they were saving money and planned to buy an apartment in the county seat. "Zouping's economy is doing well and the schools here are much better than those in the village," she told me, "so we plan on staying here for a long time."

Entrepreneurial Household I

This was a reconstituted family in which the father had divorced and remarried. I interviewed them in 2011. The father had twin 9-year-old boys with his first wife and a one-year-old daughter with his second wife, who was again pregnant. The second wife was 23 at the time of my interview, beautiful, and ten years younger than her husband. She was an only child from a village not far from the county seat. The first wife still worked in Wei Mian and came from a village near that of the father. The second wife had also worked at Wei Mian for a year or two, but after she married this wealthy, divorced, older man, she quit her job to focus on the children. All three children lived with this couple at the time of my interview. The second wife told me, "Because I am a stepmother, I really want to focus on developing warm relations [*ganqing*] with my stepchildren. I also will soon have two children of my own." The second wife also told me that as an only child she was very close to her own mother. Her home village was only a 15-minute bus ride from the county seat, so her mother often came to their apartment to visit her and her children. The twins said nothing, even when I asked them questions directly, but giggled at each other constantly. Their teacher had told me that the twins often were awkward and that this behavior was because of their parents' divorce.

One day after the interview, the second wife called me and asked if I would be willing to meet her mother, who wanted to ask me questions about the twins' behavior. I met both women at a small restaurant in the Development Zone. The mother said that she had been very worried about her daughter marrying a divorced man, even though he was wealthy and took good care of her: "Of course it is good that my daughter does not have to work at Wei Mian any more, can you imagine if his first wife tried to take revenge on her in the factory? I think that the twins act strangely because his first wife tells them bad things about us. Is divorce common where you are from?" While I could tell her that many children did grow up in families split by divorce in Australia, I had no clue about the twins' behavior. The mother then told me she had been unable to conceive more children after the birth of their daughter and their only source of income now was farming the land that she and her husband controlled back in their village. "I am very worried about the future," she said, but her daughter comforted her, saying, "Don't worry, Mom, I'll find a way to take care of you in the future."

The wealthy husband was in the business of buying, selling, and transporting corn starch. He owned several specialized trucks and had a few drivers working for him. He did a lot of business with the Xiwang Group and said he could make 30,000 yuan a month, though he would not explain to me how he was able to develop so profitable a business. They lived in a very large and beautifully decorated apartment in the nicest complex in the Development Zone. Including interior decorating, the apartment had cost over 450,000 yuan. The father did not know how much he would be fined because of the birth control policy for what was to be his fourth child but said that whatever the amount was it would be inconsequential to him. "My new wife should also have the opportunity to have a son," he explained.

The husband was born in a village in northern Zouping township where his father had been Party secretary of the village. He graduated from a technical school (*zhongzhuan*) in transportation. He had one younger sister, who had also married a wealthy man and who was also now a housewife living in a nice apartment in the county seat. The paternal grandparents lived in their village home but did not do much work. Though they still had a rather large allotment of land (13 mu, an amount that suggests the household registration of the father and his three children was still in the village with the paternal grandparents), they rented this land out instead of farming it themselves. The father gave his parents 1,000 yuan a month, and the paternal grandparents came to live in their son's county seat apartment during the winter. Overall, this was one of the wealthiest households that I interviewed. The father's ability to use either his money or his connections to disregard the birth control policy, to have all of his children receive an allotment of land in his village home, and to have started a very successful business all suggest that this is a household where political capital has been put to strategic economic use. Given the father's wealth, political connections, and slightly above average educational level, this household could have been discussed in the chapter on the middle classes, but I opted to place it here because neither the mother nor the father attended university or had a white-collar job, and both grew up in villages. As with any classificatory scheme, some people straddle the borders between categories.

Dissatisfied Entrepreneur J

While the vast majority of local migrants seemed relatively satisfied with their lives in Zouping, I met one local migrant woman who was extremely disgruntled. She was from Zhou Cun, a city about 15 kilometers from Zouping in the neighboring county and prefecture. She had been laid off from a factory job there and in 2009 sold clothing and small decorative items from a cart in a Development Zone shopping arcade. I introduced her in chapter 3 as the women who spoke of "work-unit people." Her husband was unemployed, and her only son was a migrant worker in Jinan. She commuted every day by bus from what she described as an old, dilapidated Zhou Cun apartment, storing her cart in the shop of a friend. She claimed that all officials were corrupt and that their only function was to collect fees and taxes from small vendors like her while never paying any taxes on all of their "gray income" (*huise shouru*, i.e., bribes and kickbacks). She said she made less than 800 yuan a month but had no other options. I spoke to her several times in 2009, but she stopped selling clothes in the same place, and I was not able to locate her during my 2010, 2011, and 2012 visits.

CONCLUSION

The ten case studies in this chapter introduce a number of aspects of Development Zone and village life, as well as the variety of kinship and living circumstances enjoyed and endured by local migrants. Economically, the vast majority of local migrant families were doing quite well. Most had access to two or more incomes in the range of 2,000 to 3,000 yuan per month. Most lived in apartments with decent facilities, and many owned cars and took family vacations. While some of their wealth was attributable to the general socioeconomic context of Zouping—the level of wages at Wei Mian, the affordability of housing, and the easy access to good schools—some of it was also the result of their very practical kinship relations. By pooling income, resources, and labor across three generations, these households managed child care and elder care efficiently and were able to purchase apartments and cars that may have otherwise have been out of reach. This pooling of income, labor, and resources was usually viricentric. For those households that lived in the city but continued to involve themselves in farming, this viricentricity could be said to derive from the virilocal manner in which land rights were allocated in Zouping villages. But even in those households that no longer farmed, a tendency toward viricentricity prevailed.

Other aspects of patrilineal thinking or patriarchy also appeared in the lives of the nearby migrants. Though many of the couples reported meeting at factory social events, the cases of marriage in which the wife was two years older than the husband suggest the continued use of matchmakers in the marriage process and an unknown but likely significant degree of parental involvement. While the border between "arranged" and "free love" marriages is often fuzzy (Kipnis 1997) and while the extent to which marriages are arranged in rural China is probably declining (Yan 2003b), it does not appear to be the case that urbanization in Zouping has put an end to patriarchal influence in the marriage process. The wealthy entrepreneur's desire for a son with his second wife (case I) and the way in which the paternal grandfather spoke for his family (case E) could also be said to reflect patriarchal ideas. Sons are desired by some people because they signal genealogical continuity in a patrilineal imagination and because they are thought to better enable continued control of familial property than daughters.

Kinship is simultaneously a material and affective dimension of life. The emotions and property relations tied up with kinship are powerful forms of memory that re-create the past in the present. The sharing of apartments and income from farming, the provision of care across generations, and the construction of rights to farmland are practices that persist over time and generate affect, both positive and negative. These practices re-create viricentric norms and enable the reinvention of patriarchal and patrilineal imaginaries and discourse. The use of village homes for farming, as sites of summer vacations for children, and as places for elderly parents to retire enable the re-creation of wider networks of kinship relations and the production of affective memories about the countryside for young and old alike. In short, the geographic proximity of village homes to urbanized homes for nearby blue-collar migrants produces a mode of living that straddles the urban/rural divide.

SEVEN

Distant Homes or a New Life

MIGRANT WORKERS FROM AFAR

We need some imaginative stimulus, some not impossible ideal, such as may shape vague hope, and transform it into effective desire, to carry us year after year, without disgust, through the routine work which is so large a part of life.

WALTER PATER, quoted in Crapanzano, *"Reflections on Hope as a Category of Social and Psychological Analysis"*

The situations and attitudes of migrant workers from distant locales were more diverse than those of the workers of local origin. Most of the distant migrants who worked at Wei Mian accepted temporary worker status, in part because fewer of them met the company's criteria for contract workers and in part because they chose not to apply for contract worker status. None of those I met wished to purchase company housing, making contract worker status less desirable. Many saw themselves as returning one day to their distant rural homes. Those who wished to remain in Zouping preferred to invest in commercial apartments. While some saw Wei Mian as a reasonable employer, none lauded the company as a savior in the way that some of the local migrants did, and many expressed distrust of the company.

Almost by definition, the workers in this category lived too far from their rural homes to also be part-time farmers, and they hardly ever lived in three-generation households. Twenty-two of the 35 such households I interviewed came from distant parts of Shandong province, usually from the western, poorer parts about an 8- to 10-hour bus ride away. The rest came from Sichuan, Yunnan, Gansu, Henan, Hebei, or other provinces.

Their living conditions were typically much worse than the local migrants. They usually rented rooms in the villages at the fringes of the Development Zone, where the monthly rent at the time of my research was about 100 yuan per room. Given that both parents in most households worked and that factory workers by 2010 were averaging incomes of over 2,000 yuan a month, their rents were often less than 1/40th of their monthly income. They skimped on rent to save money, sometimes living with their children in a single room with no bathroom or running water (there might be a collective toilet or tap in the larger compound, but in some cases only a poorly maintained public toilet somewhere in the neighborhood). Some saved their money in order to purchase a private apartment in Zouping some day, while others planned to return home with enough money to retire after a number of years.

Perhaps in part because they tended to live in crowded conditions, the households I interviewed uniformly consisted of nuclear families. Because of the quality of schools available to the children of migrant factory workers, most migrant workers brought their school-aged children with them. Some of them even said that the only reason they stayed in Zouping was because of the quality of the schools. But none of the households I interviewed brought either the husband's or the wife's parents with them; none planned to bring them in the future. These families visited their distant village homes at most twice a year (for some of the Shandong households) or as little as once every three years (in the case of the household from Yunnan), with most making the traditional once-a-year migration home for the Chinese New Year.

Without grandparents, these households lacked child care, and even very young children had to find their own way home after school. In some distant migrant households, desperation led both parents to work rotating shifts. Consequently, the children were forced to supervise their own homework and sometimes prepare their own meals (with a hot plate and water fetched from elsewhere, as rented rooms had no proper kitchen). While some of these children did well in school, others did not, and teachers often felt that the worst troublemakers came from such households. Perhaps not surprisingly, teachers typically blamed such problems on the "lack of quality" (*suzhi di*) of the parents rather than the difficulties of their circumstances.

In short, despite coming from rural settings that were probably not that different from those of the nearby villages, the kinship arrangements of the distant migrants were much more nuclear than those of the nearby migrants. Though some of these household members spoke of learning about the types of opportunities available in Zouping through networks of people linked to their places of origin, few had the time to regularly socialize with people from the same place. They were focused on earning money and getting their children through school and acted as individuated household units. Their situations resembled the type of kinship practice that many modernization theorists would predict: a simplification of kinship ties, resulting in nuclear families. While among the local migrants economic and householding strategies led to the sorts of family dynamics previous anthropologists have associated with Chinese viricentric kinship bonds, among the distant migrants economic pressures led to rather nucleated forms of alienation. Children received less care, adults constantly complained of tiredness, trust in the company they worked for was low, and socializing with neighbors was rare. Efforts were focused on accumulating capital for the future. If these migrants become successful, however, perhaps broader forms of kin ties will emerge at a later point in their lives.

Stevan Harrell (2013) has presented Chinese patriliny as dependent on a material property base that necessitates patrilineal thinking for survival. He shows quite clearly how flexible Chinese kinship practice has been and how patriliny and virilocality disappear when the material conditions for their reproduction are negated. But his analysis cannot predict what would happen if the material conditions for patriliny and virilocality reappear after a period of disappearance; or, perhaps more important, if material conditions are such that households or men or women actually have a choice about the types of families they would like to create. While the prevalence of neolocality among the migrants from afar supports Harrell's thesis, whether patrilineal thinking or viricentricity might emerge when they return home or even after they establish themselves in Zouping is an open question. When I asked these families about their visits home they reported visiting the husband's family rather than the wife's. While women in such households often took advantage of return visits to see their own parents, they would only do so after spending a few days at their parents-in-law's house. Husbands sometimes would not visit their in-laws at all.

The alienating aspects of life as a distant migrant worker raise broader questions from the literature on the anthropology of hope. While all humans must face questions of existential meaning—what to put one's faith in, what to lay one's hope on, what to trust—leaving home and one's extant human networks, kinship or otherwise, brings these questions to the fore. Focusing on short-term economic gain, working long hours day after day, not trusting the company one is working for, and isolation from networks of kin are interrelated phenomena that act together to put distant migrants under acute levels of stress. This stress brings about moments of despair but also a deeper search for sources of hope. As Walter Pater suggests, hope sustains hard work; mental stability in such an environment requires faith in something.

In my interviews, explicit expressions of both despair and hope were much more common among the distant migrants than members of the other groups.

In *The Protestant Ethic and the Spirit of Capitalism* (2002), Max Weber argues that Calvinists worked hard because they saw their vocation as a religious calling; they hoped that by demonstrating their work ethic, they could suggest publicly their membership in the group that God had elected for salvation. While any given Calvinist could not be sure that he or she as an individual was among the saved, all placed their hope in the knowledge that some were saved and that those who were saved would act as if they were called.

Weber's analysis illustrates how hope as a future orientation is never certain but does involve forms of knowledge about how the world works, what Crapanzano (2003) terms a "metaphysics of hope." While religion can be an important source of hope, anthropologists tend to see it in much more mundane situations. The sick often are given hope that they will be cured by doctors and relatives; the stress and pain of serious illness brings the need for an explicit source of hope to the surface, a possible postulation about what may cure the ill and how their health may evolve, though the means of giving hope vary culturally (Good et al. 1990). Hirokazu Miyazaki (2006, 2013) demonstrates that dreams of and hopes for the future inform the work of Japanese financial traders. Not only are their hopes tied to shifting intellectual visions of how markets may work and what humans can know about the patterns of this working, but they are also shaped by technologies of knowing that enable particular speculative ventures.

The notion that Chinese people in general work hard is both a stereotype and a truism (Harrell 1985; Smith 1894). Of course, there are many exceptions to this stereotype, some of which will be introduced in the next chapter, but there were few to be found among the distant migrants to Zouping. As Harrell (1985) argues, the motivation for the work often links to hopes for future familial success and to a familial ethic. Visibly sacrificing for the sake of the family by working hard proves one's virtue. The ability to "eat bitterness" (*chiku*) is widely admired. While Chinese notions of prosperity (*xingfu*) are much broader than mere monetary wealth, usually involving familial happiness, monetary wealth is often understood as an important basis for this prosperity. Thus eating bitterness becomes a means of proving one's devotion to familial reciprocity, though how individual family members define both "family" and "reciprocity" can be contested (see chapter 6).

The tendency toward hard work is exacerbated by social institutions that encourage competition. The way in which the university entrance exam encourages competition among high school students is perhaps the ultimate Chinese example of such an institution. While factory workers do not compete with one another as directly as high school students do, if we understand the markets for housing and medical care as structuring elements in Chinese society, then the parallels between high school students and factory workers becomes stronger. There are only so many good apartments and good doctors to go around, and the wealthiest will always secure them. If, as in Zouping, the supply is relatively ample, then more people will secure them, but the poor certainly will not. Since all high school students in a given class study the same curriculum with the same teachers, working hard is the only way to get ahead. Since all factory workers do more or less the same jobs at similar salaries, eating bitterness is similarly the most secure way to achieve familial success or avoid failure.

The structure of hope among migrant workers in Zouping, then, revolves around a metaphysics of hope that presumes hard work can lead to some form of familial prosperity. Visibly eating bitterness demonstrates one's moral commitment to the common cause. While such structures of hope and morality might be common to many in Zouping, especially to the migrant families, the stresses that make this commitment seem less likely to succeed were more prevalent among the migrant workers from distant locales. They faced both less stable economic starting points and, given the dispersal of their families over two distant locations, more doubts about how to translate monetary wealth into familial prosperity. These stresses manifested themselves in both expressions of resistance and despair and discussions of hope.

DISTANT MIGRANT WORKER HOUSEHOLD A

This family of three (father, mother, 11-year-old son in 2010) came to Zouping from a poor part of Gansu province in 2008 because of the father's younger brother, who went to university, graduated in engineering, and entered midlevel management at Wei Mian. The younger brother married a local Zouping woman who was a teacher. He and his wife lived in the management section of Wei Mian housing. The parents in this family both grew up in villages and said that they were introduced by a matchmaker.

The father went to a technical school (*zhong zhuan*) in Gansu and studied electric machinery. When he first came to Zouping he worked as an electrician repairing faults in one of Wei Mian's housing compounds. After a year, he quit to start an electric repair shop in a shopping center in the Development Zone; his job in the housing compound had exposed him to the high demand among Wei Mian employees for repair of television sets and other appliances. "They always came looking for me to do repairs. They have the money to buy many appliances, but they do not have the time or the knowledge to fix them properly," the father told me. The father also said that his shop was never shut. "We live in the shop and are here 24 hours a day, 7 days a week. We lock the front door when we go to sleep, but if someone comes knocking on the door in middle of the night, one of us will get up and answer it. I do a careful job on my repairs and do them on time at a fair price. As long as the customers are happy, our business will thrive."

The family lived in one small room in the back of their shop without a proper kitchen or toilet. They used the public toilets in the shopping center, traveled to the public showers in a nearby village-in-the-city to wash, and cooked with a rice cooker and a hot plate in the back of their shop. The son had no desk on which to do his homework, so he sat on the floor and wrote on a small stool. They did have an Internet connection, however, and the boy was an active contributor to the class blog and one of the better students in the class. He often wrote descriptions of his father's TV repairs. He said he likes his school in Zouping because it has much better facilities than the one back in Gansu, and the teachers are nicer. "We even use computers in class," he told me. "Back in Gansu we only did math problems and character writing again and again and again." He hopes to become a soldier or an astronaut and plans on going to a military university; he seemed to me to be much more mature than most of his classmates.

The mother crushed her leg in a motorcycle accident back in Gansu in late 2007. The family spent 20,000 yuan to have her leg fixed in a hospital there, after receiving only 8,000 yuan in compensation from the truck driver who hit her, but the Gansu doctors made a mistake during the operation. "I wanted to kill myself after the operation," she told me. "I could hardly walk and thought that I had become 'handicapped' [*feiren,* lit., "useless person"]. My brother-in-law had told us about the jobs in Wei Mian and also said that he thought the doctors were better here, so we came. I would never go back to those Gansu doctors after what they did to me. I saw the doctor here, and we paid 30,000 yuan to have another surgery ten months ago [in 2009]. Now I am finally getting better and walking without a limp. I hope to look for work in one of the nearby factories soon, but for now at least I can help out around the shop and take care of all the shopping and cooking again. I no longer think about killing myself."

They had borrowed money from the father's younger brother to pay for the operation and had just managed to pay him back. Now they were saving all of their profits from the shop with the hope of one day buying a private apartment. "We are very frugal. If my wife can work again, we should have enough for a 50 percent down payment on a small apartment in five years," the father calculated.

The father's younger brother had gone back to Gansu to visit the father's parents, but neither the father nor the mother of this household had been able to afford the trip back since their first visit in 2008. The father and mother had two siblings each, so their parents had someone to take care of them. The husband's parents lived with his second younger brother, a primary school teacher, while the wife's parents lived with her older brother, who worked in construction. The mother also had an elder sister who farmed in a Gansu village not far from where they grew up. The father said, "We cannot think about our big family [da jiating] now. They are all doing better than us, but we have a way out [chulu]. After we get our own apartment, then maybe we will think of visiting Gansu again."

In many ways this was one of the poorest households I visited. Their medical debts and relatively recent migration meant that they were literally starting over from scratch. But I caught them at a moment when their hopes were reviving, and they did not hesitate to share both their plans and troubles with me. Though serious illness and injury are often causes of despair, recovery from injury generates hope. All three family members seemed resolutely focused on what they wanted to do, and the medium-range goals of the parents centered on purchasing an apartment. Through frugality and hard work, it seemed a possibility. Though the father's younger brother lived nearby, their family dreams were strongly nucleated at the moment. Perhaps other forms of family will emerge in the future.

DISTANT MIGRANT WORKER HOUSEHOLD B

This family of three (father, mother, 11-year-old daughter in 2010) came from two neighboring villages in Zaozhuang prefecture (south central Shandong province near the Jiangsu border). As is often the case with couples from rural Shandong, the mother (b. 1976) was two years older than the father. The father was a junior middle school graduate, but the mother had only graduated from primary school. They rented a large room with an attached kitchen and latrine-style bathroom in a partially torn down adobe house for 120 yuan per month. They also had running water and had rigged a shower with a curtain and a cement floor and an aboveground gulley for a drain next to the kitchen. The room was in a village slightly more distant from the factories than the most heavily populated villages in the city and was not so crowded. They rode bikes to work and school. Because of the impending threat of relocation and the fact that the village was 2 kilometers from the schools and factories, there had not been much building in this village, and some homes were adobe rather than brick, a relatively rare occurrence in 2010 Zouping. They had been renting this house since 2003.

When they first came to Zouping the parents worked for Wei Mian in cotton spinning, but they could not stand the heat (the temperature is maintained at 40 degrees Centigrade year-round) and found work in another smaller factory group at slightly less pay. Both of them had been through brief periods of unemployment since 2003, but they had never left Zouping or given up their adobe house in this period and now felt that they had stable jobs. At the time of my interview, they both worked rotating shifts and averaged at least seven 8-hour shifts a week; the father earned 3,000 yuan a month and the mother 2,000. They were saving all their money to buy an apartment in Zouping. They had accumulated over 100,000 yuan and thought that they would have enough for a 50 percent down payment and a 50 percent mortgage on a 300,000-yuan apartment in a couple more years. The wife also hoped to have a second child the next year, though she wouldn't confirm that she was already pregnant. "When our younger child is one year old and our older daughter starts junior high school would be the perfect time to buy an apartment," she optimistically pronounced.

While hopes for a second child and a new apartment drove the parents to work hard, signs of stress and despair were also apparent. Shortly after I arrived at their house, the daughter, glaring at her mother, asked me, "Do parents hit their children where you are from?" Taken aback, I mumbled in reply that some do, but others think it is improper. The daughter, sounding like a United Nations arbitrator, then loudly declared, "Violence does not resolve problems" (*Baoli buneng jiejue wenti*). The mother just frowned. Later in the interview the father told me, "We both work so many hours, and the shifts rotate. Sometimes we even unexpectedly have to work extra shifts. We can't always be at home for our daughter, and sometimes we need her to do things like cooking and shopping. Sometimes we can't even tell our daughter when we will be home. So it is hard for her too, and my wife can get upset if she spends too much money shopping or buys or cooks the wrong things. We have to be very frugal. If we have a second child, my wife will have to stop work for a while, so it is important for us to earn money now. When our daughter is in junior middle school, she won't have enough time to do all the baby-sitting, so my wife will only be able to work part-time until our second child can go to preschool."

The daughter also explained some of the disadvantages of their current living quarters: "I don't have Internet access here, so it can be hard to do my homework when we are supposed to contribute to the class blog. I have to go over to my friend's house to do that, but then my mother accuses me of wasting time playing. Also, because we live so far from the markets, I have to carry everything in my bicycle basket when we shop, and it is hard if you ever forget anything. Yes, it is nice to have our own kitchen and our own shower, but living so far from everything makes life harder."

The father especially was ambivalent about settling permanently in Zouping. He said that they returned home twice a year (a 10-hour bus trip). The mother then said that their home district was much poorer than Zouping. The paternal grandparents only had 2 mu of land to farm as the population-to-farmland ratio is much denser there. The paternal grandparents could live by farming their own land, but with neither sufficient land nor factories there was nothing for the father and mother to do. The father had a married-out elder sister (i.e., one who lived with her in-laws in another village) but no brother, so his parents were living on their own. The mother said that her parents lived with her younger brother in their village but that he had become a rural primary school teacher and therefore had a stable income. The mother then said, "Places like Zouping have a future. In the long run it will be a little better for us and much better for our children to live in a place like this." The father then summed up the dilemma from his point of view: "We already have a nice house back in Zaozhuang. It is built of brick and has plenty of room, running water, and electricity and a sunny courtyard with lots of flowers growing. Back there it is much less polluted than here. The air really makes you feel like you want to breathe. But Zouping offers better employment opportunities and better schools. Do you think our family has a better future here or there?" I had no answer but wondered if the father's seemingly greater attachment to the Zaozhuang home had something to do with the virilocal living arrangements there and the fact that the father's parents had no one to care for them. I also noted that this household especially was one in which all three members were not afraid to speak their minds.

DISTANT MIGRANT WORKER HOUSEHOLD C

This family of four (father, mother, 11-year-old daughter, 4-year-old son) came from a village in Hezi, the poorest prefecture in Shandong, in the southwestern corner of the province bordering on Henan province. The wife was two years older than the husband. Depending on transfer times, it took between nine and eleven hours to travel there by bus. The parents both worked at Wei Mian. Neither of them had completed junior middle school, though they obtained false graduation certificates to use when applying for jobs. The father is a contract employee in cotton spinning making 2,600 yuan a month on rotating shifts, while the mother just returned to day shifts as a temporary employee earning 2,000 yuan per month.

Among the distant migrant workers I interviewed, unlike the nearby migrant workers, men were slightly more likely to work rotating shifts than women. In such families, the husband usually worked longer hours outside the home, while the wife both held a job and did more child care and housework. In this household, the wife did not work from the time their son was born until he was old enough to go to preschool (age 3). When the mother was too busy with work and shopping, the daughter had to take care of her younger brother and walk him home from preschool.

As a contract employee, the father was eligible to buy Wei Mian housing, but he did not want to. He explained, "The company housing cannot be resold on the open market, and you don't even get the owner's certificate [*fangchan zheng*]. Who can trust Weiqiao? They say you can get your money back if you move out, but we don't feel comfortable with that. What if the company goes through a bad period? What if I have a fight with my supervisor? At the end of the day, we are still outsiders [*waidiren*] here." For 200 yuan a month, the family rented two smallish rooms in a rental house in an overcrowded village on the outskirts of the Development Zone. They cooked on a hot plate, fetched water from a communal tap in their compound's courtyard, and paid each time they used the toilets or the showers in a commercial bathhouse about 100 meters from their rental house.

The father said that he didn't really like it in Zouping and that similar employment opportunities were available in many mid-sized Shandong cities. "Look at the shabby way we live," he said. "Not only do we have to pay to take a crap, but these galvanized metal [*tiepi*] rooms are steaming hot in the summer and freezing cold in the winter. I've worked in Weifang and Yantai [two other Shandong cities] as well. It is always about the same." "Why do you live here then?," I asked. "We came here about five years ago," he replied, "just because we had lost our jobs in Weifang and heard about how easy it was to find work here. But the one good thing about Zouping is that they have decent schools, and they are free to migrant workers who work at Wei Mian. In other places migrants have to pay to send their kids to even terrible schools." "Well, what about renting a nicer apartment? I think you could have your own place with a kitchen and a bathroom for about 600 yuan a month," I said. "We need to save our money," he replied. "One day I really hope our children can go to university, but that is expensive. Even to go to senior middle school you have to pay a large fee if your entrance score [on the senior middle school entrance exam, *zhongkao*] is not high enough. Plus, since our house here isn't nice, our children will probably live in the dorm rooms at junior middle school—that also costs money. In addition, our son will need to get married one day and we could get sick. All of that costs a lot of money, and we can never know how much all these things will be in the future, so we have to save."

When I asked where they would live after they retired, the father said that they would definitely move back to their village home in Hezi. "We have a nice house there, and it is more comfortable to live near friends and family. In Zouping we have few friends and no relatives. Everything here is about relying on ourselves. That is why my wife had to stop working for so long. There was no one to help out with a little baby. My wife went home for a month and stayed with her mother, but then she missed our older daughter, and I missed her. I have a brother and a sister back in Hezi, and my wife also has a sister there. Everything is easier if you have friends and family around. I don't want to wait until I am old to go back there either. When our son enters junior middle school, he can just live in the school dorms. By then my daughter should be in university, so she will live in the dorms as well. Then our job will be done and we can enjoy life [*xiangshou*] again."

In this household the father did all the talking. Like the families discussed above, the hopes expressed were largely familial, but in this case they centered on the children's education rather than the purchase of an apartment. Their Hezi home and the relatives who lived there became sources of nostalgia. The lack of friends and relatives in Zouping and the pressures of working hard to save money and raising children alone generated considerable discontent. The feeling of being an outsider, regardless of whether it stemmed from treatment by locals or their own despair, made trust difficult.

DISTANT MIGRANT WORKER HOUSEHOLD D

This family of three (mother, father, 11-year-old son in 2010) came from Hunan. They were the only Hunanese migrants I discovered in Zouping. Because the father was working at the time of the interview I only spoke to the mother and the son. The mother disliked everything about Wei Mian and Zouping. She was just 31 years old and had her son at the age of 20, after getting married at 18. Her husband is the same age as she is. When I mentioned that in Zouping the minimum legal marriage ages of 22 for men and 20 for women were usually strictly enforced, she said that no one paid attention to that where she was from in rural Hunan. "All my friends got married at 17 or 18," she added.

They rented one room in an overcrowded suburban village housing complex. It cost 100 yuan per month. They cooked on a single burner and had to use the crowded and unsanitary public toilets outside of their courtyard. The three family members shared a single bed, but they were rarely at home at the same time because both the mother and the father worked rotating shifts at Wei Mian (earning about 2,400 yuan a month each). The son was known as the naughtiest child in his class. The teachers said that he was hyperactive and that no one looked after him properly. He used to stay with his paternal grandparents back in Hunan, but the grandmother died in 2009 at the age of 46 from a sudden illness. The grandfather was too busy with farming and trying to do business on the side to look after his grandson, so the boy came to Zouping when he was 10. Though both parents had been at Wei Mian for three years and both were contract workers, the mother said that she would never buy a house in Zouping. She did not trust the company, did not like working in the 40-degree heat and, moreover, thought that it was not fair that the local villagers get to earn money from rental housing and do not have to suffer working in the factories. "Why is it that they get to live in such nice rooms and rent these places to us?," she asked.

The mother was full of despair and, even when I asked, could not really explain why she worked so hard and lived so frugally or what her hopes were for the future. "I just feel tired all the time," she said. "We don't have any

DISTANT HOMES OR A NEW LIFE · 169

friends here. At the factory you work so hard, and there is barely any time to speak to anyone. The supervisors are strict, and they are frowning all the time if they are not yelling at you. Zouping is a place where everyone only cares about money. How could we be any different? With the rotating shifts and different schedules, I barely get a chance to speak with my husband. We can't talk, so how can we make plans for the future? I just survive day by day. I have no idea how much longer we will stay here or where we might go in the future. You need to have money just to survive, so if you have more money you can survive longer. I only work to get money to survive."

When I asked the son if he liked it here, he said, "Not really. I had more friends back home, and I miss my grandma. She cooked good food for me. But the teachers are a bit nicer here. They used to hit me back in Hunan." They had no computer, but he said that he could write for the class blog at one of the computers in school during lunch. He also said that it took him almost 2 hours to do his homework. Most of the other children reported finishing it in 30 minutes. His mother added that his homework took so long because he had trouble concentrating. She also mentioned that the school's principal was originally reluctant to admit her son to the school when he suddenly showed up the previous year, but she complained to people in the factory about this problem, and they told the principal that he had to accept any child of Wei Mian contract workers. Despite his trouble with his school and schoolwork, one of the only hopes the mother expressed to me was that her son would one day attend university. "My younger brother went to university, and now he has a good job for a pharmaceutical company in Beijing. It would be ideal if my son could follow this path," she said.

Before they came to Zouping, this couple had been working in a textile factory in a Beijing suburb, near where the mother's younger brother had gotten a job. "We went to Beijing when my son was 4. Before that we just farmed and did small business in Hunan. I liked the work better in Beijing. The hours were a little shorter and the pay was about the same and the factory wasn't so hot, but that factory closed, so we had to move somewhere. My younger brother was also in Beijing, so sometimes we got to see him." They came to Zouping in 2007 because a junior middle school classmate of the father had heard from a friend about the work at Wei Mian. The classmate himself, however, had never been to Zouping.

In addition to her younger brother, the mother had two elder sisters. They were also migrant laborers but had gone to Dongguan in the Pearl River Delta. The father also had a younger brother who was working as a migrant worker, but the mother didn't know where. "Last year we went home for my mother-in-law's funeral. That's when we picked up our son. But we couldn't afford to also go home for Spring Festival, and I don't know if we will go back this year either. I can't remember exactly where everyone is now."

In short, this was one of the most alienated households I interviewed. Their alienation had several interrelated sources. Their factory work, as Marx (1964) would suggest, alienated them by turning them into objects in the production process, less important than even the objects they produced. Their alienation was compounded by the fatigue and disorientation of rotating shifts. The alienation of not being valued in the production process was further aggravated by the sense of social fragmentation and isolation that came from migrating away from family and friends to a place where one was a stranger (Simmel 1971). Finally the disintegration of the home family caused by the death of the paternal grandmother and the out-migration of all the siblings added yet another layer of disorientation to this alienation and fragmentation. The only remaining hope seemed to be that the son might one day attend university, a form of hope that was universal among the parents I interviewed (Kipnis 2011a).

CONCLUSION

Hope itself might be considered a form of memory. The knowledge or metaphysics it relies on must be reproduced and sustained over time. For the distant migrants, and perhaps many factory workers in Zouping, two related forms of knowledge structure hope. The first is the knowledge that hard work and frugality might slowly accumulate into funds that can enable prosperity. The second is the knowledge that investing one's money in familial relationships might lead to long-term security and social advancement. Together these propositions of hope might also be called a morality of eating bitterness and familial sacrifice. That the propositions structuring this morality are possibilities rather than definitive relations of causality transform these propositions into a metaphysics of hope. When fatigue and alienation raise the specter of doubt, these propositions also enable despair. Such despair might also be considered a form of forgetting the hopeful futures to which eating bitterness could lead.

In her analysis of the moral worlds of three generations of family members in a rural village in Sichuan, Anna Lora-Wainwright (2013: 78–81) describes how the idea of eating bitterness is used to draw out the commonalities among three generations of people and three very different moral economies. For the grandparents, eating bitterness was a capacity for hard physical farm labor and a frugality that involved always eating the least expensive food-stuffs and sometimes enduring starvation. For the parents, eating bitterness implied migrating away from home for work. While working as a wage lab-orer could be hard physically, it also could involve activities that were monot-onous or repetitive but not so physically difficult. The bitterness involved being away from home and enduring loneliness and alienation as much as physically taxing work. Figuring out how to earn more money with less effort was much more important to the parents than the grandparents. For the children, eating bitterness involved studying hard at school. These efforts were not physically taxing but could involve drudgery and mental exhaus-tion. The term *eating bitterness* was applied by and to all three generations in order to portray all family members as morally contributing to the long-term and unchanging goal of familial prosperity. In this sense, eating bitterness can be considered a form of memory that constructs continuity while ignor-ing differences and change. The importance of a familial prosperity may remain, but the definitions of both family and prosperity may change.

Also conducting research in rural China during the mid- to late 2000s, Hans Steinmüller (2013: 99–101) depicts a similar form of moral thinking in a Hubei village but emphasizes the disjuncture between the different forms of eating bitterness. There, some old men eat bitterness by stubbornly farm-ing the land in an old-fashioned way (focusing on rice and subsistence crops) and consuming mainly their own produce. Younger men mostly out-migrate for factory work and small business. These ventures could also involve much bitterness, but the younger men devalorize the old men's farming. The younger men operated in a more fully commoditized economy and placed value on higher rates of remuneration rather than self-sufficiency. For the younger men, consumption could be a way of displaying success, so frugality was not always highly valued, at least when they were back in their villages. But the lack of self-sufficiency could be extremely alienating for those not able to display their success in this way.

In Zouping, and at Wei Mian in particular, tropes of eating bitterness linked farming to factory work quite directly. Factory work was considered physically taxing, and the heat endured by those who worked in cotton spin-ning was sometimes compared directly to the heat endured when working in the fields during the summer. For those migrants from nearby districts who had settled on careers at Wei Mian, the parallels between farming and factory work were even more direct. Both were considered lifelong endeavors; enduring the repetitive work was more important than constantly seeking more profitable forms of employment. The situations of the distant migrants resemble those of the young migrant laborers described by Steinmüller. They were reluctant to commit permanently to Wei Mian, often sought better paying or less bitter forms of employment, and suffered from higher levels of alienation. Being caught between distant homes and a potential new one brought the dialectics of hope and despair close to the surface.

EIGHT

Villagers-in-the-City

TIME FOR COMMUNITY

Former village farmers whose land was absorbed by the expanding city were usually among the wealthiest urbanites of the groups explored so far. The terms of land appropriation in Zouping have generally been quite good. Land-losing households receive annual payments equivalent to the value of the harvest at that year's market rates for thirty years. In addition, the village as a whole often receives a section of land on which it can develop its own real estate projects, passing the profits down to the individual households. In villages where the houses themselves are razed, those losing houses are given heavily subsidized apartments in new urban developments. Households that keep their houses and are located near factories can develop lucrative rental businesses by building (as many as 20) 100-yuan-per-month rental rooms on top of and inside their existing courtyard homes.

The exact routes to prosperity differ for villager-in-the city households, as does the overall level of prosperity (some such as Anjia, discussed below, are wealthier than others), but the generality of their prosperity can be seen in the fact that there were only two factory workers among the 30 villager-in-the-city households I interviewed. Though they averaged no more education or skills than the migrants working in factories, most felt factory work was too "bitter" (*ku*) and preferred to start their own business or take easier (but lower-paying) jobs. One man explained his wife's choice of a low-paying department store job as follows: "Our household has many sources of income, the money replacing agricultural income [*dunliang qian*] and rental income as well. Factory work is too tiring; retail pays less, but it is more pleasant."

In 2005, when I completed some interviews in a village in the Development Zone whose land was about to be taken by the city, I heard that all of the old bachelors in this previously poor village were now finally able to get married.

One man of 42 who had just gotten married to a 33-year-old widow and was about to have his first child told me, "Before, our family was too poor to get married. My parents had a bad time during the Cultural Revolution and could not work hard either on or off the farm because of the health problems stemming from that period. Their poverty followed me. But as soon as it was announced that our village too would receive money replacing agricultural income, and have income from rentals as well, then the village matchmakers were able to find matches for all of the remaining bachelors in our village, including me." I met another family in this village who had just moved back to Zouping from the city of Tianjin. They had been living in Tianjin for 15 years and had a stable but not extremely high income from a small restaurant they ran there; however, despite living in Tianjin for 15 years, they were not able to move their household registrations there and officially remained residents of this poor Zouping village. As soon as they heard from relatives that their village's land was going to be requisitioned, they decided to sell their Tianjin restaurant and move back to Zouping so they could receive a share of the benefits.

The villager-in-the-city households I interviewed exhibited many viricentric tendencies. Fifteen of the 30 households included paternal grandparents, while none included maternal grandparents. Pressure to live with grandparents increased in those villages with lucrative rental markets, as living in separate households wasted potential rental space. But though they economized on space, none of the rentier households I visited economized on the quality of their homes. While the rental rooms attached to the main sections of the house were quite basic, the spaces the landlords occupied, always including separate bedrooms for grandparents, parents, and children as well as a living room, a kitchen, and a private bathroom, were usually beautifully decorated, with high-quality fittings.

In these households the grandparents rarely took formal jobs. Having lost their land, there was no farming to be done, and few felt the need to find employment. They took care of their grandchildren and socialized with neighbors. Generally speaking, the villagers-in-the-city had the most active social lives of all the groups examined in this book. They still lived in relatively organic communities and had more leisure time than the factory workers, who if from nearby villages were juggling full-time factory work with farming and if from farther away juggled extensive factory work with a lack of child care and living circumstances that made cooking and washing difficult. While the households were viricentric, their socializing involved both agnatically related fellow villagers and visits to affines, who, if not from the same village, were usually within easy commuting distance. Unfortunately, my research was not detailed enough to provide quantitative data on the relative importance of socializing with different groups of friends and relatives, though I will discuss a case study that focuses on this issue.

Another aspect of viricentricity and patriliny was visible in the patterns of inheritance in these villages. One of the villages-in-the-city that I visited, Anjia, had done extremely well with its collective real estate holdings and earned enough money to provide subsidized apartments for all village households, private health insurance for all villagers, four-year tuition scholarships for all village high school graduates who were accepted to tertiary institutions, and monthly stipends, which in 2009 were 380 yuan for those under 55 years of age, 450 yuan for those between 55 and 60, and 760 yuan for those over 60. To prevent the dispersal of these rights over time, the village had decided that the rights to these benefits could be passed on to only one household in each generation. While this household could be the household of one's daughter, and had to be so in the case of households with no sons (somewhat more common as result of the birth control policy), the rights still went to sons more often than daughters. The village Party secretary told me that of the nine cases in this village where there was both a son and a daughter in the household and the rights had been formally transferred, in seven cases the rights had gone to the son. In the two cases where the daughter had received the rights, it was because the son had settled in another city and did not want to return to Zouping. Households, he explained, chose sons for this privilege because stable material resources greatly enhanced the son's marriage prospects while doing less for the daughter's. That uxorilocal marriage was relatively common in this village (households with daughters but no sons had to marry one of their daughters uxorilocally or lose their benefits) may have intensified the competition for good uxorilocal male partners. If so, this competition would have exacerbated the pressure for virilocal marriages for the households with a son and a daughter.

Just as villages in farming regions must determine rules for the allocation of land, all of Zouping's villages-in-the-city with collective real estate income must set up rules for issuing various forms of benefits and dividends. These rules were usually framed in a gender-neutral way, but in practice they often involved logics and patterns that resemble those of allocating land rights in villages where patrilineal, virilocal kinship predominates. While I did not research cases of divorce in Zouping's villages-in-the-city, given the findings of Sargeson and Song (2010) in other parts of rural China, it seems likely that the person who marries into the village will lose benefit rights after divorce and that the person is more likely to be a woman than a man.[1] If these property arrangements mean that women have more to lose from divorce than men, then they also could form the material underpinnings of continued private patriarchy, either because the husband is more able to dominate his wife or because the husband's parents manipulate the husband into using the threat of divorce to make their own demands on the wife.

TYPES OF VILLAGES-IN-THE-CITY

Most villages-in-the-city can be classified as three or four main types: those that both retain private housing and are close enough to the factories or schools to enable households to establish rental businesses, those that retain income from collective real estate holdings, and those that trade in their collective single-story homes for new apartment complexes. A final category could be those on the outermost edge of the Development Zone that at this point only receive money replacing agricultural income. The following three cases illustrate the economic conditions across these different types.

Villager-in-the-City Household A

This family lived in the dirtiest and most populated rental village, Dongfanqian, but they have had a considerable amount of luck. There were seven people in this family: two paternal grandparents, a father, a mother, an elder daughter who was 11 in 2011, and twins (a boy and a girl) who were one year old (*longfeng tai*).[2] They were the first Zouping couple I met who had given birth to three children legally. Now with seven members in their family, for the thirty years after their land was requisitioned in 2007 they will receive roughly 2,800 yuan per household member per year in money replacing agricultural income (the total came to about 20,000 yuan in 2010 for their household).[3] They had built 18 cheap and shabby rental rooms on top of and around the 7 well-built and nicely outfitted rooms they reserved for themselves in their courtyard house. The rental rooms were full and rented for 100 yuan a month each in 2011, giving the family another 20,000 yuan per year in income. The father and mother also ran a clothing business selling mostly to migrant workers. They had started off with a stall earning 2,000 to 3,000 yuan per month but by 2010 rented a shop and earned between 5,000 and 10,000 yuan a month. The grandparents looked after the children and cooked. The household owned two cars and had taken vacations to Qingdao, Shanghai, Jinan, and Beijing. Though the parents had only graduated from junior middle school and the grandparents did not work, in 2011 this family had a total income of considerably over 100,000 yuan per year.

Villager-in-the-City Household B

This family of six lived in Beifan, a village whose land had been requisitioned but, as of 2011, was too far from the schools and factories to attract significant rental business and had no collective real estate income. The six family members included the paternal grandparents, father, mother, an elder daughter in senior middle school, and an 11-year-old in fifth grade in 2011. In 2010 they received 17,000 yuan in money replacing agricultural income. The father made 3,000 yuan a month working for a construction subcontracting team organized by a village leader; the mother earned 2,000 yuan a month working five rotating shifts a week in Weiqiao. This was one of the few villager-in-the-city households that had a factory worker, and it is perhaps no accident that they were from a village where money replacing agricultural income was the only benefit. The parents had both received a junior middle school education. They owned a car and had taken vacations to Qingdao and Beijing. The grandparents retired when the family lost its farmland.

Villager-in-the-City Household C

This household came from a village that had lost both its farmland and its housing. The village then gained rights to some apartment buildings for its residents to move into as well as a commercial building, the rental of which gave the village committee a collective income stream. The household lived in a beautiful 150-square-meter apartment in the new compound that combined residents from their former village with those of two others. They bought the apartment in 2010 at the subsidized price of 150,000 yuan. They estimated that it was worth about 450,000 yuan at 2011 market prices. They also received free electricity and water as a result of the income their village receives from the collective real estate holdings. Since the grandparents lived with the father's older brother, this household only had three members. Nevertheless, they received 10,000 yuan in 2010 in money replacing agricultural income. The mother had taken a job as a saleswoman in the ritziest department store in the Old City. She made 800 yuan per month plus commissions, which varied from 500 to 1,000 yuan per month. The father drove an unregistered taxi (*heiche*) and made about 2,000 yuan per month. He said that they were too comfortable to put up with factory work and had selected occupations that afforded them relatively relaxed lifestyles. They often used the car to take short trips to the seaside, to Jinan for shopping, or to local tourist sites in the countryside. Both parents stopped going to school after graduating from junior middle school.

Villager-in-the-City Household D

This household consisted of one woman, the only extremely dissatisfied villager-in-the-city I met. I include the case here because it illuminates the potential of Zouping land deals to undermine the lives of the elderly, despite their generally favorable terms. An older woman approached me one evening in 2009 at a shopping mall. She was a janitor there and very unhappy about her employment. She had seen me interviewed on the local news and hoped that as a foreign academic, I would have the influence to do something about her situation. Embarrassed, I admitted that there was little I could do.[4] She said that she only earned 800 yuan a month. She came from a village whose land was requisitioned by the New City and was a widow. Though her son and daughter-in-law had been offered good jobs working for the village committee in the real estate businesses that managed the village's collective property, she had not been offered any job. She said, "I don't get along with my daughter-in-law, and my son only listens to her. I was the one who farmed the land before, so when they took the land I lost my job. But it was my son and his wife who were given new positions as part of the deal. I got nothing. I complained for a year, and finally they gave me this crummy job. I only make 800 a month and sometimes have to work in the evening. After work, the buses have stopped running. I'm too old to ride a bike and sometimes not even my son will come and get me, so I have to spend money on a cab to get home."

Mother-in-law/daughter-in-law conflict is ubiquitous in Chinese patrilineal kin relations, so it is not surprising that this woman complained about her daughter-in-law. But the case can serve to remind us that when compensation in land deals focus on the household as a unit, even generous compensation cannot guarantee that all members of a given household will be equally satisfied.

COMMUNITY BUILDING BY VILLAGERS-IN-THE-CITY

Despite cases like the woman in household D, villagers-in-the-city averaged more time to develop relationships outside of their families than the predominantly factory-employed migrants described in the previous two chapters. Detailing the types of these relationships enables a consideration of how processes of urbanization affect the formation of "community." Ferdinand Tönnies's ([1887] 1963) classic work of modernization theory, sometimes translated as *Community and Society,* suggests that the transition from agricultural village life to urban industrial life involves a transformation in the social groupings in which people live. Tönnies saw village society as an organic community of people linked by kinship, common customs, a common place, and a sense of belonging. He saw life in urban centers as structured around groups that were somehow more artificial and termed these groupings society (*Gesellschaft*) rather than community (*Gemeinschaft*). Later scholars (e.g., Smith 1979) have criticized this view as too simplistic: rural communities were not simply organic but required effort to keep them going and were full of divisions and conflict; moreover, urban societies could contain close groupings that engendered strong senses of belonging. Yet most people acknowledge that there is something different about living in a city rather than a village. Fei Xiaotong (1992) contrasted China's rural society to Western urban society in terms of groups and networks. Chinese society, he argued, was formed around social networks, which were structured like concentric circles moving from an individual to her close kin to distant kin to yet more distant associates. Since each person had a different network, there were no unitary groups in society. Fei termed the Chinese mode of socializing a "differential mode of association" (*chaxu geju*). In contrast, he argued, Western society was formed through well-defined individuals working together in well-defined, bounded groups. Again, while many have criticized Fei's contrast as too simplistic, most scholars acknowledge the importance of networking in Chinese society.

A subtler form of modernization theory can be seen in the work of Julia Huang and Robert Weller (1998). They depict the rise of (predominantly female) Buddhist charity organizations in Taiwan and compare the rise of this form of organization with the rise of women's Christian charity organizations in the United States and Europe during the nineteenth century. They note that in both cases "new wealth had freed [women] from many earlier responsibilities for housework and child care, yet a limited job market and a morality of feminine propriety restrain their options outside of the home. At the same time recent urbanization and the dominance of market transactions have led to a feeling that community values have been lost to individual self-interest, and that many husbands are being lost to a new world of business and bars" (1998: 380). They also find subtle differences between the two movements and discuss the links of both movements to the historical and religious environments in which they arose.

Zouping's villagers-in-the-city were not middle class (at least in terms of educational levels) and the dominant patterns of their household gender dynamics did not involve husbands working outside the home more than wives. Nevertheless, many individuals did find themselves in positions where they had time to spend on a relatively wide range of human relationships in the context of a growing urban environment in which contact with strangers was more likely than in a village. The types of relationships they formed included those that might be seen as both community and society in Tönnies's terms and both bounded groups and networks in Fei's terms; they also included religious organizations somewhat similar to those discussed by Huang and Weller.

Drawing on the work of Jean-Luc Nancy (1991), Jamie Coates (2012) uses the term *being-in-common* rather than *community* to depict forms of interacting with significant others outside of familial relationships. His formulation highlights the fact that well-demarcated, homogeneous communities are rare and that social interaction, in urban spaces especially, often involves multiple forms and political possibilities. While I have retained the term *community* here, I approach the topic with the same sense of openness and possibility that Coates's and Nancy's theorizing suggests. Below are four case studies that explore the range of processes of being-in-common that I came across.

Villager-in-the-City Case E: A Matchmaking Woman

Like the family in case A, this household came from a village with significant rental income. The paternal grandfather was dead, and the father and mother had one 11-year-old son in 2011. The paternal grandmother lived with them and did the cooking, while the father ran a small subcontracting business specializing in the installation of windows and earned over 4,000 yuan a month. They took in about 13,000 yuan in money replacing agricultural income in 2011. The mother focused on their rental business, which earned about 20,000 yuan a year. Even though that business did not take up much of her time, she was not looking for formal employment because she felt that their family had enough income. Instead, she spent a great deal of time visiting friends and relatives from her natal family and acting as a matchmaker (*meiren*). She said that she had successfully arranged more than ten marriages over the past five years. She explained:

> My home village is on the southern end of Huang Shan district [the southernmost part of Zouping city, about 10 kilometers from the village in which she currently lived]. I was born in 1978 and am the youngest of four siblings. I have two older sisters and an older brother. The older brother and my parents are still back in my natal village, while my two older sisters married into different villages-in-the-city in different parts of Zouping. I often go to visit my sisters and my parents, and since they are all living in different places I have made friends in villages in many parts of Zouping. I ride my electric bike to visit them, and I can get to most places in less than 15 minutes. I am young for a matchmaker, but because of my family situation and siblings I have good conditions for doing this work. Each time I go to visit a place, I learn about the eligible men and women and also who is falling in love [*tan lian'ai*]. Sometimes young people like to find their own partners, but they still ask a matchmaker to help negotiate the formal arrangements. Sometimes their parents will ask me to help them find a partner as the young can be too shy to look for themselves. But nowadays young people will spend a lot of time together after you introduce them and before they get married. There are no real arranged [*baoban*] marriages anymore. People trust me because I tell the truth and don't gossip needlessly. I learn about the conditions of people's families and their special characteristics, but I only divulge this information at the right time to people who are serious about getting married and who are reasonable matches. You have to match families who are socially appropriate for one another [*mendang hudui*]. You have to consider the health, the jobs, and the education of the young people as well as the circumstances of their families. Most of the time, I make arrangements between young people from different villages-in-the-city or from villages on the outskirts of Zouping [city] who have not been to university. But last year I arranged the wedding of a pair of university graduates. The wife is a now a primary school teacher and the husband is an accountant in the tax office.

When I asked if she had ever arranged the marriages of migrant workers, she said that most migrant workers want to find a spouse from their own hometown. She added that sometimes, when a wealthy villager-in-the-city had daughters but no son, there would be an uxorilocal (*nan dao nü jia luo hu*) marriage to a man from another county or from a distant village in Zouping county, but she had not arranged such a marriage yet. When I asked why she enjoyed matchmaking she replied that it was a good way of helping people and making friends: "When you arrange someone's marriage, you will be a friend to the couple and their families for life, especially the man's family. You will be invited to the wedding, and they will give you gifts. But I am not in it for the money; I do it because I like doing it, like meeting many people and talking to them."

In a sense, this woman occupied a very traditional interfamilial, intervillage social role. But much about the ways she carried out this role reflected the social and technological circumstances of contemporary Zouping. Her electric bike and mobile phone as well as the good roads in Zouping made spur-of-the-moment visits easier than ever before. Her free time and mobility enabled her to take on this role at a relatively young age. The social divisions and circumstances that she took into consideration when making her matches were those of contemporary urban Zouping rather than the farming communities of thirty years ago. Occupational and educational backgrounds are more diverse today, and more years in school enabled more young people to meet each other without matchmakers.

As a community builder, this matchmaker fits rather closely the networking type described by Fei. But hers was not the only form of community building I discovered among Zouping's villagers-in-the-city.

Villager-in-the-City Case F: A Christian Grandmother

This grandmother came from a household with six members: herself and her husband, her son and daughter-in-law, and her two granddaughters, ages 11 and 4. She also had a daughter who had married a man from the city of Jinan after going to university there. Their village had no rental income or collective assets, but they had already received nearly 20,000 yuan a year in money replacing agricultural income for four years when I interviewed them in 2011. The whole family liked food and cooking. The grandfather worked part-time for a village subcontracting business and often did the cooking at home, while the father and the mother ran a small restaurant. The grandmother did most of the housework, but since there was no farming to do anymore, she had plenty of free time and was devoting much of it to the Protestant church in Zouping.[5] "I go to church services in town every Sunday, and I also partici-pate in two Bible reading groups," she told me. "In church I meet people from all over Zouping and have made many new friends. The church is good, because it encourages us to do good deeds." When I pressed her for some examples she told me the following stories.

> One of my Bible reading groups includes people from most of the Development Zone. It is quite a large area, and we meet in different people's homes on different days. They are mostly people like me, older women from villages-in-the-city, but there are also a few men and middle-aged women, and women from some of the apartment complexes. Sometimes ten or more of us will meet at once. I go as long as the place we meet is not too far from the bus routes or if I can get a ride [the household owned a car, which both her son and daughter-in-law drove]. One time, the aunt of one of the younger women in our group broke her arm and her hip when she fell when people pressed in on her from behind as she was getting off a bus. She needed to stay in bed, and no one in her family was able to properly care for her. So we all took turns going over to visit her, cooking her simple meals, and helping her bathe and keep her house clean. Jesus tells us that it is important to care for the sick and the ill even if they are not members of your own family. Another time, one of the members of our group told us about a girl who was going to have to drop out of high school even though she was an extremely good student. She was ranked in the top ten in her class at the number one senior middle school. But her parents were in an auto accident. They needed money for the hospital, plus the father could not work for several months. We all donated money. I gave 50 yuan from my husband's earnings. We also helped take donations from people who came from their village and other people in our church. We paid for the girl's room and board and tuition at senior middle school for her last two years and gave some money to the family.

This woman's stories illustrate another side of community building in Zouping. First of all, her church and Bible study groups are formal organiza-tions of the type that Tönnies and Fei attributed to modern, Western socie-ties. That the boundaries of these organizations may be relatively open and fluid suggests there are plenty of associations that could count as both groups and networks in Fei's terms. Second, the charitable activities of the group extended well beyond particular families or villages to include people who were strangers to those who provided the assistance, at least before the acts of charity began. The charity was, however, decidedly local; it focused on Zouping people who had met with unfortunate circumstances. Some sort of networked connection to the Zouping church seemed necessary to be recognized as a victim deserving of charity. I do not know if the church as an organization also gave money to wider causes, such as victims of the Wenchuan earthquake, but if not the church did not organize the same scale of charity as those organizations described by Huang and Weller. It would thus seem to constitute an in-between form of association.

Villager-in-the-City Case
G: A Manager of Village Identity

The focal point of this case is a cadre and Party member, Assistant Party Secretary Wang (a pseudonym), who helped manage the community assets of a relatively wealthy village-in-the-city in the New City district. He was introduced to me by a higher (city district–level) government cadre in the following terms: "Secretary Wang is a *dizhu* [landlord], do you know what that means? He is the lord of a particular place [*yi di zhi zhu*]." Given the history of the term *landlord* as a dreaded and despised class identity label during the Maoist period, I did not know what to make of this introduction, but the subsequent actions of the district-level cadre, including constantly lauding the power of Party secretary Wang and flattering him at a banquet, demonstrated that he was truly concerned about keeping Wang on his good side. The cadre told me later that his district needed the approval of the village committee on which Wang sat for many of the activities it wished to undertake, including ensuring that development in that village met certain planning criteria and using some of the office space in the village's complex for district business. In a later one-on-one interview, Wang told me that his village had developed a shopping arcade on its collective land and that part of his job was to keep his fellow villagers-in-the-city united. He said, "Having collective assets is, of course, a good thing, but it also creates the possibility of conflict. Every year we need to discuss how to use and how to divide both the collective income from our real estate assets and the money replacing agricultural income. Every year we hold several meetings to determine the rules for who should count as a villager and to explain transparently all of the sources of village income. Many problems arise. People debate who should count as a villager—what to do with in-marrying and out-marrying women, what to do about children born outside the birth control policy, what to do about people who return after living in other places. People also question whether all of the income has been accurately reported. Then we also have to decide things like how much to give out as cash benefits to individual households and how much to spend on improvements to the village's collective property. I often have to meet individually with certain households to iron out problems." When I asked if he could give some more specific examples, Wang hesitated and then mentioned just a few generalities: "To keep people happy and united, I work hard on creating a sense of village identity. Now that we are rich, people are proud of our village, and I want to keep it that way. I can understand why Anjia built that memorial archway (see figure 6). A village's reputation is important. It affects the willingness of women to marry into the village and our real estate business as well. Some villages get a bad reputation for dirty business dealings. These days people all have different occupations. It's not like before when everyone was a farmer working for the collective. So I also work during the year to set up village activities, like croquet matches for the elderly. As a village-in-the-city we need to maintain a united front or we will disintegrate, and problems will arise in our collective business."

While I did not know other people from Wang's village and could not press him for details on community conflicts, Wang's efforts to smooth out village relationships and shore up village identity were apparent enough. He received a salary as a member of the village committee, but the very existence of this salaried position is the result of the village's collective wealth. Thus the time Wang had for this sort of activity related to the relative wealth of villagers-in-the-city. As a form of association, Wang's village-in-the-city was also an intermediary type. On the one hand, it was clearly a bounded group rather than a network (though the boundaries were often disputed). On the other hand, the group reproduced the identity of an older collective form—the village. Yet, again, many villages became more sharply defined, governed, and bounded groups only during the Maoist era, when formal village governments were set up for the first time and property was collectivized, so village identity cannot be considered a timeless form of sociality. In any case, Wang's efforts illustrate yet another form of villager-in-the-city association building.

Villager-in-the-City Case H: A Rentier Father and His Tenants

This household was from Mu Wang village on the northern edge of the Development Zone. The village had a significant rental business since it bordered on a number of electricity generating plants. It differed, however, from other rentier villages in terms of its cleanliness and order. Garbage was collected at a particular place near the entrance to the village. Despite all of the rental housing, lanes in the village were of uniform size and wastewater ran out of compounds in brick-lined ditches. There were several seemingly clean (pay) public toilet and shower businesses. The father in the household I interviewed told me that their village committee had designated specialized security and public health teams when villagers first started building rental housing and that the committee demanded order from the rentier households. The village housed 6,000 people at the time of my interview, including the roughly 1,000 original inhabitants.

This household had six members: paternal grandparents, father and mother, a daughter in high school (boarding at the school at the time of my interview in 2011), and an 11-year-old son. The household had 15 neatly built rental rooms in their compound, and their own house was immaculate and had a tribute to Chairman Mao and pictures of many other CCP leaders in the main room. In addition to the rental rooms, the family ran a small restaurant and a bathhouse in the village, which catered to renters. They earned 24,000 yuan a year in money replacing agricultural income, 1,500 yuan a month in rental income, and 5,000 yuan a month from their restaurant and bathhouse. They owned a car and two computers. The father, mother, and son were all extremely articulate and spoke nearly flawless standard Mandarin.

When I complemented them on their standard Mandarin, the father explained, "We always speak Mandarin at home. All of our businesses involve people from all over the country and the only way to communicate with them is in Mandarin. I always encourage my son to interact with the people living in our compound. They have a lot of diverse experiences and he can learn much from them. He goes around to the different rooms and talks to people every evening. I also learn a lot from them. I have conversations with my tenants whenever I can. I invite them over for tea and also have many long conversations at our restaurant and bathhouse. We also help them whenever we can. They are far away from home and sometimes need a hand, and, of course, it is good for our businesses. People can trust us. They know that the food at our restaurant is safe and that the water in our bathhouse is clean."

When I asked for some examples of how he helped his renters he said, "Last month, one of the women in our compound was really ill; she had a high fever. I found out because I stopped by their room for a chat. The woman kept insisting that she didn't want to see a doctor, because it would cost too much money, but we insisted that she could at least get some medicine for the fever and that missing days of work for illness would cost even more than a doctor visit. Her husband agreed with us, and then we used our car to take her to the hospital. I know a doctor of Chinese medicine at the hospital. He is my cousin [*tangdi*], and he helped us register at the clinic. In the end, she saw a doctor and got some antibiotics for less than 50 yuan. She got better in a couple of days and went back to work."

While this man clearly mixed his socializing with business, it would be wrong to reduce his efforts at being-in-common to crass material motives. He and his son and wife enjoyed their modes of making money through socializing. They were also comfortably well-off without needing to "eat bitterness" in the factories. As a form of community building, their socializing might be considered a form of networking, but unlike the networking of the match-maker, it was not a form of networking that took kin relations as its center. Of the four cases reviewed here, this one was the only example in which being-in-common bridged the divide between locals (*bendiren*) and outsiders (*waidiren*). As such, it could hardly be considered a "traditional" mode of socializing.

CONCLUSION

Urbanization offers the possibility of new modes of association, sociality, being-in-common, or, if you prefer, community. The physical proximity of large numbers of people, many of whom previously were not related to one another, creates new options; but as Simmel (1971) and others have pointed out, it also creates new possibilities for loneliness and alienation. The literature reviewed in this chapter suggests three somewhat different ways in which community building may shift with urbanization. The first is that being-in-common might come to incorporate strangers at a greater rate than before and that in so doing might come to entail more formal (artificial) rules of belonging. The second suggests, relatedly, that being-in-common might move from individually focused networking to the formation of (rule-)bound groups. The third suggests a movement from familial reciprocity to a combination of independence from family and more generalized forms of charity. The cases reviewed here suggest a recombinant process in all of these aspects. Both groups and networks are important in urban Zouping; the people involved in any form of community can include both previously familiar people and strangers, as well as people both within and without previously formed "organic" communities. More important, the types of networks and groups formed often show historical links to forms of networking and group definition that existed before Zouping's most recent bouts of urbanization. While the cases suggest recombination, I do not have the type of data that would allow me to argue against claims of percentage shift in the types of relationships people form. It may be true that a higher percentage of an "average" person's socialization occurs with strangers, or within formal groups, than before. Depicting such percentage shifts as absolute breaks, however, would be misleading.

A wide range of social relations take time to cultivate, and some people have more opportunities than others to build communities. These opportunities arise both because of the type of work one's occupation requires and because freedom from the necessity of a formal job opens up time to devote to new relationships. Such opportunities are not evenly distributed across all Zouping residents. Compared to the factory workers discussed in chapters 6 and 7 (and to be discussed in chapter 10), villagers-in-the-city enjoyed a relative abundance of them.

NINE

The Middle Classes in a Manufacturing Center

Defining class always invites controversy. Marxists draw attention to economic relations, whereas Weberians emphasize status groups. Bourdieu (1984) examines practices of distinction. Emphasizing how distinctions are drawn, Amy Hanser (2008) depicts class and status in contemporary China as processes rather than static social categories. While I share Hanser's interest in processes of drawing and embodying distinctions, my concerns with class in this book are specific to Zouping rather than motivated by abstract theoretical generalizations.[1] The five groups I identify all emerged in the process of conducting interviews and carrying out fieldwork in Zouping. I could see distinguishing aspects of each group in their lifestyles, family organization, consumer choices, and attitudes toward the city. Of the groups, however, it was the "middle classes" that I found most difficult to define. While nearby migrants, distant migrants, and villagers-in-the-city were defined by their place of origin and youth by their age and marital status, specifying what it was about this group of people that distinguished them was difficult. To demarcate the "middle classes" here, I use a modal type rather than a single characteristic. The category thus has fuzzy boundaries; some people are more middle class than others, and many can be seen as partly middle class.

The first defining characteristic of this category is occupation. The middle classes of Zouping work in white-collar jobs, usually outside of factories. Entrepreneurs may or may not work in white-collar positions, so being a successful entrepreneur does not define one as middle class. Because factory workers are relatively well paid in Zouping, especially skilled ones, those defined as middle class are not always distinguished by their income levels, which in many cases are roughly the same as Wei Mian workers. They do, however, enjoy high levels of job security and benefits. Their white-collar jobs are typically permanent positions in a proper work unit, or danwei. They usually work for the government. According to the 2011 statistical yearbook, in that year there were more than 12,000 people in Zouping working in public administration, more than 8,000 in education, about 3,000 in public health, and 2,000 in finance (Zouping 2012: 260–64). Since the schools, hospitals, and banks were almost entirely government run, the great majority of these people were public sector employees, though some of those working for the government (including schools and hospitals) would have been temporary employees whose benefits were not good enough to truly count them as members of the middle classes. Outside of manufacturing (which employed over 150,000 people), construction (which employed over 10,000), and retail (which employed nearly 4,000), these were the largest categories of employment listed in the yearbook (Zouping 2012: 260–64). The size of these occupational niches in a broad sense reflects the onset of modernity itself in China, as industrial economies both necessitate and provide the resources to fund a much larger state bureaucratic apparatus than agricultural economies.

During the 1980s and earlier, when many of the factories were run by the government as work units in a manner similar to the banks and schools of today, some factory workers also identified as government employees and thus seemed much more middle class than the factory workers of today. Long-term Zouping residents who worked in factories during the 1980s but moved into other white-collar positions over the past two decades thus also belong to the middle class. The occupational aspect of my definition here resembles that used by Luigi Tomba (2004, 2014) in his analysis of the construction of the middle class in Beijing. As Tomba points out, since the middle class is largely constituted by public sector employees, the size, occupations, and living conditions of this class are largely determined by government hiring policies.

The second aspect of middle-class identity is educational success. Securing a job in Zouping's public sector has required a relatively high level of education for over two decades. As Carolyn Hsu (2007) suggests in her analysis of class in Harbin, education seems more central to status and identity than does income level per se. The educational pathways that lead to white-collar jobs reinforce the sense of identity these occupations can create. Leaving home to attend a boarding school for three years of senior middle school and four years of university makes one's early childhood home less important to one's eventual social position than it otherwise might be. While the majority of middle-class people I met in Zouping came from nearby places, in many contexts, for both themselves and me, it was their occupation rather than their place of origin that took precedence in their social identity. For this reason, despite spending their childhood in one of Zouping's villages-in-the-city, or migrating to Zouping from a nearby town or village, or moving to Zouping from a more distant locale, I pluck them out of the place-of-origin classificatory scheme used in chapters 5 through 7 and put them in a separate category here.

The third defining aspect of Zouping's middle classes is place of residence. They are most likely to live in the New City District and least likely to live in the Development Zone. At least since the classic works of urban sociology by Robert E. Park (1952; Park et al. [1925] 1968), scholars have noted that the segregation of both residence and employment sectors divides urban areas into distinct neighborhoods and urban residents into distinct communities. Park and his colleagues tended to see this as a matter of "urban ecology," and they have been criticized for downplaying the role of politics and planning in this segregation (e.g., Martindale 1958). As Tomba (2004) points out for Beijing, Chinese cities since 1990 have been increasingly planned to have districts devoted to government, education, and cultural activities, and these are the areas that become middle class. Zouping's New City, as discussed in chapter 2, is precisely such a district. While there are also educated, white-collar households in the Development Zone, typically engineers and managers who work for the large enterprises (recall that Wei Mian built an entire living district for its managers in the Development Zone), and also villagers-in-the-city and even a few migrant workers who reside in the New City, the segregation of employment (and the housing that was often built by particular work units) matters to the feel of Zouping as a city and the way its residents experience the city.

This zoning affects the feel of the city in at least two ways. First, while the Development Zone has its schools, shopping spaces, and entertainment venues, these tend to target the needs of migrant workers. In contrast, the shopping spaces, restaurants, parks, and entertainment venues in the Old City and the New City are more varied and include the best that Zouping has to offer. Though the Development Zone has some good primary schools, the secondary schools in Zouping, at the time of my research, were located in the Old City and the New City. As a consequence of this spatial distribution of facilities, residents of the Development Zone often had reasons to go to the Old City and the New City, but residents of the Old City and the New City rarely went to the Development Zone unless they worked there. The lack of knowledge of the Development Zone and its people sometimes generated fear and loathing among middle-class residents of Zouping's New City. They warned me of the dangers of the Development Zone, of the supposedly high crime rates and the criminal tendencies of the migrant workers who resided there. In contrast, I never heard a resident of the Development Zone, including educated, white-collar residents, worry about the crime rates there. For the record, I was never the victim of crime in any part of Zouping and never felt threatened. Second, some middle-class residents of the Old City expressed a strong desire to move to the New City. Despite the fact that real estate prices were roughly similar across the three districts of the city, it was only the New City that seemed to attract residential envy (often because of its supposed lack of pollution), and this envy was only ever expressed to me by educated, white-collar residents of the Old City.[2]

Overall, Zouping could not be considered a city with strong class differences. Salaries were relatively even across occupations, and most members of even the middle classes had relatives who lived in rural villages. The presence of relatively well-paid factory workers, the connections to rural areas, and the dependence of the city as a whole on manufacturing forced a set of contradictory attitudes on Zouping's middle classes; their subjective expressions of class superiority, distance, or anxiety often had an ironic or self-deprecatory tone. But these expressions were identifiable nevertheless. In addition to the comments about crime and real estate and the jokes and rumors about Wei Mian (chapter 3), an important aspect of their class anxiety involved an extreme degree of worry about and investment in their children's education. While I have shown elsewhere how high levels of educational aspiration were ubiquitous in Zouping (Kipnis 2011a), for the middle classes these aspirations became anxieties. They didn't just hope that their children would do well in school, they desperately feared the consequences of their children not doing well. This fear related to their economic dependence on and identification with an occupation that required educational success. It was also exacerbated by the birth control policy. While all Chinese citizens have been subject to this policy since the early 1980s, those with rural household registration (including almost all of the households discussed in the previous three chapters) were allowed a second conception if the first child was a girl, or, in some districts outside of Zouping, two children regardless of the gender of the first. Zouping's white-collar public sector employees were all given an urban household registration. As a consequence they were only allowed one child. Moreover, if they violated the policy, in addition to being heavily fined, they would be fired from their jobs and lose their white-collar identity altogether. As Vanessa Fong (2004) argues, ambitions for children can be especially high in one-child families.

In sum, the middle-class households I speak of here cluster around an ideal type that is defined by highly educated parents working in white-collar, public sector occupations, living in the New City, and expressing subtle degrees of class anxiety. The sources of my knowledge about Zouping's middle classes are somewhat different from those about the groups in the previous three chapters. Because of my research in schools and my need to work with government officials to have my research approved, I knew several middle-class families quite well and had interactions with a large number of middle-class individuals in a casual way. Consequently, when undertaking formal research for this book, I targeted factory workers who worked at Wei Mian and others who lived in the Development Zone for my interviews. My knowledge of middle-class households is ethnographically deeper but less systematic than that of the groups discussed earlier. Though the number of number of middle class individuals I spoke with was large, this group was not the result of any purposeful or random sampling strategy.

Nevertheless, to maintain some continuity with the previous chapters, let me begin with a few numeric summaries, though these numbers should not be taken as statistically significant. Of the sixteen white-collar households I either formally interviewed or knew well enough to provide data, in twelve cases both spouses were from Zouping county (having grown up in villages or towns scattered throughout the county or in villages that would become villages-in-the-city), in two households one spouse was from Zouping and the other from a more distant Shandong location, and in two households both spouses were from outside of Zouping. Ten lived in the New City, two in the Old City, and four in the Development Zone. Nine of the households were nuclear; seven included one or both of the husband's parents. Overall, viricentric kin interactions seemed slightly less intense than with the nearby migrants or the villagers-in-the-city but more regular than with the distant migrants.

CASE STUDIES

I ran across three types of situations more than once. First, because of my research in schools, I knew many primary school teachers, the majority of whom were women. Several of these women were married to relatively powerful local officials, and I began viewing the handsome, powerful official and beautiful primary school teacher pairing as a sort of idealized couple in Zouping's social context. Both partners in this pairing are educated and white-collar, but the men have power, relatively high incomes, and demanding but sometimes risky careers, while the women have stable, slightly less demanding careers with moderate incomes and expertise in dealing with children. At one primary school I visited, the principal had just hired a new art teacher who graduated from a university in Jinan. She was 22, attractive, single, and originally from a village in central Zouping. Some of the other teachers in her group office teased her by speaking loudly about finding a "big official" (*daguan*) to pair off with the "beauty" (*meinü*).

Second, both of the white-collar households I interviewed that came from outside of Zouping lived in the Development Zone. In both cases the husband was an engineer with a specialty that a Zouping enterprise desperately needed. In each case the husband had negotiated a high salary (over 5,000 yuan per month), plus a relatively cushy office job for his wife. Both couples lived with their single child in a nuclear household in a commercially bought apartment, and in both cases the child was one of the top students in his class.

Third, I interviewed public official couples from one of Zouping's townships who purchased an apartment in Zouping as an investment, which enabled them to send their child to school in Zouping city rather than their township. I came across three such cases. In one household, the paternal grandparents were living with their 11-year-old granddaughter in a Development Zone apartment while she attended primary school. The parents lived in another apartment in a township where they both worked as officials in the local government. The parents used their car to pick up their daughter every Friday evening and return her to Zouping on Monday mornings so that she could spend weekends with them. Below are more detailed but individualized cases.

Middle-Class Household A

Ms. Wang[3] was a low-level official in Zouping's government. I first met her when she attended one of the public English classes I offered in 2001. At that point she had just started working for the Zouping government as a translator in the Party secretary's office after graduating from Shandong University as an English major. Over the years that I did research in Zouping, she would often attend my English classes and practice her English with me. She grew up in Mingji town (about 10 kilometers west of the county seat), where her father was a village doctor and her mother farmed.

In 2005, when I met Ms. Wang again, she was married and had a 2-year-old daughter. Her husband was an official in the police force who had gone to a specialized university for policing. He grew up in a village in another part of Zouping. They were introduced by friends who worked in the government but called in a matchmaker in the final stages of negotiating their marriage. In late 2004 they purchased a large apartment in one of the earliest subdivisions in the New City that was reserved for government officials. The parents and daughter lived there with the husband's parents in a household of five. In 2003–4, Ms. Wang had five months of paid maternity leave. Afterward, she was able to return to work easily as her parents-in-law lived with the couple and took care of their daughter. Ms. Wang had a cheerful disposition and told me that she got along well with her mother-in-law. Over the years she never mentioned a single conflict with her in-laws and often expressed gratitude for their child care, which enabled her to work evenings when necessary and even occasionally to travel for work or pleasure.

When they purchased the apartment from her government work unit, they paid about 1,000 yuan per square meter, but by 2005 it was already worth 2,800 yuan per square meter and would be worth more than 5,000 yuan per square meter in 2011. Unlike the Wei Mian apartments, government work-unit apartments were sold to their employees with full titles. While Ms. Wang sometimes complained about the lack of shopping facilities in the New City in the mid-2000s, by 2008, after new supermarkets and the pedestrian mall had been completed, she had a different problem: "Now that we have shopping here, sometimes groups of migrant workers come from the Development Zone to window-shop. I know I shouldn't feel that way, but, to be frank, it scares me to see groups of them walking together in the street. You should be careful if you have to go to the Development Zone." By 2012, when new schools and athletic facilities were completed in the New City, the migrant workers no longer bothered her. She told me that she could not imagine living anywhere else: "My daughter has good schools nearby, there is decent shopping, it is easy to get to work, the air is clean, and we will even have a swimming pool soon." In 2005 Ms. Wang's household purchased their first car, though Ms. Wang did not learn how to drive it until 2008 and usually got around on her electric bike. After 2009, though, she drove regularly, sometimes even taking an hour trip to Jinan on weekends to shop. Her salary was roughly 1,200 yuan a month in 2005 but more than doubled to 2,600 yuan per month by 2010. Her husband earned close to 4,000 yuan per month in 2010, though his duties were fairly onerous, requiring him to dine with other officials on most nights. In 2011 Ms. Wang told me, "I am happy to remain a low-level official. As a translator I occasionally get to go overseas to accompany Zouping's leaders for work. But other than that I rarely work late or on weekends, and traveling overseas is of course exciting. My husband's job is much more demanding. A few years ago we used to be able to take vacations because my parents-in-law could look after our daughter, but now it is harder to find the time."

Though Ms. Wang's life seemed carefree in many respects, the problem of how to raise her daughter caused her great anxiety. Before her daughter entered preschool, Ms. Wang often told me that she wanted to avoid putting any pressure on her to study hard. In 2006 she said, "We didn't have that sort of pressure when we were growing up in the 1980s, and I think parents and teachers are overfocused on test results these days." She planned to enroll her daughter in the public preschool closest to her house. But by 2008 she had changed her mind. She sent her daughter to an expensive private preschool (also located in the New City). "Some of my friends sent their children there and recommended it to me," she said. "The teachers there are really good at giving the children a foundation. The children do a lot of artwork, for example. In that way they can be creative, but, at the same time, the teacher can emphasize basics like the proper way of gasping and manipulating writing tools." In the autumn of 2010, when her daughter was attending second grade, she told me how competitive things had become. Almost all of the other girls in her class did three types of after-school classes (*buxi ban*): homework class three or four days a week, an oral English class on Saturdays, and piano lessons on Sundays. Ms. Wang did not want to pressure her daughter to take these classes, but as soon as her daughter saw that most of the other girls in her class were taking them, she asked her mom to sign her up. One evening, Ms. Wang told me about the parent-student conference she had with her daughter's teacher. She learned that her daughter was usually between fourth and eighth place (out of 42 students) on various tests and that there were three other girls in the class who usually did better than she did. Ms. Wang said that she encouraged her daughter to catch up with the leading girls and that her daughter really admired them and wanted to become friends with them. A few weeks later Ms. Wang told me that the teacher had invited the mothers of the top two students in the class to give presentations on their child-rearing methods. These mothers were extremely strict and organized every second of their children's free time around homework, calligraphy, piano lessons, or other activities that they gauged would raise their child's academic performance and quality, or suzhi. In 2012, the last time I spoke with Ms. Wang, I learned that her daughter was still doing well in school but had stopped attending after-school classes. "My daughter likes to read a lot after finishing her homework, and I am convinced that that is as good as anything. To set a good example, I never watch TV in the evenings anymore. I read or do housework." Ms Wang also handed me a newspaper article that explored the reason for the large number of people who were taking the public service exam. The article concluded with the aphorism "学而优则仕" (Those who are good at studies enter officialdom," half of the Confucian saying, "Good officials don't stop studying; those who are good at studies enter officialdom").

Teresa Kuan (2011) discusses the conflicting pressures on middle-class mothers in the southwestern Chinese city of Kunming. In response to the reality of intense competition in the school system and discourses that emphasized the importance of allowing children to explore and experience the world on their own terms, without excessive discipline, these mothers alternated between strictly disciplining their children and then regretting their disciplinary actions. Kuan further points out that because women were often judged on the successes of their children more than men, Kunming mothers felt this pressure more than their husbands. Similar pressures were apparent in Ms. Wang's attitudes toward her daughter's education.

In concluding this case study, I would like to emphasize how these pressures were aggravated not just by the relation of educational success to Ms. Wang's occupational position but also by Zouping's emerging social segregation. The friends from whom Ms. Wang took advice and to which she compared herself were also white-collar workers. Her neighborhood was one that was built for government employees, and the schools her daughter attended were ones in which the majority of students came from white-collar families. Though this segregation was tempered by the fact that almost all of her neighbors and coworkers had close familial ties to the countryside and that people of rural origin thus regularly visited their living compound, it was still a more extreme form of class-based segregation than had existed in Zouping before.

Middle-Class Household B

When I first met Mr. Hao in 2006, he was a 38-year-old Chinese teacher in a junior high school located in one of Zouping's townships, about 20 kilometers from the county seat. He lived in a 120-square-meter apartment located on the school grounds that he had purchased for 60,000 yuan from his work unit (the junior high school). He came from a village located halfway between the township and the county seat. He and his two brothers had all attended university, a remarkable feat for village men of his age but one that could be attributed to the fact that his father was a graduate of Peking University who had been sent down to live in his ancestral village in the early 1960s. He was married and had a 13-year-old son, but his wife was ill with cancer and was being cared for back in her home village, which was less than a kilometer from Mr. Hao's home village. His son often left Mr. Hao's apartment on weekends to return to his grandfather's village house, living there and visiting his mother. Mr. Hao went back when he could but had to teach six days a week and carry a heavy workload as a senior teacher earning more than 2,000 yuan a month (a relatively high salary in 2006).

When I met Mr. Hao again in 2010, his circumstances had changed. His first wife had died, and he had just remarried a widow the same age as himself from the county seat. Though he still worked in the township junior high school (commuting 20 minutes by car every day), he was hoping to get transferred to a primary school in the county seat, where his work duties would be easier, even if his salary would be a bit lower. In 2012 he managed to secure his transfer, in part by banqueting with and giving gifts to officials in the education department. In 2010 he told me that all teachers working in Zouping's remote townships tried to get transferred to the county seat and that even those who were unable to obtain a transfer chose to live in the county seat and commute to work. "They think," he said, "that the city will offer more opportunities for improving the quality [*suzhi*] of their children."

His new wife was an accountant who worked at a local bank and came from an old, distinguished Zouping family. She had a daughter who was two years older than Mr. Hao's son. In 2010 they lived together in the woman's apartment, originally purchased from her work unit during the 1990s, located in a complex in the Old City. They had also just bought an apartment in the New City and were waiting for it to be completed when I last saw them in 2012. They paid less than 3,000 yuan per square meter for this apartment by purchasing it before the first stone of the building was laid, but it was worth more than 5,000 yuan per square meter even before they moved in. In 2012 he took me to see this still undecorated and unfinished apartment. It was on the tenth floor of a building with an elevator in a fancy new complex on the southern edge of the New City. As we admired the view across the New City

District to Yellow Mountain, he said, "The New City is well planned, the parks are all beautiful, and the geomancy [feng shui] is good. This is by far the best place to live in Zouping." When I pointed out that some of the newer, private complexes being built in the Development Zone had apartments of similar quality, which sold at similar prices, he replied, "The people who live there just want to be near the factories. This part of the city was built for government officials, for people of high quality [*suzhi*]. The air is much cleaner over here. I will spend my old age walking in parks and breathing healthy air."

His new wife's family were eager to meet me, and I enjoyed several meals at his wife's parents' apartment. I once had to turn down an invitation to eat dinner there because I had already arranged some interviews with households in the Development Zone. The next time I saw them, Mr. Hao's mother-in-law warned me that it was dangerous for a foreigner like me to bike around the Development Zone at night. Didn't I know that crime rates were high in areas full of migrant workers?

Mr. Hao's new parents-in-law had been high achievers in Zouping's textile factories during the Maoist era. His mother-in-law won many awards for her labor in the late 1950s, and his father-in-law had been a factory manager. His eldest brother-in-law had won an award for textile machinery repair, and his skills had been in high demand before he retired five years earlier. His wife and her other two siblings, however, had secured positions in Zouping's banking sector during the late 1980s and early 1990s and still worked there in 2012. As banking had become much more prestigious than textiles, the family's move from the textile to the banking sector was well timed and most likely reflected the parents' excellent political connections. Though Zouping's matchmaking industry had done well to pair off these two white-collar workers, of similar age, each widowed, with a child of similar age, I felt that Mr. Hao had gotten a slightly better deal. Though his family was educated, they came from a village rather than the county seat and lacked political connections to local power structures. The new couple's social life seemed to revolve around the wife's family, and Mr. Hao was quite enamored of his new wife, often holding her hand when they walked together in the street, in a manner that was common among urban newlyweds but rare for couples their age.

In 2011 Mr. Hao's son was in the final year of senior middle school and his stepdaughter attended a second-tier university in Chongqing. Mr. Hao constantly fretted that his son was not hardworking enough as a student, that his test results were too low, and that he probably wouldn't succeed in testing into a top-ranking university. "It's too late now," he told me. "While his mother was sick and then passed away, I could not supervise his studies properly. He became independent in that period, which is good, but his study habits did not improve." Mr. Hao's worries turned out to be exaggerated, for his son secured entrance to a good university in Beijing. But this success only shifted the target of Mr. Hao's anxieties. In 2012 he told me, "I do not think I can raise my class position [*wode jieceng*] any further. My son is a university student in Beijing, but he will never become a Beijing citizen [*Beijing ren*]. If he wanted to marry a Beijing girl, her parents would demand that we buy an apartment for them in Beijing, and I could never afford that."

Mr. Hao's case illustrates two important aspects of processes of class distinction in Zouping. First, forms of power useful to reproducing or advancing class position can at least sometimes be reproduced across generations. Despite being banished to the countryside, Mr. Hao's father was able to transfer the high level of cultural capital that his Peking University degree demonstrated to his three sons; in turn, Mr. Hao successfully reproduced this capital in his own son. In addition, despite the devaluation of textile factory work during the reform era, Mr. Hao's parents-in-law were able to use the social and political capital they accumulated in the textile industry to secure their children good jobs in the banking sector. From a subjective vantage point, Mr. Hao's statement about being unable to further raise *his own* class position when discussing the marriage prospects of *his son* illustrates how the reproduction of family and class advancement are intertwined concerns.

Second, Mr. Hao's understanding of class position in China is heavily informed by the "power geography" (Liu 1997) legislated in China's household registration system. Place and social position overlap because China's political hierarchy is highly spatialized: the most powerful officials live in Beijing; the next tier lives in provincial capitals; the next tier, in prefectural capitals, followed by county, township, and village officials. Mr. Hao's father was sent *down* to a village as a political punishment. Mr. Hao managed to move from his village *up* to a township by becoming a teacher and then from the township to the county seat by marrying a county seat woman, making friends with bureaucrats in the education bureau, securing a transfer to a county seat school, and purchasing an expensive county seat apartment. He could not, however, envision any way of securing a move to Beijing for his son. He also suggested that all of his fellow township teachers were attempting to move to the county seat and believed that the New City was a better place to live than the Development Zone because that is where all the government officials lived. While I agree with Mr. Hao that China's political power geography is important to social position, I also believe he underestimates the extent to which economic power has developed some independence from political power during the reform era. Just as some cities in China economically outperform cities that are above them in the political hierarchy, so do salaries and apartment prices in the Development Zone sometimes reach those of the New City. Even the pinnacle of political power, Beijing, has become home to many impoverished families and individuals. In part to counter the prejudices that China's power geography has engendered, Zouping's education bureau actually pays teachers who work in the townships more than those who work in the county seat. Mr. Hao's implicit take on these issues, I would argue, reflects the social position of Zouping's middle classes. As public sector employees, they often (over)emphasize China's political power geography when assessing the social positions of themselves and others.

Middle-Class Household C

"Boss Zhang" (Zhang Laoban), as I addressed her, owned and ran a tea, coffee, beer, and wine bar in the New City on the pedestrian mall near the number one senior middle school. I first met Boss Zhang when I had a coffee there in 2009. I found her pleasant to talk to and became a regular customer. She lived with her husband, daughter, and mother-in-law in an Old City apartment. But the whole family moved to a commercially built apartment in the New City in 2011. Her daughter was in a private junior middle school in 2009 and had progressed to year three at the number one senior middle school the last time I saw them, in December 2012.

Boss Zhang was born in a village in the county just north of Zouping (Gaoqing county). She attended a specialized two-year accounting course (*dazhuan*) in the late 1980s (a high level of education for that period), where she met her husband, who was from the same county. In part because of her father's political connections as a village cadre, on graduation she and her husband were assigned urban household registrations and white-collar jobs in one of Zouping's collective textile factories in the early 1990s and then moved to the largest collective textile mill located in the county seat in 1994. After the privatization of the early 2000s, that factory became part of a moderate-sized conglomerate that still did business in Zouping at the end of my research. It was one of the few textile mills in Zouping not to be swallowed up by Wei Mian, and, like Wei Mian, this business group had diversified into many industries by the late 2000s. Boss Zhang and her husband purchased their Old City apartment from this work unit during the late 1990s. Boss Zhang quit her job in 2008 to start the teahouse, mostly because running the teahouse allowed her to spend more time supervising her daughter. Her husband had been promoted several times and had become a relatively high level manager who often traveled, sometimes overseas, for business.

During the time I knew her, Boss Zhang's highest priority was clearly her daughter's education. The private junior middle school was expensive but was directly linked to the number one senior middle school, making it easier to test into that school on the senior middle school entrance exam. Boss Zhang told me that running her own business enabled her to cook lunch for her daughter every day, so she didn't need to eat in the school cafeteria. Because the teahouse was located near the number one senior middle school, this lunch strategy became even more convenient after her daughter won admission to that school. Their purchase of a New City apartment, located near the number one senior middle school, was in part also motivated by the daughter's education. "This apartment enables our daughter to live at home without wasting any time commuting to school," Boss Zhang explained. "Besides, many other parents will think like me, so the value of apartments in this complex is bound to rise even further. The New City is the best part of Zouping to invest in because the best schools in Zouping are here."

In autumn of 2012, her daughter began the third and crucial year of senior middle school. Boss Zhang decided to take the entire year off from work and brought in a friend to run the business for her. Though her daughter was at school from before 7:00 A.M. to after 10:00 P.M. seven days a week (except for lunch and dinner), Boss Zhang thought that she needed the time to nurse her daughter at the slightest sign of illness, to cook every meal for her, to take care of any life matter that might take even five minutes away from her daughter's devotion to studying, and to help her daughter strategize about which universities and courses to select and which subjects to focus on. "My daughter is a good student but not a great one," she explained, "and the university entrance exam is a once-in-a-lifetime opportunity, so I need to help my daughter now as much as possible."

In 2011 Boss Zhang and I had a long conversation about possible university majors and careers for her daughter. At that point she favored a major in nutritional biology, which would enable her daughter to apply for jobs in the food safety bureaucracy. "The key is to get a job in a *shiye* work unit," Boss Zhang explained. Shiye work units are government agencies, like banks and utilities, that have a source of income outside of regular government budgetary allocations. These work units offer the security and benefits of government job with higher salaries than purely administrative government units. Food safety bureaus derive income from the licensing and labeling fees paid by food processing industries, a large sector in Zouping. When I suggested that these days, skilled blue-collar positions, like those in welding and auto mechanics, paid as much as even shiye work units, Boss Zhang replied, "In China everybody wants status [*yao timian*]. No matter how much they pay, welding and auto mechanics will never give you status. Only government jobs give you status. Welding also requires you to work in the Development Zone, which isn't as safe as the New City. You should be careful when you go there, some migrants [*waidi ren*] are into bag snatching now. If you ride there on your bicycle and put your bag in the front basket, be sure to wrap the straps around the handlebar so it is harder to steal."

Though her daughter's education was clearly her highest priority, Boss Zhang also had time for community activities, similar to those of the Christian woman discussed earlier. She participated in a group devoted to "the science of humans in the cosmos" (*renyu kexue,* 人宇科学). They believed that a scientifically advanced society of extraterrestrial beings communicated with certain humans in their dreams, giving them knowledge about how to cure diseases and solve problems that current earthly technologies could not handle.[4] Humans who communicated with these beings could also channel curative thought waves to the ill. Group members did meditation exercises to enable better communication with these beings and also helped people in Zouping's hospitals who were incurably ill. Such efforts in themselves were thought to make the charitable more receptive to communication with the extraterrestrials. Boss Zhang had first joined this group when her own mother had an inoperable cancer (from which she recovered) and went with other group members to comfort and cure sick people whenever she could. In many respects, Boss Zhang's efforts here mirror those of the middle-class housewives analyzed by Huang and Weller (1998). Perhaps these efforts reflect another side of middle-class subjectivity in Zouping.

CONCLUSION

Ending the last case study with a paragraph on Boss Zhang's religious practice is meant as a reminder that the people analyzed in this chapter were not simply snobbish social beings solely concerned with their own class positioning. My emphasis on this aspect of their subjectivity is a means of exploring how the category "middle class" can be useful to understanding a significant segment of Zouping's growing population. Processes of distinction, including those of accumulating and passing on social and cultural capital and those of verbally distinguishing people, occupations, and parts of the city as having higher and lower degrees of status, enable class differentiation to occur in Zouping, despite its relatively egalitarian income distribution.

These processes of distinction themselves involve the recycling, remembering, and reinventing of those extant in Zouping's preurban past. Historically, education has had a convoluted relationship to social position. During the imperial era it could lead to government positions, though such positions were extremely rare. Nevertheless, the vast array of stories, plays, poems, artwork, and aphorisms written by China's imperial literati provide resources for imagining the current relationships between educational success and officialdom, as well as the relationship between social positioning in today's China and social positioning in China's past (see Kipnis 2011 for examples). The policies of early reform-era China (and to a certain extent, Maoist China), when graduation from a four-year university, a short-course university (*dazhuan*), or even a specialized high school (*zhongzhuan*) almost guaranteed a state sector job, also provide memories of how education might link to public sector careers.

The specific power geography defined through the People's Republic of China's household registration system, perhaps informed by earlier power geographies (higher-level officials generally resided in the most central places), increases sensitivity to the relationship of place to social status throughout China. This continuity, however, disguises the ways in which the residential segregation of today's Zouping differs from that of the past. Before Zouping's twenty-first-century urban growth spurt, housing segregation was the result of the separation between various villages and work units. As work units often employed people in many different jobs, these separations were not simply matters of occupation or purchasing power. While villages and work units are still important to the distribution of housing in Zouping, the division of the city into districts in which industry and government, educational and cultural work units are to concentrate separately, as well as the creation of private housing complexes in which all of the apartments might be relatively expensive, invites the imaginative reinvention of power geographies. These new imaginaries, however, recycle aspects of ideas generated in the older environment.

TEN

Youth between Factories
and Services

Consider the ways in which the social category of youth is itself a product of modernity. In Zouping's villages a hundred years ago, though young people might have been taught various skills, there would have been little formal schooling for the majority. Given populations of a few hundred people in most villages, there would at most have been a handful of other children the same age for a given child. These peers along with everyone else in the village would have been considered a familial relative in one way or another rather than a "friend" or a "schoolmate" (Kipnis 2013). Marriages were arranged and often occurred at a very young age, 12 for boys and 14 for girls. After marriage, the young couple would reside with and be subservient to the boy's parents. Occupations for all would revolve around village agriculture and be determined by the resources that the boy's parents could command. In such a village, the category "youth," meaning a group of unmarried young people of roughly the same age, not related to one another, somewhat independent of their parents, who had completed several years of schooling but not yet entered stable occupations, would lack significance.[1]

The category of youth (*qingnian*) first reaches a high degree of visibility in China with the publication of the magazine *New Youth* (1915–26), first in Shanghai and then in Beijing. Targeting the young and educated in these metropolises, the magazine advocated left-wing politics, with a penchant for critiquing the familial institutions of village life, such as arranged marriage, which negated the social significance of being "a youth." In 1923 it became the official journal of the young Chinese Communist Party.

In places like Zouping, the sorts of modernity that give rise to journals like *New Youth* arrive later than in Beijing and Shanghai and are not exactly the same as the modernities of the early twentieth century, though the political campaigns and changes in family law that shaped Zouping's modernity were inspired directly by the ideas expressed in *New Youth*. In today's Zouping, children average close to fifteen years of schooling (including three years of preschool), in large schools with classrooms of unrelated children of the same age (Kipnis 2011a). After graduation, those who do not go to university often find themselves living in Zouping's Development Zone, where spaces of entertainment, like the roller-skating rinks mentioned in part 1, enable them to congregate. Peers in service sector workplaces also organize social gatherings, like birthday parties, to which only other "youth" are invited. As elsewhere, the social (self-)segregation of youth is common. Completely arranged marriages are outlawed, and young people often attempt to find their own spouses, though matchmakers or nosy friends, relatives, and acquaintances are usually involved in some way. Youth also struggle with uncertainty about their future occupations as they experiment with various jobs.

The social category of youth, as it exists in Zouping and most of the rest of the world today, is existentially marked by a double uncertainty and openness: uncertainty about marital partner and uncertainty about occupation. These forms of uncertainty are experienced as both freedom and a burden or problem. As one's chronological age progresses, pressures from family elders to resolve these problems increase. The precise age at which youth ends cannot be specified; it varies from place to place and seems to increase as "modernity" progresses. That is, as the average number of years spent in educational institutions increases, so does the average age of marriage and the average age of becoming a parent. In places like Australia, one hears young people declare that "the thirties are the new twenties," and older people wonder if this statement simply represents a desire to endlessly defer the responsibilities of adulthood. In places like Zouping, where heterosexual marriage is practically mandatory and a four-year university degree is considered a high level of education, pressures to end one's youth and enter adulthood are already quite high by the age of 24. As the case of the attractive art teacher discussed in the previous chapter demonstrates, when one enters a stable occupational niche, Zouping's collective matchmaking apparatus exerts social pressure through both the enthusiasm of its agents and its efficacy in identifying socially appropriate potential partners. The problems of occupational niche and marriage thus interrelate. Matchmakers demand that one find a spouse of appropriate occupation and status; before one's occupation and status are determined, it follows, finding a spouse can be difficult.

The social openness that defines youth increases the importance of social imaginaries, desires and fantasies. As Brad Weiss (2002: 97) puts it in his discussion of youth in urban Tanzania, "fantasy" is a crucial component of attempting to fabricate life from "possible lives." The way in which social theorists have analyzed fantasy depends very much on their views on how "open" or changeable the social world actually is. For theorists like Bourdieu, who emphasize the reproduction of extant social structures through habitus and the conservation and conversion of various forms of capital, these fantasies are dismissed as unachievable delusions: "An inventory of thinly disguised expressions of a sort of dream of social flying, a desperate effort to defy the gravity of the social field" (Bourdieu 1984: 370). For ethnographers like João Biehl and Peter Locke (2010), who invoke the work of Gilles Deleuze, desires are far more crucial than any extant social field. Desires form the starting point for an analysis of *becoming,* which is all that the world is: "History amounts only to the set of preconditions, however recent, that one leaves behind in order to 'become,' that is, to create something new" (Deleuze, in Biehl and Locke 2010: 317). Like Biehl and Locke, I wish to take the dreams of youth seriously as world-building forces, but like Weiss, I do so without denying the importance of certain habitual modes of existence. To differentiate myself from Bourdieu, I focus on habituation more than habitus.

I take the notion of habituation from the long-term Wei Mian contract workers depicted in chapter 6. These workers responded to my reports of complaints, often made by youth, about working conditions in the factories, such as that factory work is too hot, too noisy, too tiring, and so on, by saying that they had already habituated to those conditions (*xiguanle*) and that their concerns were elsewhere. As Anna Lora-Wainwright (2013: 154) observes, "*Xiguan* implies a habit that has been fostered by long-term experience, but it also suggests the ability and willingness to engage in a particular activity." As an act of will, this sort of habituation requires accepting some aspects of the world, of taking the repetitive nature of factory work as well as what Bourdieu calls the gravity of the social field as an acceptable truth, and getting on with the process of bodily accustoming. What a strict mind/body dualism might see as either a simple, unconscious bodily process of acclimatization or a conscious mental decision to accept or reject a particular social circumstance is a deeply interwoven fabric of both.[2]

In Zouping, having not yet habituated to factory work is almost a defining element of the category of youth. In part this is because two common types of young Chinese people, often categorized as youth, are rare in Zouping. In large Chinese cities like Beijing, hordes of impoverished, underemployed university graduates are known as the "ant tribe" (*yizu*), because of their large population and their small and humble living arrangements (Si 2009). But Zouping does not have any academic universities, and most of the university graduates who come or return to Zouping do so because of the offer of a middle-class, white-collar job, the taking of which effectively ends their youth. Second, because it has not been a city that attracts migrant workers for long and because it is a city with a relatively relaxed household registration regime, youth in Zouping are generally not "second-generation" migrant workers. Second-generation migrant workers are those who have grown up in cities that refuse them urban household registration status. They are both alienated from their so-called rural homes (which they barely know) and denied full citizenship rights in the cities where they feel they belong (Liang 2013: 196–98; Pun and Lu 2010). Overall, three characteristics differentiate Zouping youth from those in places like Beijing or the Pearl River Delta. First, they are generally working class. Second, if they are not from Zouping, unlike second-generation migrant workers, they often express a desire to return to their places of origin. Third, if they do habituate to factory work in Zouping, they generally become permanent (contract) factory workers, get married, and cease to be youth.

I got to know Zouping's youth in three ways. I met young people working in the factories of the Development Zone by going to the roller-skating rinks and other places where at least some of them congregate in the evenings. Those in this group who chose to speak with me cannot be considered a representative sample, but I did manage to conduct unstructured interviews with twenty of them. Next, I interviewed over 30 young people who worked in hotels, restaurants, and retail stores. This group likewise cannot be considered a representative sample, though I did make sure to include youth who worked in venues located in all three parts of the city and a variety of service occupations. Finally, I interviewed and attended classes with two cohorts of 15- to 19-year-old students at a Zouping technical high school (*zhiye xuexiao*) whose mission was to prepare students for the local workforce. The school had close links with various business groups and work units in Zouping, and most graduates received offers of blue- or pink-collar jobs in the county seat on graduation. Roughly two-thirds of the students in this school came from Zouping county; the rest were recruited from other parts of the province or country and tended to come from particular places (Xingtai in Hebei province or Guyuan in Ningxia province, for example) where the school had managed to set up relationships with local education officials. The majors at the school were quite segregated by gender, and I asked to attend the classes of one male-dominated major and one female-dominated major. I was granted access to a class of 35 machine electronics (*jidian*) majors, 30 of whom were men, and a class of 20 kindergarten teaching majors, all of whom were women. I conducted 15-minute interviews with everyone in these classes, so in total I interviewed more than 100 Zouping youth.

FACTORY WORKING YOUTH

The roller-skating rinks in the Development Zone could be sites of some risk taking. Skaters crowded the available space, and beginners struggling to keep their balance created a natural obstacle course for the daring and more experienced, who weaved in and out of the slower skaters at high speed, sometimes executing spins and skating backward. No one wore helmets, elbow pads, or knee pads. Accidents resulting in cuts and bruises happened often enough, though I never witnessed or heard of a serious injury. As depicted in chapter 4, some of my interviewees spoke of the physical exhilaration they felt when skating fast. I came to see this sort of exhilaration not as a form of defying "the gravity of the social field," as suggested by Bourdieu, but as a form of flying nonetheless. What was negated here was the physical constriction and discipline of factory work. In other words, the gravity defied was that of habituation rather than habitus.

Factory Worker A

This woman was 23 when I interviewed her in 2009. She came from a village in Dezhou, a relatively poor prefecture in northwestern Shandong. She had an older brother and a younger sister. Her father left them when they were young, and she was raised by her mother. "Do you know what it means to be a single-parent family [*danqin jiating*] in the countryside?," she asked rhetorically. She came to Zouping eight years before, when she was 15, with an older girlfriend from her home village. She managed to get a job spinning cotton at Wei Mian, despite not having finished junior middle school (management told me they only hired junior middle school graduates). She remained a temporary worker, rejecting many offers to become a contract worker. "I make about 2,000 yuan a month working rotating shifts, which is the same as I would make as a contract worker; besides I always dream of leaving here, so I don't want to be a contract worker," she said. Even after eight years, she told me, she had not become accustomed to (*xiguan*) working at Wei Mian. She found it too hot and noisy and tiring. But she did it anyway because of her family's poverty: "My younger sister is still in school, my mother's health is not great, and my older brother needs to get married. I have to help out. I just hope one day all of these crises will end."

She lived in a Wei Mian dorm room and said that it took a long time to make friends: "I was here for three years before I really trusted anyone. You have to work so hard that you have no time for friends, and then some people leave on a moment's notice. Sometimes the company lays people off. I am a good worker so they never lay me off. I started skating three years ago, and I only first dared to go because I had a few friends who went at the time. But I really like it now. I go fast and it makes me feel excited [*xingfen*]." Though the group of friends I saw her with at the rink included several boys, she said that she did not have a boyfriend. Her dream was to be able to go back to Dezhou and marry someone there. That way she could be near friends and family. Once the lives of her brother and sister were settled, she wouldn't have to worry about making so much money and could move back home.

Factory Worker B

This man came from a village in the neighboring city of Zibo (about 30 kilometers from Zouping) three years before I met him in 2010, after graduating from junior middle school but failing to gain entry to senior middle school. He was 19 when I interviewed him and had an older sister who was already married. He made 2,000 yuan a month working six or seven days a week in one of the smaller textile factories in the Development Zone. He said that the money was okay, but he was always tired and had to work seven shifts a week whenever things got busy or his manager wanted something done quickly. If he didn't work whatever shifts his boss wanted, he would lose his job. He lived in the small dormitory built by his factory. He had not thought much about marriage and did not know whether he would rather settle in Zouping or move back to Zibo. He said, "Overall, my situation isn't good, to make money I have to take a job I hate; if I move back home, I won't make money and I'd never have a family." He elaborated that his parents did not have the money to help him get married and start a family, so that he was saving money for marriage, though he did not know when he would do that.

He was a daring but not too skillful skater, and I saw him fall several times. His knee was bleeding when I interviewed him. When I asked him about it he said, "That's nothing, one time I fell so hard I was limping afterward for a month. This is my only way of venting my feelings [*chuqi*]. Working in the factory is too repressive [*bieqi*]."

YOUTH IN SERVICE POSITIONS

Between 2009 and 2011, one could see help wanted advertisements for waiters and waitresses, salespeople, and hotel workers posted in the windows of service businesses all around Zouping. These ads typically mentioned salaries in the range of 1,000 to 1,500 yuan a month. Almost any of the thousands of young people working in these jobs knew that she or he could have earned more money working in a factory. They consciously chose lower-paying service work because they saw some aspect of factory work intolerable.

Service Worker C

This woman was born and raised in Zouping, though she had left town for two years to obtain a short-course university degree in machine electronics. When I met her in 2010, she was 20 and worked at her aunt's soft-serve ice cream shop, making 900 yuan a month. After receiving her degree, she had worked for three months at Wei Mian. Though her electronics degree seemed to suit her for a position in their electricity plants, she was only offered a job in cotton spinning. "They like to put women in cotton spinning and men in electronics for some reason," she explained. She had earned over 2,000 yuan a month working day shifts on the factory floor, but she didn't like it. Because of her degree, Wei Mian then offered her 1,300 yuan a month to take a relatively easy pink-collar job in one of the factory's back offices, but she turned that down as well. She explained that working at Wei Mian "turned one into a robot [*jiqiren*]. The people there never speak to one another and never have any of their own ideas. They just listen to orders. The management at Wei Mian doesn't want to develop anybody's ability and doesn't like people who are independent thinkers." She added that the Xiwang Group was much better in this regard and always encouraged worker input but that it was hard to get a job there. "Serving ice cream is also better than working at Wei Mian," she concluded, because it gave her the chance to interact with customers and use her brain to think about how to respond to different types of people. "I want to talk to people, to use my brain, to think about the most appropriate thing to say in a given situation."

A few days later she told me that if she had stayed at Wei Mian, she probably would have already been engaged to another worker there. "Once you settle in Wei Mian, people start introducing you to potential partners [*gei ni jieshao duixiang*]. Before you know it, you are married, have a baby, and live in the Wei Mian housing compound, and then that's it; your whole life is over. That is what happened to my older sister. She lives in the number four Wei Mian apartment compound. She is so boring; it is hardly worth talking to her anymore. I want to develop myself and do something with my life. The only people my age who work at Wei Mian all come from desperate situations."

When I met this young woman again in 2012, she had gotten engaged to a manager at a wedding celebration company (*hunqing gongsi*). They had been introduced by a mutual friend and after a brief courtship had a matchmaker work out the arrangements between their families. They were waiting for her fiancé to save another 20,000 yuan before they got married so they could afford a down payment on an apartment. Her fiancé had already saved 20,000 and had another 60,000 promised to him by his parents as part of the brideswealth (*caili*). They planned to take out a mortgage of 100,000, which they would pay off with their joint earnings.

She had stopped working in her aunt's shop and had gotten a job in a clothing store selling dresses. She made 800 yuan a month plus commissions, which varied from 200 to 600 yuan a month. She said that she and her husband hoped one day to open their own business in catering or retail. Like before, she was optimistic and ambitious, but she had added a note of caution to her hopes: "My aunt's fast-food place has now gone bankrupt; they raised the rent in the mall, and the high school placed more restrictions on the student's lunchtime, so she lost some of her business. If we decide to go into business for ourselves, we will really have to watch the timing. But I really like the idea of running my own business. I don't like to listen to the boss's orders."

She was also concerned about her mother's future. She gave half of her earnings to her mother and still lived at home. Her father had died a few years earlier, and her elder sister had already married out. Her worries about her mother were another reason she did not want to marry right away. "What will my mom's life be like if she has to live alone? I am encouraging my mother to get married again. Would you like me to introduce you to my mother?"

Service Worker D

This man was 21 when I interviewed him in 2009. He was born in a village about 15 kilometers from the county seat and had obtained a chemical engineering degree from a short-course university in Jinan. Despite the demand for workers with his expertise in factories all over Shandong, he decided to come back to Zouping to work as an art teacher for kids at a local art store/studio that was owned by one of his relatives. He earned about 1,600 yuan a month and slept in a back room of the shop. He explained that chemical engineering was extremely dangerous. One of his classmates had already died in an explosion, and another had suffered second-degree chemical burns on his face in a separate incident. He said that the industries making the biggest profits were the most dangerous because money was to be made cutting corners in safety regulation and compensation for workers after accidents. We then discussed the infamous accident at Wei Mian's aluminum refinery in 2007. He said that 100 workers had died (see chapter 3) and added that he would never work for Wei Mian, no matter how good the pay, as it was too dangerous.

He had no plans for marriage at the time I interviewed him. He hoped to one day start his own chain of art schools for children and did not want to contemplate marriage before he had launched his business. He said that he did not often go back to the village where his parents lived precisely because he feared that they would pressure him to get engaged to a woman introduced to him by village matchmakers.

Service Worker E

This man came from a village in Manchuria (*dongbei*) at the age of 19 in 2009 to work at Wei Mian but quit after two months because he couldn't stand the heat and noise. Many Shandong people had migrated to parts of Manchuria during the Maoist decades, as had his parents. He had relatives in the county just to the north of Zouping. When I met him in 2010 he earned 1,100 yuan a month working as a doorman at a hotel where I stayed for a while. He lived in one of the dorms the hotel provided for single workers. He said, "Earning money isn't everything; I have to live my life. If work is torture, then how can you continue? Now I feel free. I think I will go to Shanghai soon and try my luck there. I've been to Beijing, but I really want to see what Shanghai is like."

As the hotel's doorman, he once approached me about the hotel's "massage" business. Though I politely turned down his request to use their services, when we were chatting a few days later he told me about some of the dilemmas Zouping's sex industry posed for both young women working at hotels and sexually conservative young men like himself. He said that the hotels always hire attractive young women in service positions and that the hotels also all have some form of sex business. While the hotel service positions only pay about 1,100 to 1,200 yuan a month, sex workers can earn three, five, or even ten times that much. "So all the young women working here have to decide how much their purity [zhencao] is worth to them." Those who do work as prostitutes, he said, usually avoid working in their home counties to try to preserve a bit of their reputations. "I, myself, am quite conservative [hen baoshou]," he added. "When I am ready to get married I will go back home and ask my parents to help me find someone. Given what I've seen working here, I don't think I could trust any woman I met while working as a migrant laborer [dagong]."

TECHNICAL SCHOOL YOUTH

In this discussion of youth, I include students at the technical school but not those from the academic schools, for both existential and practical reasons. Academic high school students were supposed to put everything else in their lives aside and focus on preparing for the university entrance exam. They were reprimanded if caught indulging romantic inclinations and had no time to work in part-time jobs. Every waking second of every day was supposed to be devoted to study. Consequently, the forms of openness and uncertainty I define as characteristic of youth were stifled for this group. In contrast, the technical school encouraged students to work part-time (during school breaks and on weekends) and even helped arrange temporary positions for them. Gaining work experience, even at jobs not directly related to their majors, was considered an important part of their preparation for the workplace. While it did not encourage its students to become romantically involved with one another, neither did the technical school take any measures to prevent student romance. A minority of students openly conducted relationships, holding hands or even kissing between classes. At the time of my research, roughly 80 percent of Zouping's 16- to 18-year-olds attended academic senior middle schools, roughly 10 percent attended the technical school, and roughly 10 percent did not attend any school (Kipnis 2011a). Numerically, the technical school youth were thus a somewhat exceptional category, and they were considered by most in Zouping as only quasi-students rather than the real thing.

Of the 35 students in the machine electronics class, 30 were boys and 5 were girls; 17 were from Zouping, 11 from other Shandong counties, and 7 from other provinces. This class was the only place where I found young people saying positive things about factory work. In part, their positive attitudes can be attributed to the fact that they had not yet experienced full-time factory work. But perhaps some of these youth would be able to habituate to factory life quickly, accept contract worker status, marry, and settle down. Most of the nonlocal students told me that they hoped to find factory work in their hometowns but worried that the opportunities for factory work were not so numerous there. Most of the Zouping students were aiming to get work in Zouping's industrial conglomerates. Thirty-one of the students grew up in villages, and most of them disliked academic schooling. During their more academic classes, on topics like the physics of electricity or the principles of wiring machines, some of the students slept at their desks, while others kept their heads up but played with their mobile phones or read items not related to the lesson.[3] But the students all enjoyed the practical classes, during which they would move to the school's workshops and wire various machines. Forty percent of the curriculum was devoted to practical classes; the head teacher said they would like to make it 60 percent, but that would require more workshop space and equipment.

Electronics Student F

This 17-year-old boy hated regular school but liked fiddling with electric machines, so this major was good for him. He was from a village near Handian (about 10 kilometers north of the county seat), and his father worked at the Xiwang Group in an unskilled position while his mother farmed. He hoped to get a job at one of the electricity-producing factories in the Development Zone. He said the pay was good—over 2,000 yuan a month—but it was not only the money that motivated him. He told me that many of his former junior middle school classmates were now attending academic senior middle school and that most of them would go on to university. "Attending university, however," he said with a smile, "does not guarantee a job, and most of them won't find one." As a result they will have to come back to Zouping's factories for employment. Since he will already have had five or six years of experience by the time his former classmates went to work at the factories, he could end up training them. "I'll make them call me 'Master' [*shifu*] for the rest of their lives," he concluded.

Electronics Student G

One of five girls in the class, this 17-year-old was from a village in the county just to the north of Zouping. Her father was a temporary worker at Wei Mian, and her mother farmed the land. She also had a younger sister. Her original ideal would have been to become a doctor, but she didn't do well enough on the senior middle school entrance exam to get into senior middle school without paying an extra fee, and her parents could not afford that. So now she hoped to find a job at one of the larger factories in the county seat as an electrical worker. She explained, "I know they don't like to hire women in electrical work; they fear that there is too much heavy lifting involved. But I can do that, and I think they will change their policies in the future. But even if I work in textiles, sometimes you have a chance to use your electronics knowledge to repair machines." She concluded by saying that any factory job was better than farming and that living in the county seat would be better than living in a village.

Electronics Student H

This 16-year-old boy came from a village in Ningxia province. His parents both farmed, and he said that it was very difficult for anyone in his village to gain entry to an academic senior middle school. He was introduced to the school by one of the teachers at his junior middle school, who knew teachers from the Zouping technical school from a recruiting trip they had made to Ningxia. His teacher and parents saw the school and its links to factory employment in Zouping as a real opportunity and convinced him to come here, but he wasn't so sure. He often felt homesick (*xiang jia*), couldn't stand the food in the school cafeteria (especially the lack of Ningxia-style noodles), and would much rather find a job in the prefectural city near his home village than stay here for the rest of his life. However, he did like wiring machines and was also thinking about setting up his own machine repair shop.

. . .

The kindergarten teaching class differed from the machine electronics class in several respects. Not only was the latter class entirely female, but the attitudes of the students toward studying were different. The students all said they liked school and remained alert during classes. Many of the students also had fond memories of their academic junior middle schools but (at least those from Zouping) simply could not compete with their classmates in terms of test scores and were encouraged by teachers to go to a technical school. Their attitudes may simply indicate that those who selected the kindergarten teaching major desired an academically oriented white-collar occupation. In addition, none of the classes for these students was as academically challenging as the electrical physics course of the electronics majors. Practical classes focused on singing, playing a keyboard instrument, drawing, handwriting, and dancing—activities learned in order to teach or entertain the kindergarten students. The more abstract classes focused on child psychology and development.

Another difference was that 14 of the 20 students said that their ideal job would involve being a kindergarten teacher in a big city like Beijing or Shanghai. Only 2 of the students expressed a desire to have a career in their hometowns to remain near family. Arguably, this difference relates to gender and traditional kinship arrangements. Girls imagine marriage as moving away from their natal families; boys do not. Consequently, girls are more likely to imagine a future away from family in a desirable, distant locale. Of the 20 students in the class, 14 were from Zouping, 3 were from Ningxia province, and 3 were from other Shandong locations. All of the girls had rural household registrations, though three of them had grown up in relatively urban locations because their families had had their land requisitioned for urban development either in Zouping or elsewhere.

Kindergarten Student I

This student came from a village in the northern part of Zouping county where her mother farmed and her father was a temporary worker in one of the county's steel conglomerates. She was 16 at the time of the interview in

2011 and had an 8-year-old sister. She visited her parents every other weekend, and they gave her about 150 yuan each visit to purchase food at the school cafeteria. While she was quite careful with her money when she first arrived at the school, she said that she had recently become "naughtier" (*tiaopi*). Between the money her parents gave her and the money she earned at her school-arranged job, she had already bought a mobile phone and some clothes.

Like several of the girls in this class, she had actually left her academic junior middle school during the second semester of the second year (more than a year before graduation) to enroll in this kindergarten program. At that time, the technical school had sent recruiters to all of Zouping's junior middle schools to recruit girls who were academically near the bottom of their classes and had little chance of success on the senior middle school entrance exam. Her junior middle school teachers then convinced her parents that the kindergarten teaching program offered more opportunities for their daughter than continuing on the academic track.

Like my other interviews with these girls, I conducted this one in the classroom during break periods with several classmates listening in. This student took the opportunity to launch a monologue that was directed more at the other students than at me. She said that she was dismayed by the behavior of some of the other students in her school and that she disliked girls who engaged in underage romance (*zaolian*) (one of the girls present had been holding hands with her boyfriend an hour earlier) and boys who smoked and drank in the toilets. Such behavior was not tolerated at her old junior middle school, and she was not sure why it was allowed to go on here.

She said her ideal job would be a kindergarten teacher in as large a city as possible. Beijing or Shanghai would be perfect. It would be okay if she ended up working at a kindergarten in the county seat, but she definitely did not want to work at one of the kindergartens in the township where she was from. "Big cities are fashionable and exciting, and I would like to live in as big a city as possible," she insisted.

Kindergarten Student J

This student had grown up in an urban district in Guyuan city, Ningxia province. She was 18 and had a 17-year-old brother who was working at a factory in Shanghai. Her father had been a truck driver and her mother a housewife when they were growing up, but now both of her parents had left

Guyuan to work (*dagong*) in Yinchuan, capital city of Ningxia province. She was the only second-generation migrant worker I met in Zouping. It took her two days to return to Ningxia by train, and at this point the family only got together once a year, during Spring Festival. She would get homesick when she first arrived in Zouping but had gotten over it now. She was even starting to understand Zouping dialect and enjoy Zouping food. Her parents electronically transferred 400 yuan to her local bank account once a month. She had not started working yet but was planning to take a job the school promised to arrange for her during the upcoming summer vacation.

Her ideal would be to work in a kindergarten in Shanghai. That way she could be near her brother and enjoy life in the big city. "Big cities," she said, "are where you can see handsome guys, beautiful women, and celebrities [*shuaige meinü mingxing*]."

CONCLUSION

If youth is a relatively new social category in Zouping, it is not one that appeared instantaneously. It emerged slowly over the twentieth century as the educational system expanded (Thøgersen 2002) and slightly more quickly after 1949 when the marriage laws were changed to increase the minimum age of marriage and discourage arranged marriages. The post-2000 rapid urbanization of the county seat has further increased the importance of youth as a social category. Not only has the number of years spent in educational institutions continued to expand, but even those young people who leave the academic track at a relatively young age continue to spend years living away from home as singles in environments where they socialize more often with other youth than with their family members. Like the secondary schools of Zouping, the factories and service industries provide dormitory space for young people. Moreover, unlike the academic secondary schools, the technical school, the factories, and the service sector all provide young people with at least some time to socialize without adult supervision.

The gradual emergence of the category of youth has enabled those who live it to experiment with their independence while re-creating their dreams, practices, and subjectivities from the dreams and practices of previous periods. Consider the domain of sexuality. In the Zouping of a hundred years ago, before mass education, when most marriages were completely arranged and occurred in the early teenage years, concerns about underage romance and even the virginal purity of brides would have been rare. But that does not mean that the relatively conservative discourses on youth sexuality enunciated by the teenagers in cases E and I are recent inventions. Patriarchal discourses about the value of female chastity have a long history in China (Evans 1997). During earlier eras, however, they were most frequently applied to widows rather than unmarried teenage girls and young women.

Other aspects of the dreams of becoming expressed by the youth likewise draw on earlier discourses and long-extant social dynamics. The desire of almost all of the men interviewed for this chapter (as well as some of the slightly older women) to get married and settle down in the place where they were raised simultaneously reflects memories of familial relationships experienced during childhood, practical understandings of the pressures of raising a family far from the help of relatives, and nostalgic understandings of hometown living. The dreams of many of the kindergarten students (as well as service worker E) to move to a big city like Beijing or Shanghai are perhaps less mature, but they also draw on the long-extant power geographies of the PRC discussed in the previous chapter. For these young women, such dreams also arguably involve long-standing understandings of the possibilities of hypergamy for women in China's viricentric kinship imaginary. They also fit Bourdieu's category "social flying" more clearly than most of the other dreams expressed in this chapter. The social gravity defied is that of China's household registration system. Other visions of socioeconomic success, whether they involved starting one's own business (cases C and D), making something of oneself (case C), or placing oneself socially above one's former classmates in factory hierarchies (case F), draw on long-standing but continually evolving imaginaries of social hierarchies in Zouping, discourses of the superiority of mental (academic) labor over manual labor, and strategic assessments of Zouping's current fields of social possibility.

Processes of habituation are a crucial aspect of the experience of youth, and these processes necessarily entail a bodily resistance to habituating to lives that do not fit one's dreams. Pun Ngai (2005) argues that the regimentation of factory labor, at least as it is currently administered in China, necessarily gives rise to bodily resistance. Though I agree with Pun's assessment, I would add that the contract workers discussed in chapter 5 demonstrate that at least some degree of habituation is possible and that the social imaginaries of youth can either speed or delay the processes of habituation. Student J's successful habituation to Zouping food and dialect is arguably related to the flexibility her dreams of physical and social mobility to even grander locales required. Student F's desire to succeed in factory settings may lead to his rapid habituation to factory life. Worker A's inability to become accustomed to factory life even after eight years may well reflect her desire to find work closer to her natal home.

The ease with which Zouping youth are able to habituate to factory life matters greatly to Zouping's future. Its prosperity is built on manufacturing. Its distinctiveness and the relative fairness of its regimes of governance (relaxed household registration requirements, subsidized housing for factory workers, good schools for factory workers) derive from the fact that Zouping's leaders imagined that those who would work in Zouping's factories were locals. But if Zouping residents stop seeing factory work as a desirable future, then the place will either lose its manufacturing industry or be forced to rely primarily on workers from elsewhere. In the latter case, Zouping could come to resemble the Pearl River Delta in its extremely exploitative regimes of governance for outside workers.

Student F exemplifies one type of person who could be a source of local factory workers. Zouping's education system encourages people to pursue academic success rather than factory careers, and some part of the prosperity that Zouping's manufacturing sector provides has been devoted to expanding the availability of a decent education to everyone in the county. On the surface, then, it would seem that youth's pursuit of academic success over factory work should be increasing. But though the education system can clearly produce people who disdain factory work, it also produces rebels and dropouts who disdain academic values (Kipnis 2011b).

As of 2011, Zouping had roughly 9,000 students a year entering junior middle school and over 150,000 people working in manufacturing (Zouping 2012: 337, 260). To make a prediction based on some rough assumptions, if I assume that manufacturing workers average 30-year careers, then 5,000 workers would retire a year; consequently, to maintain a workforce of the current size, 5,000 new workers a year would need to be hired. Given the rate at which Zouping's children attend academic senior middle schools (over 80 percent) or enter academically oriented technical school majors like kindergarten teaching, it is unlikely that there could be much more than 1,000 students a year who resemble student F. Thus, in addition to people like student F, to maintain a workforce that is at least half local, Zouping will need a portion of its youth who initially dreamed of white- or pink-collar careers to habituate to factory work. Whether they will do so is an open question.

ELEVEN

Recombination Reconsidered

In chapter 1, I suggest that several types of theories about modernity illuminated Zouping's urbanization. These might be called classic modernization theory, which analyzes the societal transformations linked to industrialization and urbanization; second wave modernization theory, which emphasizes postindustrial social transformations (especially those related to globalization and new communications technologies); alternative modernization theory, which sees the importance of prior social and historical contexts to the ways in which modernization proceeds; compressed, late, or East Asian modernization theory, which emphasizes the importance of the contemporary global context to late modernizing countries; and cyclical modernization theory, especially as articulated by Jonathan Friedman and Kajsa Ekholm Friedman (2013), which contrasts modernity with postmodernity and suggests that the two relate to cyclic movements of capital around the world and the consequent cycles of economic development and decline in any given place.

Let us consider how these theories illuminate Zouping's urbanization, beginning with the Friedmans' perspective. Zouping is clearly a place on the economic upswing, and this economic development has been accompanied by a "modern" cultural ethos in the Friedmans' terms. The planning discussed in chapter 2, as well as the interrelationships between government and business and between Capital and locality, discussed in chapter 3, reflect this modernity. Moreover, as the Friedmans would point out, the rise of Zouping's industrial economy is linked to deindustrialization in other parts of the world, and, concomitantly, Zouping's industrialization and economic ascent are reversible rather than permanent transformations. Not only might Zouping face deindustrialization at some point in the future, but even Zouping's urbanization could be reversible. In deindustrializing Detroit, for example, "wild" spaces have emerged around abandoned homes, and even upscale urban neighbourhoods in wealthy cities have made room for the cultivation of urban gardens and establishment of farmer's markets.[1] Though the Friedmans' affirmation of the cyclic aspects of economic development are important, I am less convinced of the usefulness of their sharp contrast between a modern cultural ethos and a postmodern one. In Zouping, the importance of progress, planning, and government is clear to many actors. But alongside this optimistic modernism, there are various expressions of alienation and despair. The Friedmans link postmodernity to both cosmopolitanism and xenophobia, but upswings of both cosmopolitanism, in the form of the variety of foodstuffs consumed and their marketing as nonlocal (see chapter 4), and nativism, in the form of fear of and prejudice against migrant workers from distant locales, are constitutive elements of Zouping's urban expansion. As almost all forms of urban expansion involve the incorporation of people and products from outside locales, I have difficulty imagining any form of urbanization that would not involve both cosmopolitanism and nativism, both the appreciation for and the fear of the exotic.

Classic modernization theory also has something to offer to an understanding of Zouping's urbanization, precisely because Zouping's urbanization has been led by industrialization and accompanied by so many of the transformations associated with classic interpretations of modernity—nation building, educational expansion, a growth in bureaucracy, a demographic transition, increased consumer spending, and the rise of advertising. While nation building, educational expansion, and a demographic transition have progressed gradually over many decades rather than sharply coinciding with Zouping's more recent industrialization and urbanization, these transformations have continued and even accelerated over the past two decades. Many of the subtler aspects of social transformation analyzed by classic theorists, including a rise in social interaction with strangers, the social segregation of space, and a simplification of kin ties, have also progressed but never in a simplistic black or white manner.

As those second wave theorists who redefine modernity in terms of the global sweep of new communications technologies would note, mobile phones and Internet access are ubiquitous aspects of life in contemporary Zouping. But this book suggests that classic modernization theory illuminates Zouping's urbanization more brightly than the second wave theorists. As part 2 demonstrates, issues stemming from factory work, or working in an economy where most people are factory workers, dominate the concerns of Zouping residents. As chapter 4 suggests, for linguistic, technological, and political reasons, the cosmopolitanism and worldliness that new communication technologies enable are largely defined by the space of the Chinese nation-state rather than the world at large. This form of spatialization tightly links the "new," second wave modernity defined by the arrival of mobile phones and the Internet to the classic forms of modernity defined by the rise of the nation-state. In short, though the past twenty years of industrialization and urbanization in Zouping are not the first cycle of economic growth ever experienced there and though they have been accompanied by aspects of what some theorists have seen as postindustrial historical ruptures, it would be hard to deny that Zouping's simultaneous industrialization and urbanization constitute a major historical transformation. As the theorists of East Asian modernity would point out, Zouping's modernization is a late and compressed one in which there has been plenty of room for government actors to implement practices and policies learned from studying other places around the world.

But if classic modernization theory illuminates aspects of Zouping's industrialization, there has been little "rupture" or "break" with the preindustrial or preurban past in terms of practices of kinship, metaphysics of hope, patterns of association, dynamics of social distinction, and dreams of becoming. Rather, there have been various forms of re-creating the past in the present, replicating and reinventing tradition, selectively drawing on and unconsciously reproducing memories from a different time. These forms of continuity could be said to define Zouping's present as an alternative modernity, in which modern forms first tangible in the West are fully intertwined with local culture.

Thus all of these perspectives on modernity can illuminate some aspect of Zouping's urbanization but also have limitations. To illustrate the intersection of the realities these theories illuminate and to go beyond their individual limitations, this book has developed the idea of recombinant transformations rather than historical ruptures, revolutions, or categorical distinctions between separately defined social types. Recombination implies the simultaneous recycling of the old and the absorption of the new in the process of social transformation. Let us review the recombinant transformations explored in each chapter.

Chapter 2 depicts the most radical urbanization Zouping has witnessed: the building of the New City and the Development Zone from scratch on formerly village land during the early 2000s. The plans for this process were largely created in other parts of China, which had absorbed capacities for urban planning from many locations around the world. The building techniques utilized were likewise absorbed from other parts of China, through both the hiring of outside construction firms and the study of those techniques by local contractors. But continuities with the past, even in the built landscape, remain. Yellow Mountain's importance in the city was reinforced by the building of Yellow Mountain Plaza. In fact, in terms of geomancy, it became even more important because it occupied the space at the center of the city rather than its edge.[2] Villages-in-the-city reasserted their collective identities, sometimes architecturally, with varying degrees of success. Government employees who lived together in the government housing compound of the 1990s were relocated to government housing compounds in the New City in the early 2000s, and their social and material privilege as well as their central location was effectively reproduced. Factories from the 1980s and earlier still produce beer, liquor, and mineral water in the Old City, despite the desire of planners to remake this part of town as an entirely commercial district. But more important than these continuities of built space and neighbourhood identities are the ways in which the dreams of government planners were informed by concerns from the past even when they designed completely new physical spaces. The geometric and geomantic layout of the New City reflects long-standing imperial apprehensions of the need to declare the power of the state architecturally and to assert the privilege and prestige of those who work for it. Its form incorporates both the ancient symmetries of imperial power and design features prevalent in socialist-era parks, plazas, and government headquarters. Zouping's imagined past is also reiterated in the names of its streets, parks, and landmarks.

Chapter 3 demonstrates that the major industrial conglomerates of contemporary Zouping both grew out of local collective industries and retained aspects of the ethos of earlier eras of production. The industrial sectors these conglomerates occupy involve the agricultural crops grown in Zouping at the beginning of the reform era, though they have now expanded to involve production techniques learned from many sources around the world. Their work-unit-like forms and the attitudes they take toward their workers reflect the founding of these enterprises in an era when development and providing jobs for local workers were overlapping political goals. The work-unit form of social organization also reproduces the lack of separation between home and work, private and public, that is common in agricultural societies. As these businesses privatized and the problematic of Capital (the continual need for profit) became more pronounced, they did not lose the ties that embedded them in local society. Whether they will do so in the future is an open question.

Chapter 4 examines the continuities in the purposes to which consumption is put alongside the rapid change in the products and technologies available for consumption as well as the amount of wealth available for spending. Most consumption in Zouping involves familial reproduction, male bonding, and, in the case of youth especially, an appreciation of "hot and noisy" atmospheres. The processes by which these recombinant continuities emerged were both a matter of conscious structural nostalgias and a relatively unreflective habitual practice. Chapter 5 explores the way in which the new, modern, urban public spaces of parks, plazas, shopping malls, and advertising make room for the recombination of old and newly imported phantasmagoria.

Kinship, the focus of chapter 6 and part 2 more generally, is a starting point for much of the habitual practice underlying the continuity this book has explored. In Zouping, both before and after recent rounds of urbanization, almost all children have been born in two-parent families where the parents take household responsibility for rearing the children. Adult children are still expected to take care of their aging parents, and grandparents often help with child-rearing, though, as part 2 demonstrates, there can be considerable variation in these practices. Nevertheless, the importance of the household as a basic economic unit and the site of long-standing kinship ideologies, dynamics, and practices in the production of households means that few in Zouping can shift their hopes and dreams or their despair and alienation away from familial concerns.

The pressure for marriage in Zouping is quite high. It comes not only from parents and elder relatives but also from a range of people who see themselves as matchmakers and any unmarried person in a stable job as a potential target for their matchmaking efforts. Youth sometimes appreciate or at least tolerate matchmaking efforts, but, in a few cases, young people fear them enough to refuse job offers in order to avoid the subsequent pressure to get married. That such pressure is heteronormative almost goes without saying, and I never met a person in Zouping who openly identified as gay or lesbian. I suspect that the majority of people from Zouping who would be inclined to do so leave Zouping to settle in larger urban areas. In Boellstorff's (2004) terms, Zouping is strongly heterosexist without much homophobia.

For the majority of married couples in Zouping, kinship tends to be viricentric, though the exact forms of viricentricity vary among the groups of people examined in this book. Long-distance migration can shock family structures and sharply disrupt viricentric practice. But for those who are not from distant locales, the land rights regimes of both agricultural villages and villages-in-the-city, expectations in the marriage market, and the layers of sentiment and expectation that build up in ongoing relationships create a social context conducive to the production of viricentricity. This viricentricity, however, is not exactly the same as past virilocality; it has been adapted to the realities of apartment purchase, ownership, and living, the moneymaking opportunities available to relatively young people (factory hiring discriminates against the elderly), and the importance of school in the lives of children. In short, Zouping's modernity has involved a recombinant transformation of kinship practices. The variations of kin practices among the four groups of married households explored in this book as well as among the individual households within each group suggest that social transformations never move from one singular state to another singular state but rather involve shifts in configurations from a multipatterned past to a multipatterned future. To reiterate the terms of Ferguson (1999), a "full house" of kinship practice continues to exist.

In addition to being a form of habitual practice, kinship provides models for explicitly imagining social continuity. Children become youth, youth become married couples, married couples become parents, and parents become grandparents. Examining the lives of one's own parents is an important source of ideas about what to do or not do in the future. The moralities derived from these imaginings have also transformed in recombinant fashion. The language of familial sacrifice, of "eating bitterness" for the sake of some larger familial goal, is applied to the very different forms of activity experienced by family members separated by age, gender, occupation, and opportunity. As in the past, this trope can be invoked in an inclusive way, to emphasize the sacrifices of all, or in an exclusive manner, to claim the sacrifices of some are greater and more worthy than the sacrifices of others.

Cities, as large spaces of high population density, create new opportunities to meet strangers, to hide from the surveillance of relatives, to suffer from loneliness, and to create associations. Mobile phones, the Internet, a well-built transportation infrastructure, and the creation of relatively public spaces for social gathering all facilitate the construction of associations and egocentric social networks. Though these technologies, spaces, and opportunities may be relatively new, the practices through which social relationships are constructed draw on past practices and past imaginings of community.

Developing and maintaining an extensive social network, however, requires time, and those who do so tend to have either relatively undemanding jobs or jobs that allow or require them to devote time to such networking. The majority of Zouping residents examined in this book—married factory workers with children—did not have the time to create large extrafamilial networks. But some villagers-in-the-city, middle-class residents, and youth did. The types of interconnections they created—village collectives, matchmaking networks, business-centered communities of customers, and religious forms of charity—emerged organically from previously imagined social groupings. The means by which these networks and associations were constructed—talking, commensality, entertaining, and working together on particular projects—evolved gradually from earlier forms of "producing guanxi."[3]

Class struggle was a central dimension of the Maoist revolution in China. Mao famously applied the analysis of class to the Chinese countryside in his writings (1975: 1:13–21), in his practice of guerrilla warfare, and in the governing of China after the People's Liberation Army secured power for the Chinese Communist Party. Mao's ability to conceptualize and manipulate the continuities between class distinctions in the urban capitalist societies typically analyzed by Marxian thinkers and those of the peasant societies of early twentieth-century rural China resonates with the analysis of class distinction in chapter 9. Though a significant population of middle-class people could only exist in a fully modern, industrialized, and bureaucratized society, the forms of class imaginary by which they distinguish themselves as well as the methods by which they attempt to pass on their class identities and advantages to their children were present in Zouping long before the rapid twenty-first-century urbanization analyzed in this book. Some in Zouping obsessed about providing educational opportunities to their children long before the past two decades. Ideas about society as a hierarchical structure in which different people have different extents of "face" have also long existed.[4] In short, as Mao's analysis implies, the processes of class distinction in contemporary Zouping emerged from a recombinant transformation rather than a historical rupture.

The category "youth" has likewise emerged as a recombinant transformation. The expansion of schooling over the course of the twentieth century and the legal and social campaigns against arranged marriage have been important to this emergence. Schools provide children with a space to socialize away from their parents, while choosing a marital partner gives them an important life domain in which to exercise agency. The emergence of youth, however, has accelerated during Zouping's recent round of urbanization as urban jobs, vocational schools, and new recreational arenas have expanded the space available for their socializing and agency. The forms of socializing youth engage in as well as their dreams for marriage and jobs in the future, however, draw on preexisting imaginings of both what is possible and what is desirable.

In addition to involving recombinant transformations in Zouping's spaces of living, organization of work, and forms of consumption, urbanization in Zouping has necessarily effected changes in the categories "rural" and "urban" themselves. As Williams (1973) argues, the meaning of the rural/urban (city/country) contrast evolves alongside the physical, social, and ideological distinctions between rural and urban places. How have and will conceptions of rural and urban transform in Zouping as utilities, infrastructure, and services in rural areas improve and as more and more villages become suburban commuting communities? While China's wider ideological environment (especially the household registration policy and the way it is implemented in large cities) will ensure a continued reification of rural/urban difference, I suspect that in Zouping a conceptual emphasis on rural/urban difference will lessen. Most Zouping residents have experienced living in both rural village houses and urban apartments, and many own one of each. Moreover, under the New Socialist Countryside program, Zouping's government is attempting to bring urban planning and infrastructure (and even high-rise housing) to Zouping's villages.[5] Though China's wider power geographies will continue to color the dreams of the ambitious, for many Zouping residents the distinction between rural and urban will lose significance. Perhaps ambition itself will become synonymous with urbanity.

In a book on everyday ethics in rural China, Steinmüller (2013) shows how various theorists of classic modernization imagined that urbanization and industrialization led to a new concern with the "everyday." These theorists felt that premodern "cyclic" understandings of daily life became untenable in the face of the irreversible linear changes of modernity. As a consequence, new urbanites in early modernity (such as Proust, quoted at length in chapter 1) obsessed over everyday objects, practices, and memories that could one day become obsolete. Steinmüller goes on to argue that in contemporary rural China rapid change has led to the emergence of a focus on the everyday, and he applies this insight in his analysis of rural modes of ethical reasoning about everyday sociality. In making this argument, Steinmüller suggests yet another way in which the rural/urban distinction has disappeared. This book, with its emphasis on recombinant transformation in newly urban areas, supports Steinmüller's insights but twists them in a slightly new direction. While it accepts that rapid social change can lead to a heightened concern with everyday ethics, in both rural and urban settings, it does not suggest a complete demise of the cyclical in urbanization. As the second half of this book demonstrates, the problematics of kinship still matter in urban settings and these problematics are above all cyclic. In short, not only has everyday ethics become important in rural areas, but cyclical moralities remain strong in cities, at least in cities like Zouping.

Many of the recombinant urban transformations that have taken place in Zouping may be understood metaphorically as the opening up of new spaces for human practice. While the spaces are new, the practices that are redeployed there inevitably draw on previous practices. Sometimes, as in the case of public parks and plazas, these are literal spaces. Sometimes they are metaphorical spaces of opportunity (or perhaps simply of necessity), such as advertising or youth or class or stranger sociality, in which recombinant practices are newly deployed. New technologies as well, especially the Internet and mobile phone, can be understood as spaces for recombinant practice.

In depicting urbanization in Zouping as part of a broader social transformation, I suggest that the multiple changes that have made up this transformation are in some sense interrelated. How to characterize these interrelations is a crucial theoretical issue. If the interrelations are conceived as being too tight and monolithic, then we are left with a stereotypical black/white theory of modernity in which the transformations of a concomitant industrialization and urbanization yield the same result everywhere. If they are seen as too loose and various, then industrialization and urbanization become simply two more forms of social change in a world where everything is changing all the time anyway; they are no more significant than, say, a shift from 6-story to 17-story apartment buildings, or the latest upgrade in computing technology. The concept of new spaces for the redeployment of recombinant practice suggests one intermediary way of depicting these links. Even if the spaces created for recombinant practices are interlinked in a similar manner in many places, the practices themselves may still differ. Other forms of linkage raise problems of temporal and spatial scale.

The social transformations usually associated with modernity do not always take place simultaneously or on the same time scales. The number of years children spend in school, for example, increased in Zouping during most of the twentieth century as well as the first decade of the twenty-first century (Kipnis 2011a; Thøgersen 2002), while Zouping's urbanization has been most rapid during the twenty-first century. Though there is some overlap between the two types of change, they are not absolutely simultaneous. But that these transformations have not been absolutely simultaneous does not imply that they are completely unrelated. Rather the relationships between these two changes should be seen as multiple but not infinitely variable. Education, in Zouping and elsewhere, feeds a desire for off-farm employment and urban jobs, but this desire could only be accommodated when the economic resources for rapid urbanization and industrialization became available. It also could be argued that increases in educational levels across the nation—and the resultant rises in literacy, numeracy, and fluency in standard Mandarin—facilitate the incorporation of migrant workers into Zouping. In short, I see these two forms of change as intertwining in ways that recur in many places without arguing that the relation between urbanization and the number of years spent in school will always occur in the same way everywhere.

The two changes might also be seen as relating differently to spatial scale. Both are embedded in processes that are unfolding at the national and even global level. The increasing availability and length of education has reflected national policies across a range of regimes (Nationalist, Maoist, and post-Mao) as well as international ideas about the value of education to youth. During the twenty-first century the national government has also promoted urbanization in various guises, and for a longer period urbanization could be seen as a global trend. But despite the fact that both urbanization and education involve national and global policies and trends, the way in which the local, national, and global interact in these two processes differs. The spread of education has received more material subsidies from higher levels of government than urbanization, with the result that the extent of this spread is more even across China than that of urbanization. The differential timing of the two processes in Zouping also reflects the differential timing of the related national and global processes.

That Zouping's urbanization and industrialization have occurred historically later than in many parts of the world influences the spatial and temporal scales of Zouping's modernization. Zouping has been able to draw on plans and models and practices from other parts of the world for the layout of the city itself, the design of its buildings, the structure of its bureaucracy, the laws of its zoning requirements, the organization of its education system and classrooms, the advertising campaigns of its businesses, and just about every other aspect of its "modern" urban, industrial, business, and bureaucratic infrastructure. The availability of such plans, models, and practices enabled the rapidity and relative simultaneity of Zouping's modernization in so many dimensions. Some of this borrowing was even forced on Zouping through national laws and regulations. But the existence of such plans and models does not reduce Zouping's urbanization to a purely mimetic exercise. For one, many of these plans have a distinctive "Chinese" feel rather than a generically global one. But more important, in choosing which plans to use and how to adapt them to Zouping, Zouping's modernizers have exercised as much agency and creativity as any governing agent anywhere. Robinson (2006) points out that survival in impoverished cities involves forms of creativity that wealthy cities should study and learn from. I argue that late modernizations require just as much creativity as survival in impoverished circumstances.

Memory, crucial to the recombinant practices deployed in newly urbanized spaces, occurs across completely different temporal scales than the twentieth- and twenty-first-century processes of urbanization and educational expansion. In their epoch study of an Inner Mongolian Buddhist monastery, Caroline Humphrey and Hürelbaatar Ujeed (2013: 3–5) discuss the difficulty of blending the temporality of their seventeen event-filled years of fieldwork (1992–2009) with the temporality of the traditions narrated by the lamas whom they studied. The lamas would often explain contemporary events in terms of a history that could, depending on the circumstance, stretch back decades, or centuries, or millennia. In Zouping too, the period of urbanization (corresponding roughly to the period of my fieldwork) yields an event structure that does not neatly map onto the long durée histories invoked by practices like geomancy, patrilineal kin reckoning, Confucian styles of education, or representations of Minister Fan's image. The merging of time frames in various forms of memory work, whether explicit or implicit, forms yet another layer of connection among the processes that make up Zouping's modernity.

What might the future hold for Zouping? Consider three possibilities. The first is continued economic growth and expansion. Zouping's excellent transportation infrastructure, its social embedding of local capital, its highly educated population and good schools could make room for such growth. As suggested in chapter 2, the metropolitan area could come to stretch from Handian in the north to Zhoucun in the southeast and include over a million people. Such overall economic growth would enable an increase in the number of white-collar positions, and it seems likely that these positions would be filled primarily by locals while the factory jobs would be taken by outsiders, though locals who disliked education would also take blue-collar jobs. In such a scenario, as suggested in chapter 9, the Development Zone could become a part of town that is imagined to be inhabited by recent migrants while the New City becomes the neighborhood of choice for locals. This residential segregation could lead to growing levels of fear and loathing of migrant workers and of the Development Zone itself by Zouping's middle classes. Given that these middle classes also make up Zouping's governing bureaucracy, perhaps this fear and loathing will finally give the government the impetus it needs to risk the ire of the villagers-in-the-city and crack down on the shantytowns that have been built on the fringes of the Development Zone. Though a scenario of continued growth is in some ways the rosiest, in addition to the downsides of segregation and growing prejudice, such growth might bring even higher levels of pollution and traffic congestion than were apparent the last time I visited Zouping before completing this book.

The second scenario is economic stagnation and urban stasis. The fact that the majority of Zouping's workers labor in the textile industry makes this scenario a real possibility. While wages rose rapidly during the 2000s, given the global competition in this sector, the potential for further wage growth requires Zouping's conglomerates, especially Wei Mian, to upgrade to more profitable sectors. Whether they can do so is unknown. Without further wage growth it seems unlikely that Zouping's middle class can continue to grow, and it is likely that a portion of Zouping's youth will either have to work in factories after having attended university or leave Zouping altogether. While a future without economic growth may seem disastrous to some, the presumption that economic growth is a panacea is a bit too easy. Though an economically stable but nonexpanding future would not result in white-collar jobs for all locals, at least it would offer Zouping residents the continued option of an in situ industrial sector, of off-farm employment without needing to move too far from home.

In terms of a comparison with other Chinese urban areas, especially the larger ones of Beijing, Shanghai, and the Pearl River Delta, Zouping's industrialization has proceeded in a relatively humane fashion. In many ways, this relatively humane industrialization is typical of China's smaller urban areas. As is the case in Zouping, it is in such places that real estate prices are lower and workers can afford apartments, that household registration policies are more relaxed, and that in situ industrialization regimes, which frame workers as locals rather than outsiders, emerge.

The third scenario is economic decline and perhaps population loss and re-ruralization. Many factors could push Zouping down this path. Perhaps China's massive pollution problems will lead to a national crackdown on both polluting industries and automobile ownership, and perhaps such a crackdown will lead to bankruptcy for some of Zouping's major employers. Or perhaps China's rapid demographic transition will lead to a shortage of workers, which will push manufacturing out of China. In either case, the majority of migrants from distant locales would leave, the shantytowns on the edges of the Development Zone would shrink in population, and a larger proportion of those growing up in Zouping's villages would either have to work on the farm or leave Zouping to find work. If they are not too badly polluted or scarred, perhaps even some of Zouping's newly urbanized spaces could be farmed once more.

Scenarios are always simplified guesses of how life might evolve. Whatever the overall economic future holds for Zouping, we must acknowledge that this future will be multiple rather than singular; that is to say, just as different individuals, households, and groups of people experienced the transformations of the 2000s in a variable manner, so will different individuals, households, and groups experience future transformations variably. In addition, future transformations will continue to be recombinant, and thus future social analysts will still be able to point to continuities with the Zouping presented in this book.

A final, both cyclic and linear aspect of Zouping's urbanization is raised by the dislike of and inability to habituate to factory work of many of the youth depicted in chapter 10. What is the future of a factory town in which many, perhaps the majority of people do not wish to accustom themselves to factory work? Imagining an answer to this question suggests that some of the seeds of deindustrialization are planted in the very process of industrialization. If the transformation from a society in which the majority of people are farmers to one in which the majority work in factories itself transforms factory work from a desired to a despised occupation, then can any industrialization be permanent? Such a cycle of transformation is in some aspects also linear, as a place that has first industrialized and then deindustrialized is never exactly the same as it was before industrialization. Perhaps one of the few fates more difficult than *becoming* a factory worker in an industrializing city is *being* a factory worker in a deindustrializing one.

NOTES

CHAPTER 1

1. Robinson herself mentions China in her book only when she lumps it together with India as a place of impoverished urbanization (2006: 128). Such a categorization again ignores the rapidly expanding infrastructure and consumer spending in places like Zouping. In this manner, she reproduced the very dichotomy that is the focal point of her critique. Jankowiak (2004a) also notes the lack of attention to urbanization in China, especially outside of China's "global cities," Beijing, Shanghai, and Shenzhen, and attributes this lack of attention in part to a focus on urban inequality.

2. The critique of tree metaphors for evolution by Gould and its implications for social theory have been discussed at length by J. K. Gibson-Graham (1996). I formerly discussed Gould's work in terms more favorable than I do here (Kipnis 2003, 2008).

3. See, e.g., the edited volume *Alternative Modernities* (Gaonkar 2001).

4. On the lack of simultaneity of industrialization, urbanization, and the growth of rational government in England, see Wrigley 1981; Short 2012: 53–55.

5. S. N. Eisenstadt (2000, 2003) is one of the foremost theorists of alternative modernities in this latter sense. Lisa Rofel (1999) shows how multiple understandings of modernity can emerge among different generational cohorts in a single time and place.

6. I have analyzed this problematic at length elsewhere. See Kipnis 2003, 2008.

7. Bruno Latour restaged the 1903 debate between Tarde and Durkheim and, for the benefit of English-language readers, put an English-language transcript online. See www.bruno-latour.fr/sites/default/files/downloads/TARDE-DURKHEIM-GB.pdf (accessed March 3, 2014).

8. The adjective *recombinant* here is thus used to emphasize a *perspective* on transformation that is applicable to all transformations rather than to differentiate one type of transformation from another. The complete, black/white succession of one sort of reality for another is theoretically possible but does not count as a "transformation." It is, rather, a form of replacement.

9. The Chinese scholars Qiu Feng and Zhang Lin (2014) also argue that county-level cities are vastly understudied even among the huge number of scholars and government researchers studying urbanization China. In the discipline of anthropology, many recent books discuss life in Beijing, Shanghai, the Pearl River Delta, and other large metropolises (Chan et al. 2009; Chang 2009; Chen et al. 2001; Dutton 1998; Farquhar and Zhang 2005; Farrer 2002; Fong 2004; Hoffman 2010; Jacka 2005; Jankowiak 1993; Zhang 2001; Zhang 2010; Zheng 2009). Urban studies scholars like Gaubatz (1996, 2008) and Airriess (2008) likewise suggest an excessive focus on the largest metropolitan areas, but their "correctives" focus on second- and third-tier cities with populations of well over a million. There are too many books on rural villages to list and even some on the topic of "rural urbanization" (Guldin 1997, 2001), as well as the topic of "in situ" urbanization in rural areas (Zhu 1999), but very little on places with a population in the range of 100,000 to 1,000,000. In a recent study of a town smaller than Zouping, Beatriz Carrillo (2011) also argues that the urbanization that occurs in midsized metropolises has been an understudied phenomenon, especially over the past decade.

10. For the period of my research, rural residents in Zouping were permitted to have a second child (several years after the first) if the first was a girl, but urban residents were restricted to one child. In general, in other rural areas around the country the policy was implemented in at least as permissive a fashion as it was in Zouping. In some rural areas two children were allowed no matter what the gender of the first child. The birth control policy continues to evolve, and urban parents can now also legally have two children. For a recent article that references much previous work on the policy, see Wei and Zhang 2014.

11. Recently the central government has demanded that localities offer places in primary and junior middle school to migrant workers' children (these two levels of schooling are compulsory). Though this demand has increased access to these levels of schooling in many parts of the country, some places continue to prevent migrant children from attending local schools. Even where children can attend primary and junior middle school, in many places they are blocked from attending senior middle school, which thus blocks access to university. For an exploration of how this latter sort of policy works in Shanghai, see Ling 2015.

12. The minimum livelihood allowance (*dibao*) is the most important form of welfare in China. In places with large numbers of laid-off workers, this allowance, despite its relatively low level, can be crucial to entire neighborhoods. In Zouping, employment opportunities are numerous and the number of people deemed eligible for the minimum livelihood allowance few. They include only those who cannot work for health reasons and who also have no relatives to support them. For more on the minimum livelihood insurance scheme and its impact on governance in areas with large numbers of laid-off workers, see Solinger 2008; Tang 2015.

13. Whether or not the issuing of collective or temporary household registrations also affects land rights in one's home village depends in part on the policies of the home district. Some of the strategies migrants use to maintain land rights in their home villages are explored in chapter 6.

14. The classic ethnography on this topic is *Chen Village* (2009) by Anita Chan, Richard Madsen, and Jonathan Unger. Other recent work includes Chung and Unger 2013; Tomba 2012.

1. Zouping was the site of a large Sino-American research project on rural China. For more on the project, see Kipnis 1997: 11–15. Other research on Zouping has been published in Farquhar 2002; Oi 1998; and Walder 1998. Work by Michel Oksenberg and Guy Alitto is forthcoming.

CHAPTER 2

1. March 8 is International Women's Day in China. I never discovered when or why the reservoir was named for this day.

2. For a sarcastic, fictional discussion of how to build a development zone, see the Han Han novel, *Tade Guo* (2011: 64–66).

3. In many of China's larger urban areas, shequ have emerged as important sites of governance. While Zouping has shequ, their importance is diminished for three reasons. First, as a newly urbanized area, Zouping does not have an entrenched urban underclass, one of the typical targets of shequ governance. Second, as described above, villages-in-the-city have resisted joining shequ, so village government structures remain under the jiedao. Third, factory workers who live in factory housing (the majority of Development Zone residents) are governed by their work units (the factories) rather than the shequ in which they live. The lack of an entrenched underclass, the wealth of the villages-in-the-city, and governance of factory workers by their work units has also meant that there is much less welfare work for shequ governments to do in Zouping than in China's larger, older cities. For more on shequ in other parts of China, see Heberer and Göbel 2011; Tang 2015.

4. A discussion of how the duties of county government employees are shifted according to the priorities of the county Party secretary may be found in Smith 2009. Party secretaries use the concept "core task" (*zhongxin gongzuo*) to justify the shifting.

5. For a summary of some of the literature on political modernization, see Heper 1976. Whyte (1973) usefully reviews how Mao's critique of bureaucracy involved different assumptions about how bureaucracy functioned than are made in many forms of modernization theory.

6. See Gupta 2012 for a detailed ethnography of bureaucracy in India that emphasizes the more negative aspects of bureaucratic functioning.

CHAPTER 3

1. Many local governments have been accused of making some task the central work (*zhongxin gongzuo*) of the government, to the point of ignoring everything else. Graeme Smith (2009) describes this process in detail.

2. During the 1960s and 1970s a large number of Chinese urban youth were sent to the countryside as part of the Maoist movement to temper youth through revolutionary experiences. A more economic government goal of the program was to reduce unemployment in urban areas. See Chan et al. 2009 for a detailed description of the experiences of some of these young people.

3. The quote and information on being sent to the countryside come from an interview published in the internet journal *Week in China,* June 1, 2012, edition, www.weekinchina.com/msingle/?mpage=14438 (accessed July 31, 2013). For the latest scholarship on the down-to-the-countryside movement, see Bonnin 2013.

4. Several overlapping sources of information are used in constructing this biography. The best is the Zouping county almanac of 1986–95 (Zouping 1997: esp. 304–6, 497), but this is supplemented by online bibliographies, especially that of Baidu Baike (http://baike.baidu.com/view/335945.htm; accessed 31 July 2013), and various newspaper and journal interviews (Fen 2007; Yin, Sun, and Zhang 1999; Zhongguo 2000a, 2000b; Xu 2009). In the text I cite the county almanac where various sources give the same information.

5. See Chan and Unger 2009 for a discussion of one work-unit-like enterprise in the twenty-first century.

6. Originally reported in the *Shandong Evening News* (Qilu Wanbao). Downloaded from Sina Net, http://news.sina.com.cn/o/2009–10–24/021316490275s.shtml (accessed August 6, 2013).

7. For more detail, see Kipnis 2011a.

8. See the article titled "Shandong's Wealthiest Man Zhang Shiping" (Shandong Shoufu Zhang Shiping), on the *New Fortune Magazine* website, www.xcf.cn/zhuanti/ztzz/xwzt/2012zt/sdsfzsp/images/neirongo.html (accessed August 9, 2013).

9. See www.forbes.com/profile/zhang-shiping/ (accessed August 9, 2013).

10. Neither the best newspaper reporting on this incident nor the most critical blogs I collected in 2007 and 2008 are still available on the Chinese Internet. The best press coverage was on Sichuan News Net (Sichuan Xinwen Wang, www.newssc.org). A year after the incident, on August 28, 2008, it ran a detailed analysis of the accident under the title "Shandong Weiqiao Pioneering's August 19 Incident—Explosion from the Leakage of Molten Aluminum" (Shandong Weiqiao Chuangye "8.19" Lüye Waiyi Baozha Zhongda Shigu), http://aqsc.newssc.org/system/2008/08/28/011073001.shtml (accessed August 29, 2008). Blogs were collected from Bokee Net, www.bokee.net/bloggermodule/blog_viewblog.do?id=985748) (accessed October 16, 2008, no longer available) and Baidu (http:tieba.baidu.com/f?kz=363392828, still available as of

August 14, 2013). As of August 14, 2013, official news coverage was still available at www.chinasafety.gov.cn/wangluocankao/2007–08/22/content_258776.htm and http://news.163.com/07/0822/03/3MFK5KV40001124J.html.

11. See Zouping Bureau of Statistics 2008: 162; 2009: 159; 2012: 149.

12. See Laura He, "China Mints Another Billionaire, Wang Yong, as Consumption of Food Sweeteners Grows," January 30, 2013, article on the *Forbes Magazine* website, www.forbes.com/sites/laurahe/2013/01/30/china-mints-another-billionaire-wang-yong-as-consumption-of-food-sweeteners-grows/ (accessed August 22, 2013).

CHAPTER 4

1. For an analysis of this process elsewhere in China, see Gaubatz 2008.

2. For excellent studies of Chinese consumption that discuss its rise at the beginning of the reform era in China's largest metropolises, see Davis 2000; Croll 2006a, 2006b. As a place that developed its consumer market later than China's metropolises, Zouping in the years 2005–13 arguably shares something with the places and times depicted in these works.

3. While seminal essence is not exactly the same as semen, in examples such as that of Chinese medical doctors advising teenage boys and young men against excessive masturbation, they amount to more or less the same thing.

4. For more on the nationwide and even global effects of automobile culture in China, see Gerth 2010: chapter 1.

5. For more on the thrift of migrant workers, especially in terms of "eating bitterness," see Loyalka 2012: 185–88.

6. Elsewhere I have discussed the rise of roller skating as a common pastime in China in relation to the ubiquity of smoothly paved plazas as an architectural form (Kipnis 2012a).

7. For more on the consumption of educational services, see Kipnis 2012c.

8. The general topic of suzhi discourse has attracted a great deal of attention. See Anagnost 2004; Bakken 2000; Cao 2009; Greenhalgh and Winckler 2005; Jacka 2009; Judd 2002; Kipnis 2006, 2007, 2011a; Lin 2009; Sigley 2009; Sun 2009; Tomba 2009; Woronov 2009; Yan 2003a.

9. For a discussion of this phenomenon in larger Chinese metropolises, see Jing 2000.

10. See Adrian 2003 for the wedding photography business in Taiwan.

11. Investing most of a family's resources in the purchase of the apartment is perhaps the highest manifestation of this value. For more on the centrality of purchasing apartments to urban family life, see below and Zhang 2010.

12. In Zouping I did not see any cosmetic surgery clinics, though certainly some Zouping women could have gone to larger cities like Jinan for these services. For more on cosmetic surgery in China, see Wen 2013.

CHAPTER 5

1. Pile's use of the term *real* here takes a cue from the psychoanalysis of Jacques Lacan, who uses the term to refer to a certain form of psychic reality. But Pile's use differs radically from Lacan in that Lacan opposed the "real" to both the "symbolic" and the "imaginary," whereas Pile's real includes all psychic phenomena. The term *structure of feeling* comes from the work of Raymond Williams (e.g., Williams 1973).

2. Pile (2005: 20) also emphasizes the relation of phantasmagoria to modernity for Benjamin. For a taste of how the past haunts the present in Benjamin's work, read his essay on the flâneur in *The Arcades Project* (1999: 416–55).

3. As Susan Gal and Gail Kligman (2000) note, the categories of public and private almost always internest in a fractal pattern; that is to say, within a "private space" like a home, there are further divisions of public and private space like the living room and the bedrooms; the extent of privacy of a given space is related to the size of the "public" granted access to it.

4. In large cities in China, sexualized images of Han women emerged during the 2000s, but at least in Zouping, as late as 2013, foreign women were overrepresented in sexualized advertising. The sexualization of Chinese minority women often involved minorities from Yunnan province. Northern minority women were rarely presented in this way, though other stereotypes were commonplace (Bulag 2008).

5. For an English translation, see Roy 1997–2013.

6. For an analysis and translation of this series, see Su and Wang 1991.

7. For more on social heat in such environments, see Chau 2006; Sangren 2000.

CHAPTER 6

1. Here I refer primarily to what Silvia Walby (1990) called "private patriarchy." Power relations within the family and the types of desires they generate both affect and are affected by gendered power relations outside of the family, or what Walby calls "public patriarchy."

2. These sorts of businesses are becoming more and more common in China. Their popularity reflects both a loosening of the regulation of "superstitious" activity and the fact that many people seek advice when facing life decisions in China's rapidly changing economy and society. For research on such businesses in another part of Shandong, see Li 2015.

3. Deng Xiaoping was the first leader of China after Mao Zedong. He is commonly credited, in both China and the West, with beginning the economic reforms that have brought China its current prosperity. Recent scholarship suggests that the hagiography of Deng has been overdone and that other, sometimes relatively despised or forgotten leaders deserve equal credit (Teiwes and Sun 2013).

4. The Chinese marriage law states that the minimum age for marriage is 22 for men and 20 for women. In Shanghai in 2010, the average age of first marriage was 26.5 for women and 28.8 for men (Jacka, Kipnis, and Sargeson 2013: 49–52).

CHAPTER 8

1. Lihong Shi (2009) argues that women in northeastern rural China retain a significant amoung of property after divorce. Her findings, however, are contradicted both by Sargeson and Song and by recent court rulings on the division of property after divorce, which say that property brought to the marriage by one party (including the parents) returns after divorce to the party that originally supplied it. See Jacka, Kipness, and Sargeson 2013: 48–51.

2. In all, I met six pairs of twins during my research, four of whom were boy-girl (dragon-phoenix) pairs. Five of these pairs of twins were born after 2009. The number of twins I met during the last few years of research seemed high to me, and I suspect that the use of fertility treatments was a factor, though I have no concrete evidence.

3. The exact amount depends on the market value of grain (wheat) on July 31 of each year and the total number of eligible recipients in the household and village as a whole.

4. Steinmüller (2013: 234–36) translates the story the local television station broadcast about him during his fieldwork in Enshi county, Hubei province. My experiences broadly resonate with Steinmüller's. During my years in Zouping, I was the subject of one local news story and was interviewed by TV journalists three other times. My words were always edited to make it sound like I was enthusiastically endorsing the local Party. Though I found this presentation of my opinions hard to take, I felt that I could not avoid giving such interviews since my fieldwork had been officially approved by the local government. Moreover, the media exposure usually helped my research. Those who saw me on TV often approached me to initiate conversation if they saw me in public. In addition, even disgruntled people, such as this woman, did not seem to interpret my televised words as representing my actual opinion or a blind commitment to support the local government. Rather they took me as someone who could speak to the local government and thus did not hesitate to share their dissatisfaction with me.

5. For a discussion of the Zouping church in 1995 and its earlier history, see Kipnis 2002.

CHAPTER 9

1. I once offered my own definition of class (Kipnis 2008) but will not explicitly rely on that here.

2. Middle-class fear of the dirt and crime of the lower classes is a common phenomenon. Stallybrass and White (1986) argue that the categorization of dirt and crime as "lower" is how middle classes distinguish themselves everywhere.

3. All the names used in this chapter are pseudonyms. Some minor details of their lives have also been altered to disguise their identities.

4. The emphasis on science in religious belief systems in China can be a way of claiming legitimacy. To the members of this group, being "scientific" simply implies that an activity is based on careful thought and long-term experience. Members of this group also emphasized how their basis in science differentiated them from groups like Fa Lun Gong, which is labeled by the government as a heretical (and certainly unscientific) sect and strictly outlawed. For more on the place of science in popular religion in China, see Li 2015; Lora-Wainwright 2013: 234–35.

CHAPTER 10

1. Philippe Aries (1962) famously argued that the category "childhood" did not exist during the Middle Ages in Europe and thus must be analyzed historically. His work has been criticized for missing some of the ways in which childhood was marked in the Middle Ages, though he certainly demonstrates that the advent of modernity led to a proliferation of discourse about the category. A similar and perhaps even stronger argument about the category "youth" could be made.

2. That some permanent workers claim to have habituated to factory work, however, does not imply that the work has no ill effects. It might be better to say that some workers claimed habituating to factory work as a form of sacrifice to their families and wished this sacrifice to be recognized.

3. For an even more extreme example of dysfunctional vocational school education in China, see Woronov 2011.

CHAPTER 11

1. For a discussion of the "ruralization" of the urban, see Krause 2013.

2. On the importance of centering to place making in China, see Feuchtwang 2004a, 2004b.

3. *Producing Guanxi* (Kipnis 1997) examines the means of constructing relationships in a village in Zouping county. John Osburg (2013) has discussed the evolution of practices of constructing relationships during the reform era in Chengdu.

4. Elsewhere I have written about educational desire in Zouping (Kipnis 2011a) and the hierarchical concept of face (Kipnis 1995).

5. For more on the New Socialist Countryside campaign, see Abramson 2006; Bray 2013; Rosenberg 2015.

REFERENCES

Abramson, Daniel. 2006. "Urban Planning in China: Continuity and Change: What the Future Holds May Surprise You." *Journal of the American Planning Association* 72(2): 197–215.

Adrian, Bonnie. 2003. *Framing the Bride: Globalizing Beauty and Romance in Taiwan's Bridal Industry.* Berkeley: University of California Press.

Airriess, Christopher. 2008. "The Geographies of Secondary City Growth in a Globalized China: Comparing Dongguan and Suzhou." *Journal of Urban History* 35(1): 134–49.

Alpermann, Bjorn. 2011. "Class, Citizenship and Individualization in China's Modernization." *Protosociology* 28: 7–24.

Anagnost, Ann. 2004. "The Corporeal Politics of Quality (Suzhi)." *Public Culture* 16(2): 189–208.

Appadurai, Arjun. 1996. *Modernity at Large: Cultural Dimensions of Globalization.* Minneapolis: University of Minnesota Press.

Aries, Philippe. 1962. *Centuries of Childhood.* London: John Cape.

Bach, Jonathan. 2010. "'They Come in Peasants and Leave Citizens': Urban Villages and the Making of Shenzhen, China." *Cultural Anthropology* 25(3): 421–58.

Bakken, Børge. 2000. *The Exemplary Society: Human Improvement, Social Control, and the Dangers of Modernity in China.* New York: Oxford University Press.

Bauman, Zygmunt. 2000. *Liquid Modernity.* Cambridge: Polity Press.

Beck, Ulrich, Anthony Giddens, and Scott Lash. 1994. *Reflexive Modernization: Politics, Traditon and Aesthetics in the Modern Social Order.* Cambridge: Polity Press.

Beck, Ulrich, and Edgar Grande. 2010. "Varities of Second Modernity: The Cosmopolitan Turn in Social and Political Theory and Research." *British Journal of Sociology* 61(3): 409–43.

Benjamin, Walter. 1999. *The Arcades Project.* Cambridge, MA: Harvard University Press.

Biehl, João, and Peter Locke. 2010. "Deleuze and the Anthropology of Becoming." *Current Anthropology* 51(3): 317–51.

Billiter, Jean-François. 1985. "The System of 'Class Status.'" In *The Scope of State Power in China,* ed. S. R. Schram, 127–69. London: School of Asian and African Studies.

Boellstorff, Tom. 2004. "The Emergence of Political Homophobia in Indonesia: Masculinity and National Belonging." *Ethnos* 69(4): 465–86.

Bonnin, Michael. 2013. *The Lost Generation: The Rustication of China's Educated Youth (1968–1980).* Hong Kong: Chinese University Press.

Bourdieu, Pierre. 1984. *Distinction: A Social Critique of the Judgement of Taste.* Trans. R. Nice. London: Routledge & Kegan Paul.

———. 1990. *The Logic of Practice.* Cambridge: Polity Press.

———. 2005. *The Social Structures of the Economy.* New York: Polity Press.

Boyer, Dominic, and Alexei Yurchak. 2010. "American Stiob: Or, What Late-Socialist Aesthetics of Parody Reveal about Contemporary Political Culture in the West." *Cultural Anthropology* 25(2): 179–221.

Bray, David. 2005. *Social Space and Governance in Urban China: The Danwei System from Origins to Reform.* Stanford, CA: Stanford University Press.

———. 2008. "Designing to Govern: Space and Power in Two Wuhan Communities." *Built Environment* 34(4): 392–407.

———. 2013. "Urban Planning Goes Rural: Conceptualizing the 'New Village.'" *China Perspectives* 3: 53–62.

Bulag, Uradyn E. 2008. "Contesting the Words That Wound: Ethnicity and the Politics of Sentiment in China." *Inner Asia* 10(1): 87–111.

Buyandelger, Manduhai. 2013. *Tragic Spirits: Shamanism, Memory, and Gender in Contemporary Mongolia.* Chicago: University of Chicago Press.

Campbell, Colin. 1987. *The Romantic Ethic and the Spirit of Capitalism.* New York: Blackwell.

Cao, Nanlai. 2009. "Raising the Quality of Belief: Suzhi and the Production of an Elite Protestantism." *China Perspectives* 4: 54–65.

Carrillo, Beatriz. 2011. *Small Town China: Rural Labour and Social Inclusion.* London: Routledge.

Castells, Manuel. 1998. *End of Millennium.* Oxford: Blackwell.

Chakrabarty, Dipesh. 1998. "Afterword: Revisiting the Tradition/Modernity Binary." In *Mirror of Modernity: Invented Traditions of Modern Japan,* ed. S. Vlastos, 285–96. Berkeley: University of California Press.

———. 2000. *Provincializing Europe: Postcolonial Thought and Historical Difference.* Princeton, NJ: Princeton University Press.

Chan, Anita, Richard Madsen, and Jonathan Unger. 2009. *Chen Village: Revolution to Globalization.* Berkeley: University of California Press.

Chan, Anita, and Jonathan Unger. 2009. "A Chinese State Enterprise under the Reforms: What Model of Capitalism?" *China Journal* 62: 1–26.

Chang, Leslie T. 2009. *Factory Girls: From Village to City in a Changing China.* New York: Spiegel and Grau.

Chau, Adam Yuet. 2006. *Miraculous Response: Doing Popular Religion in Contemporary China.* Stanford, CA: Stanford University Press.

Chen, Nancy N., et al., eds. 2001. *China Urban: Ethnographies of Contemporary Culture*. Durham, NC: Duke University Press.

Chiu, Fred Y. L. 2003. *Colours of Money, Shades of Pride: Historicities and Moral Politics in Industrial Conflicts in Hong Kong*. Hong Kong: Hong Kong University Press.

Cho, Mun Young. 2013. *The Specter of "The People": Urban Poverty in Northeast China*. Ithaca, NY: Cornell University Press.

Chung, Him, and Jonathan Unger. 2013. "The Guangdong Model of Urbanisation: Collective Village Land and the Making of a new Middle Class." *China Perspectives* 3: 33–41.

Cliff, Thomas. 2012. "Oil and Water: Experiences of Being Han in 21st-Century Korla, Xinjiang." PhD diss., Australian National University.

Coates, Jamie. 2012. "Being-with Others: An Existential Anthropology of Recent Chinese Migration in Tokyo, Japan." PhD diss., Australian National University.

Coronil, Fernando. 1997. *The Magical State: Nature, Money, and Modernity in Venezuela*. Chicago: University of Chicago Press.

Crapanzano, Vincent. 2003. "Reflections on Hope as a Category of Social and Psychological Analysis." *Cultural Anthropology* 18(1): 3–32.

Croll, Elisabeth J. 2006a. *China's New Consumers: Social Development and Domestic Demand*. London: Routledge.

———. 2006b. "Conjuring Goods, Identities, and Cultures." In *Consuming China: Approaches to Cultural Change in Contemporary China,* ed. K. Latham, S. Thompson, and J. Klein, 22–41. London: Routledge.

Davis, Deborah S., ed. 2000. *The Consumer Revolution in Urban China*. Berkeley: University of California Press.

De Brauw, Alan, et al. 2008. "Feminization of Agriculture in China? Myths Surrounding Women's Participation in Farming." *China Quarterly* 194: 327–48.

Dean, Mitchell. 1999. *Governmentality: Power and Rule in Modern Society*. London: Sage.

Debord, Guy. 1977. *Society of the Spectacle*. Detroit: Black & Red.

Dikotter, Frank. 2010. *Mao's Great Famine: The History of China's Most Devastating Catastrophe, 1958–1962*. New York: Walker and Company.

Ding Haitang, Zhang Zhiyong, and Li Yunxiang. 2005. "Guanyu Shandong Weiqiao Chuangye Jituan Zuoda Zuoqiang de Jingyan he Qishi" (Lessons to Be Learned from the Growth and Strength of Shandong Wieqiao Pioneering Group). *Qiye Guanli* (Enterprise Management) 6: 36–38.

Doron, Assa, and Robin Jeffrey. 2013. *The Great Indian Phone Book: How the Cheap Cell Phone Changes Business, Politics, and Daily Life*. Cambridge, MA: Harvard University Press.

Durkheim, Émile. 1952. *Suicide: A Study in Sociology*. Trans. J. A. Spaulding and G. Simpson. London: Routledge and Kegan Paul.

———. 1956. *Education and Sociology*. Trans. S. D. Fox. Glencoe, IL: Free Press.

———. 1960. *Division of Labor in Society*. Trans. G. Simpson. Glencoe, IL: Free Press.

———. 1973. *Moral Education: A Study in the Theory and Application of the Sociology of Education*. New York: Free Press.

———. 1979. *Durkheim: Essays on Morals and Education*. Trans. H.L. Sutcliffe. London: Routledge and Kegan Paul.

———. 1992. *Professional Ethics and Civic Morals*. Trans. C. Brookfield. New York: Routledge.

Dutton, Michael, ed. 1998. *Streetlife China*. Cambridge: Cambridge University Press.

Eisenstadt, Shmuel Noah. 2000. "Multiple Modernities." *Daedalus* 129(1): 1–29.

———. 2003. *Comparative Civilizations and Multiple Modernities*. Leiden: Brill.

Evans, Harriet. 1997. *Women and Sexuality in China: Dominant Discourses of Female Sexuality and Gender since 1949*. Cambridge: Polity Press.

Farquhar, Judith. 2002. *Appetites: Food and Sex in Post-Socialist China*. Durham, NC: Duke University Press.

Farquhar, Judith, and Qicheng Zhang. 2005. "Biopolitical Beijing: Pleasure, Sovereignty, and Self-Cultivation in China's Capital." *Cultural Anthropology* 20(3): 303–27.

———. 2012. *Ten Thousand Things: Nurturing Life in Contemporary Beijing*. New York: Zone Books.

Farrer, James. 2002. *Opening Up: Youth Sex Culture and Market Reform in Shanghai*. Chicago: University of Chicago Press.

Fei Xiaotong. 1992. *From the Soil: The Foundations of Chinese Society, a Translation of Fei Xiaotong's "Xiangtu Zhongguo."* Trans. G. Hamilton and W. Zheng. Berkeley: University of California Press.

Fen He. 2007. "Ji You Weiqiao" (Exceptional Results by Weiqiao). *Zhongguo Fangzhi* (China Textiles) 3: 148–49.

Ferguson, James. 1999. *Expectations of Modernity: Myths and Meanings of Urban Life on the Zambian Copperbelt*. Berkeley: University of California Press.

Feuchtwang, Stephan. 2004a. "Curves and the Urbanisation of Meifa Village." In *Making Place: State Projects, Globalisation and Local Reponses in China,* ed. S. Feuchtwang, 163–79. London: University College London Press.

———. 2004b. "Theorising Place." In *Making Place: State Projects, Globalisation and Local Reponses in China,* ed. S. Feuchtwang, 3–30. London: University College London Press.

Fong, Vanessa L. 2004. *Only Hope: Coming of Age under China's One-Child Policy*. Stanford, CA: Stanford University Press.

Foucault, Michel. 1979. *Discipline and Punish: The Birth of the Prison*. New York: Vintage Books.

———. 1991. "Governmentality." In *The Foucault Effect: Studies in Governmentality,* ed. G. Burchell, C. Gordon, and P. Miller, 87–104. London: Harvester Wheatsheaf.

Frank, Andre Gunder. 1998. *ReOrient: Global Economy in the Asian Age*. Berkeley: University of California Press.

Friedman, Jonathan. 1994. *Cultural Identity and Global Process*. London: Sage.

Friedman, Jonathan, and Kajsa Ekholm Friedman. 2013. "Globalization as a Discourse of Hegemonic Crisis: A Global Systemic Analysis." *American Ethnologist* 40(2): 244–57.

Friedman, Kajsa Ekholm, and Jonathan Friedman. 2008. *The Anthropology of Global Systems*. Lanham, MD: AltaMira Press.

Gal, Susan, and Gail Kligman. 2000. *The Politics of Gender after Socialism: A Comparative-Historical Essay*. Princeton, NJ: Princeton University Press.

Gaonkar, Dilip Parameshwar, ed. 2001. *Alternative Modernities*. Durham, NC: Duke University Press.

Garnaut, Ross, et al. 2005. *China's Ownership Transformation: Process, Outcomes, Prospects*. Washington, DC: International Finance Corporation/World Bank.

Gaubatz, Piper Rae. 1996. *Beyond the Great Wall: Urban Form and Transformation on the Chinese Frontiers*. Stanford, CA: Stanford University Press.

———. 2008. "New Public Space in Urban China: Fewer Walls, More Malls in Beijing, Shanghai, and Xining." *China Perspectives* 4: 72–85.

Gerth, Karl. 2010. *As China Goes, So Goes the World: How Chinese Consumers Are Transforming Everything*. New York: Hill & Wang.

Gibson-Graham, J. K. 1996. *The End of Capitalism (as We Knew It): A Feminist Critique of Political Economy*. Cambridge, MA: Blackwell.

Gladney, Dru. 2004. "Representing Nationality in China: Refiguring Majority/Minority Identities." *Journal of Asian Studies* 53(1): 92–123.

Good, Mary-Jo DelVecchio, et al. 1990. "American Oncology and the Discourse of Hope." *Culture, Medicine, and Psychiatry* 14(1): 59–79.

Graeber, David. 2001. *Toward an Anthropological Theory of Value: The False Coin of Our Own Dreams*. New York: Palgrave.

———. 2011. "Consumption." *Current Anthropology* 52(4): 489–511.

Greenhalgh, Susan, and Edwin A. Winckler. 2005. *Governing China's Population*. Stanford, CA: Stanford University Press.

Griffiths, Michael B., Malcolm Chapman, and Flemming Christiansen. 2010. "Chinese Consumers: The Romantic Reappraisal." *Ethnography* 11(3): 331–57.

Guldin, Gregory Eliyu. 1997. *Farewell to Peasant China: Rural Urbanization and Social Change in the Late Twentieth Century*. Armonk, NY: M. E. Sharpe.

———. 2001. *What's a Peasant to Do? Village Becoming Town in Southern China*. Boulder, CO: Westview Press.

Gupta, Akhil. 2012. *Red Tape: Bureaucracy, Structural Violence, and Poverty in India*. Durham, NC: Duke University Press.

Halbwachs, Maurice. 1992. *On Collective Memory*. Chicago: University of Chicago Press.

Han Han. 2011. *Tade Guo* (Another's Country). Shenyang: Wanjuan Chubanshe (Wanjuan Publishers).

Han, Sang-Jin, and Young-Hee Shim. 2010. "Redefining Second Modernity for East Asia: A Critical Assessment." *British Journal of Sociology* 61(3): 465–88.

Hanser, Amy. 2008. *Service Encounters: Class, Gender, and the Market for Social Distinction in Urban China.* Stanford, CA: Stanford University Press.

Harrell, Stevan. 1985. "Why Do the Chinese Work So Hard: Reflections on an Entrepreneurial Ethic." *Modern China* 11(2): 203–26.

———. 2013. "Orthodoxy, Resistance, and the Family in Chinese Art." In *The Family Model in Chinese Art and Culture,* ed. J. Silbergeld and D. C. Y. Ching, 71–90. Princeton, NJ: Princeton University Press.

Harvey, David. 1989. *The Condition of Postmodernity: An Inquiry into the Origins of Social Change.* Oxford: Blackwell.

Heberer, Thomas, and Christian Gobel. 2011. *The Politics of Community Building in Urban China.* London: Routledge.

Henderson, Gail E., and Myron S. Cohen. 1984. *The Chinese Hospital: A Socialist Work Unit.* New Haven, CT: Yale University Press.

Heper, Metin. 1976. "Political Modernization as Reflected in Bureaucratic Change: The Turkish Bureaucracy and a 'Historical Bureaucratic Empire' Tradition." *International Journal of Middle East Studies* 7: 507–21.

Herzfeld, Michael. 1991 *A Place in History: Social and Monumental Time in a Cretan Town.* Princeton, NJ: Princeton University Press.

———. [1997] 2005. *Cultural Intimacy: Social Poetics in the Nation-State.* 2nd ed. New York: Routledge.

Hobor, George. 2007. "Post-Industrial Pathways: The Economic Reorganization of the Urban Rust Belt." PhD diss., University of Arizona.

———. 2012. "Surviving the Era of DeIndustrialization: The New Economic Geography of the Urban Rust Belt." *Journal of Urban Affairs* 34(1): 1–18.

Hobsbawn, Eric, and Terence Ranger, eds. 1983. *The Invention of Tradition.* Cambridge: Cambridge University Press.

Hoffman, Lisa M. 2010. *Patriotic Professionalism in Urban China.* Philadelphia: Temple University Press.

Horkheimer, Max, and Theodor W Adorno. 1972. *The Dialectic of Enlightenment.* Trans. J. Cumming. New York: Herder and Herder.

Hsing, You-tien. 2010. *The Great Urban Transformation: Politics of Land and Property in China.* Oxford: Oxford University Press.

Hsu, Carolyn. 2007. *Creating Market Socialism: How Ordinary People Are Shaping Class and Status in China.* Durham, NC: Duke University Press.

Hua, Wen. 2013. *Buying Beauty: Cosmetic Surgery in China.* Hong Kong: Hong Kong University Press.

Huang, Chien-Yu Julia, and Robert P. Weller. 1998. "Merit and Mothering: Women and Social Welfare in Taiwanese Buddhism." *Journal of Asian Studies* 57(2): 379–96.

Humphrey, Caroline, and Hurelbaatar Ujeed. 2013. *A Monastery in Time: The Making of Mongolian Buddhism.* Chicago: University of Chicago Press.

Jacka, Tamara. 2005. *Rural Women in Urban China: Gender, Migration, and Social Change.* London: M. E. Sharpe.

———. 2009. "Cultivating Citizens: Suzhi (Quality) Discourse in the PRC." *positions: east asia cultures critique* 17(3): 523–35.

Jacka, Tamara, Andrew B. Kipnis, and Sally Sargeson. 2013. *Contemporary China: Society and Social Change.* Cambridge: Cambridge University Press.

Jankowiak, William R. 1993. *Sex, Death, and Hierarchy in a Chinese City: An Anthropological Account.* New York: Columbia University Press.

———. 1995. *Romantic Passion: A Universal Experience?* New York: Columbia University Press.

———. 2004a. "Introduction." *Urban Anthropology* 33(2–4): 115–37.

———. 2004b. "Market Reforms, Nationalism, and the Expansion of Urban China's Moral Horizon." Urban Anthropology 33(2–4): 167–210.

Jia Pingwa. 2000. *Huainian Lang* (Remembering Wolves). Beijing: Zuojia Chubanshe.

Jing, Jun, ed. 2000. *Feeding China's Little Emperors: Food, Children, and Social Change.* Stanford, CA: Stanford University Press.

Jin Ri Zouping. 2008. *Meili Zouping Huihuang 30 Nian 1978–2008* (30 Years of Glorious History for Beautiful Zouping, 1978–2008). Zouping, Shandong, China: Jin Ri Zouping (Zouping Today).

Judd, Ellen R. 1994. *Gender and Power in Rural North China.* Stanford, CA: Stanford University Press.

———. 2002. *The Chinese Women's Movement between State and Market.* Stanford, CA: Stanford University Press.

Kipnis, Andrew B. 1995. "'Face': An Adaptable Discourse of Social Surfaces." *positions: east asia cultures critique* 3(1): 110–35.

———. 1997. *Producing Guanxi: Sentiment, Self, and Subculture in a North China Village.* Durham, NC: Duke University Press.

———. 2002. "Zouping Christianity as Gendered Critique? The Place of the Political in Ethnography." *Anthropology and Humanism* 27(1): 80–96.

———. 2003. "Post-Marxism in a Postsocialist Perspective." *Anthropological Theory* 3(4): 457–80.

———. 2006. "Suzhi: A Keyword Approach." *China Quarterly* 186: 295–313.

———. 2007. "Neoliberalism Reified: Suzhi Discourse and Tropes of Neoliberalism in the PRC." *Journal of the Royal Anthropological Institute* 13(2): 383–99.

———. 2008. *China and Postsocialist Anthropology: Theorizing Power and Society after Communism.* Norwalk, CT: Eastbridge.

———. 2011a. *Governing Educational Desire: Culture, Politics, and Schooling in China.* Chicago: University of Chicago Press.

———. 2011b. "Subjectification and Education for Quality in China." *Economy and Society* 40(2): 261–78.

———. 2012a . "Constructing Commonality: Standardization and Modernization in Chinese Nation-Building." *Journal of Asian Studies* 71(3): 731–55.

———. 2012b. "Introduction: Chinese Modernity and the Individual Psyche." In *Chinese Modernity and the Individual Psyche,* ed. A. B. Kipnis, 1–18. New York: Palgrave Macmillan.

———. 2012c. "Private Lessons and National Formations: National Hierarchy and the Individual Psyche in the Marketing of Educational Programs." In *Chinese Modernity and the Individual Psyche,* ed. A. B. Kipnis, 187–202. New York: Palgrave Macmillan.

———. 2013. "Education and Inequality; Education and Equality." In *Unequal China: The Political Economy and Cultural Politics of Inequality,* ed. W. Sun and Y. Guo, 111–24. London: Routledge.

Krause, Monika. 2013 . "The Ruralization of the World." *Public Culture* 25 (2): 233–48.

Kuan, Teresa. 2011. "The Heart Says One Thing but the Hand Does Another: A Story about Emotion-Work, Ambivalence, and Popular Advice for Parents." *China Journal* 65: 77–100.

Latour, Bruno. 1993. *We Have Never Been Modern.* New York: Harvester Wheatsheaf.

Li, Geng. 2015. "Fate Calculation Experts: Diviners Seeking Legitimation in Contemporary China." PhD diss., Australian National University.

Liang Hong. 2013. *Chu Liangzhuang Ji* (Records of Those Who Left Liangzhuang Village). Guangzhou: Huacheng Chubanshe (Flower City Publishers).

Lin, Qinghong. 2009. "Civilising Citizens in Post-Mao China: Understanding the Rhetoric of *Suzhi.*" PhD diss., Griffith University.

Ling, Minhua. 2015. "'Bad Students Go to Vocational Schools!': Education, Social Reproduction and Migrant Youth in Urban China." *China Journal* 73: 108–31.

Liu, Xin. 1997. "Space, Mobility, and Flexibility: Chinese Villagers and Scholars Negotiate Power at Home and Abroad." In *Ungrounded Empires: The Cultural Politics of Modern Chinese Transnationalism,* ed. A. Ong and D. Nonini, 91–114. New York: Routledge.

———. 2002. *The Otherness of Self: A Genealogy of the Self in Contemporary China.* Ann Arbor: University of Michigan Press.

Lora-Wainwright, Anna. 2013. *Fighting for Breath: Living Morally and Dying of Cancer in a Chinese Village.* Honolulu: University of Hawai'i Press.

Loyalka, Michelle Dammon. 2012. *Eating Bitterness: Stories from the Front Lines of China's Great Urban Migration.* Berkeley: University of California Press.

Macdonald, Sharon. 2013. *Memorylands: Heritage and Identity in Europe Today.* London: Routledge.

Mao T'se-tung. 1975. *Selected Works of Mao T'se-tung.* 5 vols. Beijing: Foreign Languages Press.

Martindale, Don. 1958. "Prefatory Remarks: The Theory of The City." In *The City,* ed. M. Weber, D. Martindale, and G. Neuwirth, 9–62. New York: Free Press.

Marx, Karl. 1964. *The Economic and Philosophical Manuscripts of 1844.* New York: International Publishers.

Marx, Karl, and Friedrich Engels. 1886. *Capital: A Critical Analysis of Capitalist Production.* London: William Glaisher.

Miller, Daniel. 1998. *A Theory of Shopping.* Ithaca, NY: Cornell University Press.

Miyazaki, Hirokazu. 2006. "Economy of Dreams: Hope in Global Capitalism and Its Critiques." *Cultural Anthropology* 21(2): 147–72.

———. 2013. *Arbitraging Japan: Dreams of Capitalism at the End of Finance*. Berkeley: University of California Press.

Moskowitz, Marc L. 2010. *Cries of Joy, Songs of Sorrow: Chinese Pop Music and Its Cultural Connotations*. Honolulu: University of Hawai'i Press.

Nancy, Jean-Luc. 1991. *The Inoperative Community*. Ed. Peter Connor and Lisa Garbus, trans. Peter Connor, Michael Holland, and Simona Sawhney. Minneapolis: University of Minnesota Press.

Nappi, Carla. 2009. *The Monkey and the Inkpot: Natural History and Its Transformations in Early Modern China*. Cambridge, MA: Harvard University Press.

Notar, Beth E. 1994. "Of Labor and Liberation: Images of Women in Current Chinese Television Advertising." *Visual Anthropology Review* 10(2): 29–44.

Oi, Jean C. 1998. "The Evolution of Local State Corporatism." In *Zouping in Transition: The Process of Reform in Rural North China,* ed. A. G. Walder, 35–61. Cambridge, MA: Harvard University Press.

Osborg, John. 2013. *Anxious Wealth: Money and Morality among China's New Rich*. Stanford, CA: Stanford University Press.

Park, Robert E. 1952. *Human Commuities: The City and Human Ecology*. Glencoe, IL: Free Press.

Park, Robert E., et al. [1925] 1968. *The City*. With an Introduction by Morris Janowitz. Chicago: University of Chicago Press.

Pile, Steve. 2005. *Real Cities: Modernity, Space and the Phantasmagorias of City Life*. London: Sage.

Proust, Marcel. 1923. *Remembrance of Things Past: Part 1, Swann's Way*. Vol. 1 New York: Henry Holt and Co.

Pun, Ngai. 2005. *Made in China: Women Workers in a Global Workplace*. Durham, NC: Duke University Press.

Pun, Ngai, and Huilin Lu. 2010. "Unfinished Proletarianization: Self, Anger, and Class Action among the Second Generation of Peasant-Workers in Present-Day China." *Modern China* 36(5): 493–519.

Qiu Feng and Zhang Lin. 2014. "Xianxia Shi: Xinxing Chengzhenhua de Tupokou" (County-Level Cities: An Opening for Understanding New Forms of Urbanization). Jingjin Guancha Wang (Economic Survey Net), www.eeo.com .cn/2014/0812/264821.shtml. Accessed 26 August 2014.

Robinson, Jennifer. 2006. *Ordinary Cities: Between Modernity and Development*. London: Routledge.

Robison, Richard, and David S. G. Goodman. 1996. "The New Rich in Asia: Economic Development, Social Status and Political Consciousness." In *The New Rich in Asia: Mobile Phones, McDonald's, and Middle-Class Revolution,* ed. R. Robison and D. S. G. Goodman, 1–16. London: Routledge.

Rofel, Lisa. 1999. *Other Modernities: Gendered Yearnings in China after Socialism*. Berkeley: University of California Press.

Rosenberg, Lior. 2015. "Why Do Local Officials Bet on the Strong? Drawing Lessons from China's Village Redevelopment Program." *China Journal* 74: 18–42.

Roy, David Tod, trans. 1997–2013. *The Plum in the Golden Vase, or, Chin P'ing Mei.* 5 vols. Princeton, NJ: Princeton University Press.

Sangren, Paul Steven. 2000. *Chinese Sociologics: An Anthropological Account of the Role of Alienation in Social Reproduction.* London: Athlone.

Sargeson, Sally. 2012. "Why Women Own Less and Why It Matters More in China's Urban Transformation." *China Perspectives* 4: 35–42.

Sargeson, Sally, and Yu Song. 2010. "Land Expropriation and the Gender Politics of Citizenship in the Urban Frontier." *China Journal* 64: 19–45.

Scott, James C. 1998. *Seeing Like a State: How Certain Schemes to Improve the Human Condition Have Failed.* New Haven: Yale University Press.

———. 2009. *The Art of Not Being Governed: An Anarchist History of Upland Southeast Asia.* New Haven, CT: Yale University Press.

Shepard, Wade. 2015. *Ghost Cities of China.* London: Zed Books.

Shi, Lihong. 2009. "'Little Quilted Vests to Warm Parents' Hearts': Redefining Gendered Performance of Filial Piety in Rural Northeastern China." *China Quarterly* 198: 348–63.

Short, John Rennie. 2012. *Globalization, Modernity, and the City.* London: Routledge.

Si Lian, ed. 2009. *Yizu: Daxue Biyesheng Juju Cun Shilu* (Ant Tribes: True Reports on the Residential Districts of College Graduates). Nanning: Guangxi Shifan Daxue Chubanshe (Guangxi Normal University Press).

Sigley, Gary. 2009. "*Suzhi,* the Body, and the Fortunes of Technoscientific Reasoning in Contemporary China." *positions: east asia cultures critique* 17(3): 537–66.

Simmel, Georg. 1971. *On Individuality and Social Forms: Selected Writings.* Ed. Donald N. Levine. Chicago: University of Chicago Press.

Siu, Helen F. 2007. "Grounding Displacement: Uncivil Urban Spaces in Postreform South China." *American Ethnologist* 34(2): 329–50.

Smith, Arthur. 1894. *Chinese Characteristics.* New York: Fleming H. Revell.

Smith, Graeme. 2009. "Political Machinations in a Rural County." *China Journal* 62: 29–60.

Smith, Michael P. 1979. *The City and Social Theory.* New York: St. Martin's Press.

Solinger, Dorothy J. 2008. "The *Dibao* Recipients: Mollified Anti-Emblem of Urban Modernization." *China Perspectives* 4: 36–46.

Song Geng and Tracy K. Lee. 2010. "Consumption, Class Formation, and Sexuality: Reading Men's Lifestyle Magazines in China." *China Journal* 64: 159–77.

Sontag, Susan. 1979. *Illness as Metaphor.* New York: Allen Lane.

Stallybrass, Peter, and Allon White. 1986. *The Politics and Poetics of Transgression.* Ithaca, NY: Cornell University Press.

Steinmuller, Hans. 2013. *Communities of Complicity: Everyday Ethics in Rural China.* New York: Berghahn.

Su, Xiaokang and Wang Luxiang. 1991. *Deathsong of a River: A Reader's Guide to the Chinese TV Series "Heshang."* Trans. Richard W. Bodman and Pin P. Wan. Ithaca, NY: Cornell University Press.

Sun, Wanning. 2009. "*Suzhi* on the Move: Body, Place and Power." *positions: east asia cultures critique* 17(3) :617–42.

Tang Beibei. 2015. "Deliberating Governance in Chinese Urban Communities." *China Journal* 73: 84–107.

Tapp, Nicholas. 2000. "The Consuming or the Consumed: Virtual Hmong in China." *Asia Pacific Journal of Anthropology* 1(2): 73–101.

Teiwes, Frederick C., and Warren Sun. 2013. "China's Economic Reorientation after the Third Plenum: Conflict Surrounding 'Chen Yun's' Readjustment Program, 1979–80." *China Journal* 70: 163–87.

Thøgersen, Stig. 2002. *A County of Culture: Twentieth-Century China Seen from the Village Schools of Zouping, Shandong.* Ann Arbor: University of Michigan Press.

Thornton, Patricia M. 2009. "Crisis and Governance: SARS and the Resilience of the Chinese Body Politic." *China Journal* 61: 23–50.

Tomba, Luigi. 2004. "Creating an Urban Middle Class: Social Engineering in Beijing." *China Journal* 51: 1–26.

———. 2009. "Of Quality, Harmony, and Community: Civilization and the Middle Class in Urban China." *positions: east asia cultures critique* 17(3): 591–616.

———. 2012. "Awakening the God of Earth: Land, Place, and Class in Urbanizing Guangdong." In *China's Peasants and Workers: Changing Class Identities,* ed. B. Carillo and D. S. G. Goodman, 40–61. Cheltenham: Edward Elger.

———. 2014. *The Government Next Door.* Ithaca, NY: Cornell University Press.

Tonniës, Ferdinand. [1887] 1963. *Commmunity and Society.* Trans. and ed. C. P. Loomis. New York: Harper and Row.

Walby, Silvia. 1990. *Theorising Patriarchy.* Oxford: Blackwell.

Walder, Andrew G. 1986. *Communist Neo-Traditionalism: Work and Authority in Chinese Industry.* Berkeley: University of California Press.

———. 1998. "The County Government as an Industrial Corporation." In *Zouping in Transition: The Process of Reform in Rural North China,* ed. A. G. Walder, 62–85. Cambridge, MA: Harvard University Press.

Wang Jianxin, ed. 2006. *Jizhe Yan Zhongde Xiwang* (Xiwang in the Eyes of Reporters). Beijing: Zhongguo Wenhua Chubanshe.

Weber, Max. 1978. *Economy and Society: An Outline of Interpretive Sociology.* Ed. G. Roth and C. Wittich. Berkeley: University of California Press.

———. 2002. *The Protestant Ethic and the Spirit of Capitalism.* Los Angeles, CA: Roxbury.

Wei, Yan, and Li Zhang. 2014. "Re-examination of the Yicheng Two-Child Program." *China Journal* 72: 98–120.

Weiss, Brad. 2002. "Thug Realism: Inhabiting Fantasy in Urban Tanzania." *Cultural Anthropology* 17(1): 93–124.

Whyte, Martin King. 1973. "Bureaucracy and Modernization in China: The Maoist Critique." *American Sociological Review* 38(2): 149–60.

———. 2010. "The Paradoxes of Rural-Urban Inequality in Contemporary China." In *One Country, Two Societies,* ed. M. K. Whyte, 1–25. Cambridge, MA: Harvard University Press.

Whyte, Martin King, and William L. Parish. 1984. *Urban Life in Contemporary China.* Chicago: University of Chicago Press.

Williams, Raymond. 1973. *The Country and the City.* London: Chatto and Windus.

Wolf, Margery. 1968. *The House of Lim: A Study of a Chinese Farm Family.* Englewood Cliffs, NJ: Prentice-Hall.

———. 1972. *Women and the Family in Rural Taiwan.* Stanford, CA: Stanford University Press.

———. 1992. *A Thrice-Told Tale: Feminism, Postmodernism, and Ethnographic Responsibility.* Stanford, CA: Stanford University Press.

Woronov, Terry E. 2009. "Governing China's Children: Governmentality and 'Education for Quality.'" *positions: east asia cultures critique* 17(3): 567–89.

———. 2011. "Learning to Serve: Urban Youth, Vocational Schools and New Class Formations in China." *China Journal* 66: 77–99.

Wrigley, E. A. 1981. The Process of Modernization and the Industrial Revolution in England. In *Industrialization and Urbanization: Studies in Interdisciplinary History,* ed. T. K. Rabb and R. I. Rotberg, 23–57. Princeton, NJ: Princeton University Press.

Xu Haiyun. 2007. "Weiqiao: Xuxie Shenhua" (Weiqiao: Continuing to Write a New Legend). *Zhongguo Fangzhi* (China Textiles) 2: 110–12.

Xu Yi. 2009. "Weiqiao Fangzhi: Chuangxin Zhi Lu Shang Puxie Xin Pianzhang" (Weiqiao Textile: Writing New Pages in the Progress of Information). *Fangzhi Daobao* (Textile Reports) 8: 28–29.

Yan Hairong. 2003. "Neoliberal Governmentality and Neohumanism: Organizing *Suzhi*/Value Flow through Labor Recruitment Networks." *Cultural Anthropology* 18(4): 493–523.

———. 2008. *New Masters, New Servants: Migration, Development, and Women Workers in China.* Durham, NC: Duke University Press.

Yan, Yunxiang. 2003. *Private Life under Socialism: Love, Intimacy, and Family Change in a Chinese Village, 1949–1999.* Stanford, CA: Stanford University Press.

———. 2009. *The Individualization of Chinese Society.* New York: Berg.

———. 2010a. "The Chinese Path to Individualization." *British Journal of Sociology* 61(3): 489–512.

———. 2010b. "Introduction: Conflicting Images of the Individual and Contested Process of Individualization." In *China: The Rise of the Individual in Modern Chinese Society,* ed. M. H. Hansen and R. Svarverud, 1–38. Copenhagen: NIAS Press.

Yang, Jie. 2011. "*Nennu* and *Shunu:* Gender, Body Politics, and the Beauty Economy in China." *Signs: Journal of Women in Culture and Society* 36(2): 333–57.

Yin Zongyuan, Sun Weiqi, and Zhang Tongliang. 1999. "Shandong Weiqiao Fang-zhi Jituan Kaituo Shichang Qiu Fazhan" (Shandong Weiqiao Textile Group Explores the Market and Looks for Possibilities for Development). *Zhongguo Mianhua* (China Cotton) 26(11): 42–43.

Yurchak, Alexei. 2006 . *Everything Was Forever, Until It Was No More: The Last Soviet Generation*. Princeton, NJ: Princeton University Press.

Zhang, Everett Yuehong. 2007. "The Birth of *Nanke* (Men's Medicine) in China: The Making of the Subject of Desire." *American Ethnologist* 34(3): 491–508.

Zhang, Li. 2001. *Strangers in the City: Reconfigurations of Space, Power, and Social Networks within China's Floating Population*. Stanford, CA: Stanford University Press.

———. 2010. *In Search of Paradise: Middle-Class Living in a Chinese Metropolis*. Ithaca, NY: Cornell University Press.

Zheng, Tiantian. 2009. *Red Lights: The Lives of Sex Workers in Postsocialist China*. Minneapolis: University of Minnesota Press.

Zhongguo Shangban Gongye Staff. 2000a. "Shandong Weiqiao Fangzhi Jituan Gongsi" (Shandong Weiqiao Textile Group Co.). *Zhongguo Shangban Gongye* (China Commercial Industry) 6: 1.

———. 2000b. "Weiqiao Fangzhi Jituan" (Weiqiao Textile Group). *Zhongguo Shangban Gongye* 9: 17–18.

Zhu, Xiaoyang. 2014. *Topography and Political Economy in Rural China: The Story of Xiaocun*. Singapore: World Scientific.

Zhu, Yu. 1999. *New Paths to Urbanization in China: Seeking More Balanced Patterns*. Commack, NY: Nova Science Publications.

Zouping Bureau of Statistics, ed. 2005. *Zouping Tongji Nianjian 2004* (Zouping Statistical Yearbook 2004). Zouping: Zouping Bureau of Statistics.

———. 2007. *Zouping Tongji Nianjian 2006* (Zouping Statistical Yearbook 2006). Zouping: Zouping Bureau of Statistics.

———. 2008. *Zouping Tongji Nianjian 2007* (Zouping Statistical Yearbook 2007). Zouping: Zouping Bureau of Statistics.

———. 2009. *Zouping Tongji Nianjian 2008* (Zouping Statistical Yearbook 2008). Zouping: Zouping Bureau of Statistics.

———. 2012. *Zouping Tongji Nianjian 2011* (Zouping Statistical Yearbook 2011). Zouping: Zouping Bureau of Statistics.

Zouping, Gazeeteer Office. 1992. *Zouping Xianzhi* (Zouping County Gazeteer). Beijing: Zhonghua Shuju.

———, ed. 1997. *Zouping Nianjian 1986–1995* (Zouping Yearbook). Jinan: Qilu Chubanshe.

———. 2004. *Zouping Nianjian 1999–2003* (Zouping Yearbook). Binzhou: Shandong New China Printers.

Zuo Mingyu. 2010. "Weiqiao Changye Jituan: Weiguo Chuangye, Weimin Zaofu" (Weiqiao Pioneering Group, Creating Employment for the Country and Prosperity for the People). *Jin Ri Zouping* (Zouping Today), 30 December, 1–2.

INDEX

consumption *(continued)*
  the local, national, global, 122–25;
    consuming the urban, rural,
    modernity, tradition, 125–29; and
    distinction, class, 110–13; and familial
    relations, 104–108; and male bonding,
    108–110; and time space compression,
    99–102; and young migrant workers,
    102–104. *See also* recombinant
    consumption
cosmopolitanism, 3, 8, 10, 27, 224–25
Crapanzano, Vincent, 158, 161
cultural capital, 201, 205

Death Song of the River (He Shang), 128
Debord, Guy, 135
DENG Xiaoping, 150, 242n3chpt.6
despair, 160–62, 164–65, 169, 171, 173, 224,
  227
Discipline and Punish (Foucault), 13
dissatisfied entrepreneur, 155
distinction, 27, 110–14, 139, 190, 201, 205,
  225, 229–30
divorce, 13, 148, 152, 154, 176–77,
  243n1chpt.8
dormitories, 40, 57, 80, 81*fig.*, 102, 150
Durkheim, Emile, 7, 13, 237

eating bitterness *(chiku)*, 161–62, 171–72,
  228
education, 7, 8, 9, 10, 42, 55, 63, 76, 80,
  85–86, 100, 105, 138, 168, 183, 191–93,
  198–99, 203, 207, 220, 229, 232–34,
  241n7, 244n4chpt.11; and class, 86, 138,
  191–93, 198–99, 205; and consumption,
  105; and modernity, 7, 8, 9, 10, 229,
  232–34; and Wei Mian managers,
  85–86; and youth, 229
electricity generation, 75
entrepreneurial households, 152–55, 162–
  64, 177–78, 186–88
entrepreneurial local migrants, 152–55
erasures of memory, invocations of
  tradition, 129–32

factory housing, 57
factory workers, 143–52, 164–71, 210–12
factory working youth, 210–12

familial sacrifice, 171, 228
farm and factory, lives between, 141–52;
  for local migrants outside of Wei Mian
  apartments or of nonrural origins,
  149–52; for migrant workers, 141–43;
  for Wei Mian apartment dwellers of
  rural origins, 143–46
Farquhar, Judith, 12, 14, 15, 109, 122, 127
FEI Xiaotong, 180, 183, 184
Ferguson, James, 4, 5, 24, 228
Forbes Magazine, 83, 94
Fortune Plaza, stores, 105*fig.*
Foucault, Michel, 7, 13, 62
Friedman, Jonathan, 8, 9, 10, 25, 223, 224
Friedman, Kajsa Ekholm, 8, 10, 223
full house, 5–6, 228

Gansu province, 75, 158, 162, 163, 164
Geng Song, 110
geomancy, 43, 115, 150, 200, 226, 233
ghost city, 17
gifts, 80, 93, 110, 112, 183, 199; to
  matchmakers, 183; to officials, 110, 112,
  199; to workers, 83, 93
gossip, 17, 70, 71, 84–87; and Weiqiao
  Pioneering Group, 83–87, 89
Gould, Stephan Jay, 4, 5
government headquarters, 32, 38, 41, 41*fig.*,
  42, 43, 44*fig.,* 47*fig.,* 51, 54, 69, 109,
  226
Graeber, David, 82, 96
Griffiths, Michael, 125, 126
Guldin, Greg, 19, 238

habituation, 139, 208, 210, 221–22; and
  youth, 208, 210, 221–22
Halbwachs, Maurice, 11
Harrell, Stevan, 2, 160, 161
Hebei province, 2*map,* 75, 158, 209
Herzfeld, Michael, 129
highway billboard, 130*fig.*
Hobor, George, 95
hope, 40, 139, 158, 160–65, 168–71, 173, 225,
  227
Horkheimer, Max, 96
household registration policy, 20–21, 230
Hsing, You-tien, 40
Hsu, Carolyn, 191

HU Jintao, 78
Huang, Julia, 180, 181, 185, 204

individuality, 128, 141–43, 180, 181–82; and
    community, 181–82; and marketing
    strategies, 128
industrial accidents, 87, 210, 214
industrial safety, post-financial crisis
    decline, 87–89
Internet, 10, 41, 71, 75, 80, 88, 89, 99–100,
    102–103, 224, 225, 231

Jankowiak, William, 19, 114
Jia Pingwa, 11, 100
Jinan, 2*map*, 36, 101, 111

kinship, 4, 113, 114, 141, 143–44, 146, 148,
    156–57, 159–60, 227–28, 231; and
    distant migrants, 158–60; and middle
    classes, 194; and nearby migrants,
    144–58; and villagers-in-the-city,
    175–76
Kuan, Teresa, 198
Kunming, 52, 198

land bureau, 24, 58, 63
Latour, Bruno, 14
LI Shizhen, 15
local dialect, 125, 220
local migrants, 141–157
local social embeddedness, 71, 86
local state corporatism, 95
Long Distance Bus Station, 32, 46
Lora-Wainwright, Anna, 171, 208

male bonding, 108–110
Mandarin language (Putonghua), 125, 187,
    232
Mandopop, 124
March 8 Reservoir, 34, 36, 43, 130
Marx, Karl, 7, 8, 12, 171
matchmaking, 156, 175, 181–83, 196, 200,
    207, 213, 214, 227, 229
Mauss, Marcel, 24
memory, social, 10–12, 15, 94, 96, 98, 106,
    129–132, 156, 171–72, 233; political
    manipulation of, 129–132; and
    technologies, 11, 96, 128

middle-classes, 190–205, 244n2chpt.9
migrant workers, 141–73; from afar,
    158–73; distant migrant worker
    households, 162–71; second generation,
    138, 209, 220
Miller, Daniel, 97, 108
mobile phones, 99–100, 102–103, 216,
    224–25
modernity: and class, 190–94, 229; and
    community, 180–81; and consumption,
    96–98; and kinship, 141–42; and
    phantasmagoria, 115–116; and
    production, 66–67; and the everyday,
    230–31; and youth, 206–208, 229–30
modernity, theories of, 1–10; alternative,
    7, 233; classic, 6, 234; cyclical, 8–9,
    233–34; compressed, 9, 223; East Asian,
    9, 233; political, 62–64; second wave, 7,
    224–25
myth, 4, 5–6

Nappi, Carla, 14–15
New City apartments, 42*fig.*
New City government headquarters, 41*fig.*
New City pedestrian mall, 117*fig.*
New City Plaza, 64*fig.*
New Fortune Magazine, 83
New Youth, 206, 207
Nongjiale restaurant. *See* peasant
    restaurants

official spectacles, 132–134
outdoor market, 107*fig.*

Parish, William, 18, 19, 22
Park, Robert E., 192
parks, 1, 11, 29, 40, 43–45, 48, 61, 117–18,
    129
Pater, Walter, 158
patriarchy, 141, 142, 156, 177
patrilineal reasoning, 141
Pearl River Delta (PRD), 16, 17, 18, 21, 22,
    52, 61, 63
peasant restaurants *(nongjiale),* 126, 127*fig.*
peasants *(nongmin),* 19, 72, 77–78, 139
phantasmagoria, 115–36; and erasures of
    memory, invocations of tradition,
    129–32; and official spectacles, 132–34;

Lightning Source UK Ltd.
Milton Keynes UK
UKHW012000060123
414974UK00003B/10